Spun into Gold

THE SECRET LIFE OF A FEMALE MAGICIAN

ROMANY ROMANY

To the brave, fierce souls who spin into their gold,

step by step, no matter what.

To those who, in spite of their fears, dare to say,

I AM, I WILL.

To the women that have inspired and given me courage:

Elizabeth Gilbert, Oprah, Caroline Myss, Marie Forleo,

Pink, Brené Brown, Glennon Doyle Melton, Amy Purdy

& my courageous, always red carpet ready grandmother.

Thank you for your golden teaching, inspiration and example.

.

Table of Contents

Introduction

BEHIND THE VELVET CURTAIN

"We are the magicians of our own lives."
—Eugene Burger

I am a magician.

I am nothing like David Blaine. Or Dynamo. Or even Derren Brown. I don't do children's parties. I am a manipulator of reality; a shaper of cosmic dust; a believer—a seeker.

That's not to say I don't perform tricks. I do: a whole show full of them. I'm a real life professional magician—a card-carrying member of the exclusive inner circle of The Magic Circle, no less. But don't be fooled; it's a smoke screen, a fabulous misdirection, a sparkling sequin-strewn cloth to hide what's really going on. While the audience gasps as a birdcage with a singing bird appears out of nothing, as a square of scarlet silk changes to turquoise and three ropes melt into one, my job is to distract the audience while a crack team of angels are busy topping up tired hearts with new love, courage, and hope. It's a cosmic pit stop. When the ruby curtain falls and the audience spills out into the night, they wonder curiously why it is that they feel a little lighter—a little brighter. But shhh…don't tell. It's a secret. Oh, and although I'm a magician, I am a woman—which is unusual in the world of magic. In fact, everything in this book is a little "unusual." So if you prefer "usual," then move along, nothing to see—no offence taken.

If you're wondering whether this book is going to be your cup of tea, let me be up front. My story is about magic: stage magic, real magick, and whatever other sort of magic you fancy. It contains dreams of theatre, meddling angels, love and marriage, heartbreak and divorce, a swirling sacred fire, extraordinary cosmic adventures, a helpful ancient-Egyptian Goddess, and handy detailed instructions on how to manifest the man (or woman) of your dreams. I promise to take you behind the curtain, to spill the secrets of how I became a magician, to reveal my secret rollercoaster ride caught on the paralysing barb of a cruel and persistent eating disorder while reaching, always, towards a dream of Light.

This book is about keeping hold of your vision for as long as it makes you shiver with excitement any time you come close. It's a story to convince you to ignore anyone who says "you can't," to ignore the even louder voices in your head that tell you in a million nasty ways that you're never going to be or do what you've always dreamed of.

This book is about deciding that you're going to walk stubbornly towards your heart's desire and not stop until you're there.

Where?

There.

Then deciding that same thing over and over again, *damn it,* until it's done. Or you are. Hopefully it. My story is about trusting that the next step will appear. Yes, as if by magic.

And why draw the curtain aside just now? In magic, timing is everything. It's time to share what I've learnt in the hope that it will help someone, somehow. That's what my heart wants.

There is nothing more important in the world.

Costume design and illustration by Kevin Freeman

1

HALF LADY

*I*magine this. A short film. The main character talks to her audience, looking straight into the camera like one of Alan Bennett's *Talking Heads*. From the outside, looking into the spacious room, you see the director watching the playback on his monitor, the crew filming, the bright television lights fixed on the actress talking to camera. The room is elegant, there is an expensive rug on the polished parquet floor; a large antique, gold-framed mirror on the mantelpiece reflects the light and sparkle from a crystal chandelier. A fire burns in the grate.

The woman talking to the camera sits upright, looking straight ahead. There is something odd about her. If you look closer, you notice that her body ends at her waist on the surface of the table. Under the table, under the smooth, polished wood, there is only a thick scarlet-patterned Turkish rug. She has no legs, no feet. You peer at the finely turned table legs with the little brass wheels and the space in between. Nothing. The woman is wearing a shimmering gold lamé gown. Half a gown. Her arms, torso, and head are normal. One shoulder is bare, and her arms are slender, she rests her hands gracefully on the table, her nails manicured with a simple French polish. Her dark brown hair has been set and expertly curled; she is beautiful in an old-fashioned Jane Austen heroine sort of way. She checks her face in an antique silver-backed Victorian mirror and rubs her cheeks to smooth her blusher.

The director snaps the clapperboard.

"*Half Lady.* Take three." The woman looks directly into the camera, smiles a professional smile, and takes a breath.

"Today is an exciting day—a wonderful day. As you, my loyal fans know, I've been away from the spotlight for a while. I've taken some time to rest, to recover. I'd been overdoing it a little, but here I am." She looks at her devoted fans through the camera with love. "In just a few hours, my favourite Café de Paris in the heart of London's West End is throwing a fabulous party just for me. Everyone is coming: Kylie, Robbie Williams, Elton. Elton has written a new song to celebrate my return on this special night. My driver is due to arrive any minute now." She checks her delicate jewelled watch. It is nearly time.

"And what about my new dress? It's a Renaissance. You know, one of Kevin's, my gorgeous designer—so talented." She shifts a little on the table, raising one bare shoulder coquettishly, the diamanté trim on the golden gown catching the bright television lights.

"Just a short ride to town. The paparazzi will all be waiting. I admit I've missed it: the buzz, the gossip. It's been a little quiet these last months."

A pause. She is thinking of that particular quiet in rehab: the empty hours, broken by the sound of someone weeping in the next room. And in the night, a cry, sudden and loud, then the sound of feet running down a corridor, a shout, a rush of white coats, a quick jab of steel. She is thinking of how the silence presses softly back.

She gives a slight shake of her head.

"How do I look?" She arranges her smile to camera and raises one arched eyebrow. She takes a quick gulp from a glass of red wine by her elbow and nonchalantly brushes a trace of white powder from the corner of the table. She skims her hand past her nose lightly and looks in her hand-mirror to check.

"The limo will be here any minute." On cue, the doorbell rings. "Perfect."

But she does not move to answer it; she cannot move. She is nothing from the waist down. The crew stand motionless, holding their breath. The doorbell rings again; the chauffeur must be leaning heavily on the buzzer. The camera catches a twitch under her left eye, a slight pulling down at one corner of her mouth, the beginning of a frown on her smooth forehead. The bell jangles a third time. Still, no one moves. No one helps.

When the last echo of the doorbell falls away, the silence sweeps back, filling the room.

There is a vintage telephone with a cream onyx rotary dial and a 1930s mouthpiece standing elegant and aloof on a tall occasional table nearby. If she stretches out her hand to her full reach, she can touch it. Afraid that the car will leave without her, she leans forward and, reaching out, touches the receiver with the very tips of her fingers. But feeling herself go over the limits of her balance on the table, she quickly pulls her arm back, sending the telephone crashing to the floor. It lies there as if its neck is broken. Her hands grip the edge of the table. Her eyes are fixed on the telephone sprawled on the floor, receiver askew, the tone an endless beep in the broken air. She catches her breath in short, jagged gasps.

No one will come now.

No one can reach her.

She is alone and knows it.

With a huge effort, she controls her face back to calm, fixes her expression to a half smile, quietens her breathing. Still, the crew watch, the camera turns.

Today, there will be no red carpet, no flashbulb paparazzi. Today, her friends, her fans will not see her after all.

Today has not been a good day. Tomorrow will be better. Tomorrow the voices in her head will be softer, kinder. Tomorrow she can try again.

Tomorrow.

She gives up, the corners of her mouth give in, drop down. Her shoulders start to shake; her hands grip the table, knuckles white, her head falls back, her mouth open in a desolate, soundless cry.

The light technician fades the electric bright to dark.

And cut.

2

GOLD UPON GOLD

Abracadabra: As I think, as I speak, as I feel, *so I create.* This is precisely what magic is—a universal law. Not always easy to follow, but logical and reliable. I'll explain. Step into my story.

Imagine a child: short brown curly hair, chubby little legs, wide wondering eyes. She believes in fairies, God and magic. When asked for the very first time what she would like for Christmas, she knows precisely: "Something gold and something silver."

A few years later, if you ask her what she would like more than anything, more than a puppy, more than roller skates, she tells you with shining eyes that she wants to live in a theatre with crimson velvet curtains trimmed with rich gold braid and a star on the dressing-room door. I was that child.

One Boxing Day, age six, my parents took me to see *La Fille mal gardée* at the Royal Opera House in Covent Garden. With my feet dangling and a box of jelly babies on my lap, I sat in my theatre seat and gazed up at the huge, red velvet curtain. Velvet has its own old, musky, dusty scent. I breathed it in. I was astonished, eyes wide with it all. I didn't know such colour could exist, such a deep red, so deep you could fall right in and stay. And gold—gold everywhere. The bottom of the curtains were edged with a thick, bright gold braid and heavy tassels, the letters ER embroidered in golden thread in the corners where the two halves met. Three gilded balconies full of more ruby velvet seats stretched up to the turquoise-blue and gold ceiling, with its huge sparkling crystal chandelier.

Gold upon gold.

I'd never heard a sound like the jumble of the hidden orchestra tuning up. So much expectation, yet I didn't know what to expect. The conductor, in a black tailcoat, strode on, bowed, took his applause and raised his baton. The huge curtains swept open to reveal a rich pastoral scene, all muted shades of pale pink, soft yellow and duck egg blue. A whole new world of milkmaids carrying pails of milk, farm girls chasing chickens and young men leaning on a gate following the girls with their eyes. The gentle music swelled, scene followed scene and as the real-life story book turned its pages, I leant in, enchanted. Enter a flock of dark-haired ballerinas in floaty chiffon skirts with thin, graceful arms. Enter regal young men with strong, muscular thighs, effortlessly leaping across the stage, lifting the girls into the air. The girls didn't weigh a thing. Enter a man dressed as a woman who danced in clogs. Enter colour and costume, dry ice and scenery and, best of all, the most wonderful, most fascinating thing I had ever, ever seen: the magical beam of the white spotlight.

Even at my early age, I understood the great power of that light. Everything, everyone in it became vibrant, charismatic, special.

It was my first and greatest experience of magic.

One visit and the bar was set. Nothing—nothing else would do.

In the seventh year of my grandmother's cancer, when they sliced a chunk out of the top of her mouth and sewed it up again crooked, she continued to red rouge the remaining three quarters of her lips and smile as valiantly as ever.

Born in a poor family in the East End of London, just before the start of the First World War, she wore hand-me-downs and didn't even have her own shoes. Her toes grew slanted, and doctors removed the second toe from each foot. That didn't stop her dancing. Most afternoons she would go to the local hall with her friends: Big Rose, Little Rose, Ada and June. She would dance the man's part, leading the ladies through a quickstep or a waltz; many of the husbands had been killed in the war or preferred to stay home for a quiet hour or two by the fire with the newspaper.

She could whip up a new outfit in a day or two on her Singer sewing machine, conjuring copies of Hollywood gowns out of remnants, concentrating hard with a mouthful of pins. Surveying the result in the mirror, adding a string or two of glittering beads, she would give a little twirl of satisfaction. Despite her flat shoes—which, with her four toes per foot, were the most glamorous footwear she could manage—she was always red-carpet ready for the Dagenham village hall.

When I was six, I entered the holiday camp fancy-dress competition. My grandmother dressed me in a hula-hula skirt made out of cut-up green Marks & Spencer plastic bags and covered my top half with full-blown scarlet-red roses she'd stolen from the camp's private greenhouse. Of course, I won. A man in a blue striped blazer and a straw boater hat knelt down and gave me a voucher to spend in the gift shop. I picked out a ring with a large pink plastic stone.

"Is this real, Nana?" I asked earnestly. I didn't want it if it wasn't.

"Of course it is my darling," she replied, "everything is real."

3

BANG, BANG, CLAP

$\mathcal{M}$y mother took me to my first ballet class when I was three. Question: How much ballet can you do when you're three? Answer: Not much.

I knelt with my fellow toddlers in a circle, our tambourines on the floor. We banged on them with gusto: bang, bang, clap, bang, bang, clap, our lusty efforts vibrating through our knees. I still have that tambourine: turquoise-blue tin with five orange cymbals around the sides. On the front, a dark-haired gypsy dancer with a tiny waist and full-layered calf-length rose-pink skirt—beautiful—raises her graceful arms, smiling. She dances in a circle of moonlight, a canary-yellow gypsy wagon behind her in the forest. I wanted to be her. I still do.

When I was a little older, on Saturday mornings, there were three whole hours of ballet, tap and modern dance classes with Miss Muriel in the Co-op hall. Miss Muriel had trained as a ballerina and then danced as a Bluebell girl in Paris: one of those tall, elegant showgirls glittering in diamonds and feathers. Now, her brown hair scraped back and tightly gripped in a bun, she was strict, serious and precise. One evening after class, I overheard Miss telling my mother that I had talent. I loved Miss Muriel with all the passion and devotion a little girl could have.

My mother was born in East London in 1939. She was a child through the Second World War and left school at fourteen, with only a threadbare education. She wanted me to have and to learn everything that she had missed out on. At the age of six, in addition to ballet, I was taken to elocution and drama lessons. My private teacher, Miss Wilson, had swollen old lady ankles in face-powder-coloured tights, stubby fingers covered in glittering rings and a booming, theatrical voice. I never saw her actually standing. She lived in an antique gold velvet armchair with well-thumbed copies of plays and scripts wedged down the sides.

Mum and I visited her once a week in her warm basement flat at seven o'clock on Friday evenings. The room was crowded, with books stacked from the floor to the ceiling. The smell of cat food hung in the stuffy air. The cat, following the age-old feline law to always sit on the person that likes them least, purred on my mother's lap as she sat hidden in the corner, worried that Miss Wilson would ask her for the meaning of a word she didn't know.

For nine years, Miss Wilson trained me to perform poems and pieces of theatre. Each week she gave me chunks of literature to learn by heart. I practiced sight reading and tongue twisters: *Billy bangs both bongos in the banjo band, bang de-de-la-la-la, doesn't he bang grand? Whenever the weather is good, whenever the weather is not, we'll weather the weather, whatever the weather, whether we like it or not.* I did the entire set of Llama drama exams, performing pieces of Milton, George Bernard Shaw and Shakespeare in impressive living rooms of posh houses.

"If you'd like to begin?" asked the sniffy, highly educated examiner with fascinating protruding nasal hair. He raised his eyebrows and nodded encouragingly.

Without a stage, costume or supporting cast, standing in my best dress on the plastic matting protecting the expensive rug from dirty shoes, I morphed into Eliza Doolittle, bedraggled in the rain, a tatty flower basket on my arm and a slick of mud across my nose.

"*Cheer up, Captain, buy a flow'r off a poor girl.*"

The examiner jotted a few notes on my report form.

"Thank you. And your next piece?"

This time I was Titania making love to a donkey. No costume, no change of scenery, no donkey.

"*To have my love to bed and to arise, and pluck the wings from painted butterflies.*"

I was twelve; I had no idea what that meant. But I loved the sound of the words and practiced saying them over and over in my bedroom. Soon after my final exam, Miss Wilson fell, hitting her head on a radiator, and died. Our literary Friday evenings came to an abrupt end.

In the evenings, I danced in our living room in the reflection of the window while Mum washed up and Dad tinkered with the car in the garage. I watched myself twirl in the mirror of the dark glass, expecting every moment that a talent scout would pass by, see me dancing and make me a star. While Mum locked up the house before a trip to the shops, I danced on the doorstep, just in case 'he' was passing the very moment I turned a rather fabulous pirouette. When Dad left me in the car while he bought our Friday night fish and chips, I would lip synch to Neil Diamond on the car tape player.

Cracklin' Rosie, make me a smile
Girl, if it lasts for an hour, that's all right,
We got all night, to set the world right...

"Would you believe it, that girl can sing just like Neil Diamond!" the talent scout exclaimed as he walked past our car. "Little girl, I'm going to make you a star!"

In my childhood world, talent scouts were everywhere, and it was only a matter of time before I was discovered. I was ready—ready for the bright lights and Hollywood film sets, costume fittings and flash-bulb paparazzi.

Aged twelve, I demanded to have *The Stage* newspaper delivered. I read the adverts for dancing jobs and dreamed of glamorous opportunities. In school, our mothers were expected to embroider our names on our royal-blue swimsuits. I asked mine to embroider *The Stage* in hot pink thread instead of my name. She was never very good at embroidery and ran out of room after the 'g.'

"What's The Stag?" my swimming teacher asked curiously, "your favourite pub?"

On Sunday afternoons, my mother and I cosied up on the sofa and watched Hollywood musicals: Gene Kelly, Fred Astaire and Judy Garland, Marilyn Monroe, Liza Minelli and Doris Day. At the age of thirteen, I joined the local amateur dramatic society. We learnt new show songs on Tuesday evenings and choreography on Thursdays. On Saturday afternoons, after my morning dance class, the dramatically flouncing director put the show together. I played a dancing bear in a smelly furry costume, a prancing flower in a pink-foam petal headpiece and had a real egg cracked on my head each night in *Jack and the Beanstalk* during a song about a chicken. Mum copied chunks of scripts by hand and tested me so that I knew them by heart. Dad drove me to every rehearsal and every class, waiting patiently in the Co-op hall carpark. Money was tight, but my parents paid selflessly for all the classes, exams, ballet shoes and pink cross-your-heart cardigans that I needed. Encouraged and supported by my parents, I fell passionately, irrevocably in love with show business.

When the am-dram group put on Rodger and Hammerstein's *Carousel*, I was fifteen and given the part of Louise, who has a solo ballet number. In the local professional theatre, the stage empty except for clouds of theatrical mist around my feet, the orchestra played the *Carousel* waltz just for me. As I danced, nothing else mattered in the world. I was in love with the bright shine of the spotlight, the communion with the audience in the dark, the fearless opening of my body as I spun and leapt. I had found my perfect place; everything was joy.

For a child obsessed with words and theatre, music and ballet, it was all going very well.

And then.

4

THROWING SUNLIGHT

$\mathscr{A}$nd then?

Then came the resistance training. Resistance training? You know, weights in the gym, sprints uphill, exercises designed to make you fitter, faster, stronger. As far as showbiz was concerned, age thirteen, I'd grown into the wrong shape. Professional dancers have to be lean. I'd been a chubby little girl, and now in my teenage years, I had a curvy, sturdy build. Knowing that I'd always dreamt of being a dancer, my mother started to watch what I ate. I joined her in this activity, and by the time I got to fifteen, I was down to eating—not very much.

The summer I performed in *Carousel*, I could make twenty satsumas last all day. Why satsumas? Well, if you take the time to peel them v-e-r-y slowly and take off all the teeny tiny bits of pith, they take a very long time to eat. I did that for quite a while. Not only satsumas: lettuce, cucumber, green salads, grated carrots and anything with minimal calories. When I danced through the clouds of mist, I was slim and light, with slender arms and defined shoulders. I had cheekbones. In my memory, it was my finest moment.

These days, when we know so much more about nutrition, it's widely understood and scientifically proven that if you dramatically restrict calorific intake over a long period of time, the subject will respond by not only getting obsessed by food but also piling all the weight back on as soon as normal eating resumes. When the show was over, I regained the pounds lost during my satsuma extravaganza and then piled on more. By seventeen, I was a good two stones—28 lb / 12 kg—overweight. Unpacking those unhappy years now, I remember crying myself to sleep every night, praying to be thin, desperately bargaining with God. Every day I tried to eat less but ended up eating more, hating what I saw in the mirror, looking with disgust at my pudgy face with unhappy, tortured eyes. I went on every diet I could find, although I drew the line at the 'drink your own urine' one that my mother's friend suggested and actually did. I wrote down every morsel I ate in my Jane Fonda food diary, went to Slimming World and got up early before school to exercise, but nothing worked. I hated myself for being fat but despised myself more for sabotaging my dream of becoming a dancer. I was stuck in the horrible rut of being the wrong shape and feeling powerless to change.

I stopped dance classes. I couldn't bear to see myself in the mirror. Who wants a ballerina with bouncing boobs? I didn't audition for stage school. My mother said I was too intelligent to be a dancer. She knew as well as I did that I was too 'sturdy.' There was nothing to be done. Instead, I got some decent A-levels and a place at university. I wrapped my dreams of theatre and dance and that magical spotlight in thick layers of disappointment and self-disgust and left them to gather dust at the back of the wardrobe of hope.

Fast forward two years. I was in my second year at Manchester University, studying for a degree in English and Italian literature. One afternoon, as I sat reading on a bench outside the library, I heard a curious putt-putting noise. I looked up from my book to see a bloke standing on the grass nearby, throwing shards of light up, up, up, into the air—red, silver, gold. Squinting against the sun, at first I couldn't work out what he was doing, but then I saw that he was throwing juggling clubs into the sunlight. Tall and scruffy, brown split-end hair to his shoulders, he was wearing a blue faded t-shirt, torn grey jeans and had grubby bare feet. I thought he looked beautiful.

After watching him for twenty minutes, I decided that I needed to learn how to juggle with sunlight too. Universities have clubs for students: Tai Chi, rock climbing, stamp collecting. The circus society met on Wednesday evenings at eight. At my first session, wearing my best hippy tie-dye, I stood in a circle with my new friends as we threw an imaginary ball to each other, each person shouting out their name as they caught it. We climbed on each other's shoulders to make a human pyramid. Someone farted, everyone giggled and we all tumbled down. I spent a chunk of my student grant on a large sack of clubs, balls and rings. My clubs were red, silver and gold; to me, they were beautiful splinters of light.

I spent more time learning to juggle than studying Italian in my dingy, mouldy student digs in Manchester. At the weekly circus club, I practiced balancing a long peacock feather on my nose. Afterwards, I couldn't wait to show my friends my superhuman skills. I rushed home and picked up an empty milk bottle from the kitchen. Perfect.

"Watch! Watch! This is fantastic!" Placing the milk bottle on my nose, I put my head back in the correct position, looking at the ceiling. My housemates watched curiously.

But the bottle wasn't empty, and the stinky, soured milk ran to the back of my nose and down my throat.

"Argh!" The bottle dropped and smashed on the floor. Hopping about in my socks to avoid the glass, I shook my head vigorously, still with the lumpy milk in my nose and throat. My housemates collapsed on the floor, convulsed with laughter. *Bastards.*

After two years at university, I was going to have a year out working in Italy as a teaching assistant in a school. Although the official idea was to become fluent in Italian, my real aim was to meet men—preferably sexy Italian men. In two whole years of university, I'd not had a sniff of romance; not a snog nor a fumble. There were a handful of boys on my course, but since I was two stone heavier than I should have been and felt fat and unattractive, it wasn't surprising that I was still a card-carrying virgin. Italy was my big chance. *I'm twenty, I'm available. Look out ragazzi, here I come.*

But first a little fact for you; I went to an Ursuline convent school. The Ursuline order was founded in Brescia, Italy, in 1535 by St. Angela Merici, as the first institute for women dedicated exclusively to education for girls. Why would you need to know this? Because, not knowing any better, when it came to choosing an Italian town in which to spend my year out, I didn't choose sexy Rome, or even sexier dangerous Naples; I chose dull, industrial Brescia, a town between Milan and Venice, with nothing more than a sister Ursuline convent to boast about: a feeling of familiarity, a home away from home. Worse still, I made the major mistake of asking the nuns from my school if they knew of anyone I could stay with. An Italian-Catholic couple volunteered to find me accommodation. Somehow, wires got crossed and when they picked me up at the airport, they drove me to a convent. *A convent!* A real convent, with real nuns, where I found, to my complete horror, I was booked to stay for the entire year.

My tiny room was a basic white cell with a narrow single bed and a small window too high to see out of. The evening meal was a thin, watered-down soup with a few sad slices of vegetables floating about, a white roll and a few slices of salami. The eyes of the Pope watched me undress from a framed photograph on my wall. The heavy wooden front doors were shut and bolted at ten o'clock every evening. No visitors allowed. I couldn't even go to the cinema and get home before the doors were locked for the night.

How on earth was I going to break free to find those sexy Italian men? I couldn't stay there all year, but how was I going to escape?

These days, I would simply walk out, waft my credit card about and easily find myself a better alternative, but my younger self obeyed the rules and worried about what people might think.

After two weeks of sleepless nights in my narrow bed, I had a plan. I would knock on the door of Sister Superior to tell her that it had all been a terrible misunderstanding, I wanted to leave and could I please have my passport back? I did. She invited me to sit down and leant back in her chair behind her desk. I couldn't meet her eyes. A single long dark hair sprouted from the mole on her chin.

"Booked is booked," she declared. "No, you can't have your passport back."

The hair quivered with anger. Nuns can be very frightening. But the thought of spending my year in Italy in a convent was too awful to accept without a fight.

"I really would prefer to leave," I said politely in my best Italian.

"*Disgraziata!*" she snapped, glaring at me. "*Tu sei propria una disgraziata!* You're a disgrace!" She continued in rapid Italian, which I didn't understand, but I could tell from her scowl and flying spittle that it wasn't complimentary.

I stayed where I was, resolute, glaring back at her. I'd been extremely obedient for most of my life; I'd even been head girl of my school for heaven's sake, but this was too much. Looking at me with distaste, the nun shook her head, unlocked her desk drawer and handed over my passport, saying that I had one hour to pack my bags and leave. Back in my tiny cell, I threw everything into my case; then with the energy of conflict surging through my veins, I sprinted down the corridor and out the main gate to freedom.

After two weeks of living on watery vegetable soup and worry, I'd lost seven pounds. *Wild love affairs with passionate Italians and pepperoni pizza, I'm ready for ya.*

5

BUBBLE BATHS & LINGERIE

*S*ince I was now homeless, a teacher at the school where I was working suggested that I stay with a Yugoslav friend of hers who wanted to learn English. I would speak English to her at home and, in return, live rent-free. This wasn't any way to improve my Italian, but I was desperate. Her apartment was elegant and furnished with fine antique furniture. I had my own room and my own beautifully tiled bathroom with expensive gold taps. Each afternoon, a grizzled but obviously wealthy man in his seventies came to visit my beautiful thirty-something hostess. It seemed a little strange that they had perfumed bubble baths together when he arrived. It seemed odd that he stayed for a couple of hours but never spent the night. After he left, she hung her exquisite lingerie to dry all over the apartment. It was only after a couple of weeks that I realised, of course, that she was his mistress.

He must have wanted a little more privacy because one day, my hostess suggested that I move to a one-bedroom flat that also belonged to her lover. And that is how I arrived in a little apartment with a bed that folded back into the wall during the daytime, a tiny white kitchen, and an even smaller balcony, perfect for a morning espresso watching the busy traffic below. The flat had a television, and I practiced my Italian watching dubbed episodes of *Dallas* and *Dynasty*.

"*Ciao*," said JR, lifting his Stetson hat.

"*Ciao*," I echoed back.

As the English teaching assistant, I could teach whatever I wanted, so I challenged my students to explain the lyrics of David Bowie and introduced them to the joys of English country dancing. We pushed back the desks and had a lively time doing wild do-si-dos and 'swing your partner.' I gave them exercises in how to respond to gossip, which in my opinion is always useful.

Me: "He's left his wife and taken up with that blonde."

Them: "No! That's terrible! *And* she's half his age!"

We didn't bother much with grammar.

The Italian teenagers were charming and affectionate; they linked arms with me as I walked down the corridor and invited me out to eat pizza on a Saturday night.

Then, two months later, having failed to find any social life other than Saturday night pizza with my students, I enrolled for an evening clown course that I saw advertised at the university.

"*Stare in piedi su una sedia e ruggire come un leone*," the teacher said. "Stand on a chair and roar like a lion." We hadn't covered this sentence in university, and I hadn't a clue what he was telling us to do. Everyone else leapt onto their chair and, as far as I could make out, were pretending to be lions. I jumped onto my chair and roared loudly too.

Each week, we learnt a classic clown move. First, the Comedy Fall. Do a little jump and fall backwards, ending up flat on your back. It looked simple. I did a little jump as instructed, fell back and—*wham!*—hit the back of my head hard on the floor. *Ouch!* I lay there, marvelling; it's true, you actually do see stars.

Second, the Table Prat Fall. This is the deal: you walk up

to a table, attempt to put a foot on it but instead fall face first onto the surface, apparently banging your nose, but really you support yourself by placing your hands on either side of your face. I spent the week practicing. In class, when it was my turn, I marched towards the table, slipped my foot off as we were taught, and slammed my face and both hands flat on the surface. *Bam!* Everyone laughed and applauded. As I walked away, the laughter turned to a horrified gasp. Looking back, I saw a pool of fresh bright blood spreading quickly over the surface and starting to drip onto the floor. I touched my nose, it was slippery and wet. My blood. No wonder they were so impressed. Dedicated, that's me.

In Italy, in Venice, February is the time for the famous *Carnivale di Venezia*. It was only an hour from Brescia, and I'd never been there before. Even though I had no idea what went on, I naively decided to join in and show off my still-basic juggling skills.

In the early morning, I got off the train and walked to Piazza San Marco through the still-sleeping streets. The huge square was empty except for a quiet layer of white mist and a flock of pigeons sleeping on one leg. No one was about. The echoing space was far too silent to disturb with my particular style of juggling, which included loud and frequent drops. I walked through the square and into the tiny side streets.

Finding a narrow residential street, I warmed up with two balls and one club, nothing fancy. Boff, boff, platt. Boff, boff, platt.

Then…. *Then!* A coin jingled at my feet. Someone from an upstairs window had thrown a coin! I can still feel the swoop of my heart. That first magical coin gave me courage. I packed up my kit and looked about for a bigger stage. Shops were beginning to open, and a few people had ventured out for their morning espresso. I stood in the entrance of a jewellery shop and started again. Boff, boff, platt. Boff, boff, platt.

A policeman appeared out of the mist, probably summoned by the jeweller, who understandably wasn't impressed by a novice juggler throwing things about in his doorway.

"Mi scusi, pero non se puo fare questo qua." "Excuse me miss, you can't do that here." He continued in Italian, "You should go to St Mark's square." Aha! Now, I was a professional *and* had an official instruction to perform in the main square. Still, nobody about. In the middle of the deserted piazza, I put my up-turned hat on the ground and began to juggle.

Out of the mist, out of nothing, magically, a coach-load of Japanese tourists appeared. They had come to see the famous *Carnivale di Venezia*, and so far that was me. Suddenly, I was surrounded by cameras, pointing fingers, laughter and chatter. A clatter of coins and then, as swiftly as they had arrived, they had gone.

But look! *Look!* My blue cloth cap was full of coins and notes. I picked it up carefully, found the nearest café, and counted it. Thirty thousand lire. Twenty-five British pounds! I wanted to shout, *I'm a professional street performer!* But everyone had their heads in a newspaper or were in deep conversation, so I finished my coffee and hurried back to my spot in the square. The morning sun was breaking through, burning off the mist; more people were about.

"Can I have a go?" a tall, scruffy guy asked in a strong French accent. He'd been standing watching me for a while. He had a battered leather biker jacket, shoulder-length, tangled black hair, faded grey jeans and a weary heavy-metal T-shirt.

"Sure."

He took three balls and juggled easily, throwing complex patterns into the air, obviously an expert.

"My name is Stanislaus. My parents were Russian, but I am French," he said, still juggling.

I noticed his stubble and the shadow of a Kirk Douglas dimple on his chin. I continued to stare, feeling English, awkward—the opposite of his French cool.

"My brother is starting a show in five minutes," he added, "just over there. *Tu viens?*"

"Sure," I said again. At that moment, I would have agreed to anything.

I packed my bag and followed him to the other end of the piazza, where a large circle of people stood waiting, expectant and silent. We pushed our way to the front. In the centre of the circle, two monks stood, each holding a giant unicycle. I knew they were monks because they were dressed in long brown habits and had a bald spot shaved on their heads. Six large rubber sink plungers lay at their feet. *Ah*, I suddenly realised, *that's Stanislaus' brother. They're performers, not monks, they're wearing wigs.*

On an invisible signal, they hitched their robes up to their knees, jumped into the air, then sprinted in opposite directions to the edge of the audience, before abruptly turning on their heels and running back to take a flying leap onto their unicycles, each peddling fast high up on a single wheel. The crowd burst into enthusiastic applause. A volunteer threw up the sink plungers and they passed them between each other above our heads. The crowd laughed and applauded again. I watched with both admiration and shame. There I was, juggling two balls and one club, asking for money, and these guys were doing it for free! I didn't understand that they were paid by the city council. As I watched, I felt a new sensation in my stomach: a conviction that this was what I wanted to do too. Fascinated, I studied their interaction with the crowd, the building rhythm of the show, the way the circle of their audience stayed perfect and grew stronger as more people gathered.

I was also aware of a growing tingling feeling, a quiver of electricity running through my body as I stood next to Stanislaus. I know it might seem unlikely, but at the age of twenty-one, I'd never felt that feeling before. We waited together until the crowds cleared. His brother and friend threw off their monks' robes and packed their stuff. Without their tonsure wigs, their hair was long and lank, caught up in untidy ponytails. They lounged on the step of a statue in jeans and faded black t-shirts, pigeons at their feet, smoking Gauloises. To me, they were the ultimate in cool.

The *Carnivale* was warming up as the main Piazza di San Marco began to fill. Old bewigged noblemen in exquisite brocade coats strolled by in white stockings and silver-buckled shoes; ladies with white-powdered faces and black beauty spots swished in silk crinoline gowns with cream frills of lace at the neck and cuffs. My trio of French troubadours—Stanislaus, his brother and his performing partner—headed off to a large building just off the piazza, wheeling their unicycles. I followed like a puppy. No one talked. Stanislaus seemed to be the silent type and stayed close to my side.

"We're going to the Palazzo to get our money. *Tu viens?*" his brother asked me.

We waited in a large hall inside an elegant palazzo just off the main square. The walls were lined with mahogany panelling and huge oil paintings hung in ornate gold frames. While a clerk organised the cash to settle their fee, a woman in a classic black old-fashioned servant's dress offered us *frittelle* pastries dusted with icing sugar on a silver tray. Someone else brought us chilled champagne fizzing in elegant flute glasses. I had a glass or two, and probably three, and then followed Stanislaus out onto an ornately carved stone balcony that overlooked the square. We nibbled the delicate patisserie, watching the costumed crowd below. He didn't speak. I was aware of his tall frame in battered black leather. I felt his hand gently lifting my chin, tilting my face towards his. Lips sticky with sugar, he kissed me. I forgot to shut my eyes. His were closed, his long black lashes quivering. The three glasses of champagne had made me all warm and squishy. I snuggled in closer, feeling the zip of his biker jacket against my neck, the scratch of his stubble on my skin.

Without saying a word, Stanislaus took my hand and led me

back down to the piazza to join the crowds of costumed revellers. In the Venice mist, the world was magical. I floated tipsy and content, held to earth by Stanislaus's warm hand. We drifted, arm in arm, for the rest of the afternoon, the effect of champagne slowly evaporating.

About four o'clock, when the light had begun to turn a little dull, Stanislaus casually mentioned that his brother and friend had both left and that he had nowhere to stay the night. My present self, watching my younger, thinks, *Great, grab that gorgeous silent man and take him back to yours pronto!* but my Catholic younger self, prim and proper, was shocked. *Aha! I knew it, my mother was right! Sex! That's all they want!* The last of the champagne bubbles popped.

"Well," I said, turning into my mother, "we'd better get you back to the station then, so that you can go find your brother."

We jumped on a crowded bus. Squashed together, my face against his chest, I could smell the leather of his jacket. He was bewildered by my sudden determination to get rid of him.

"At least give me your address," he pleaded. I scrawled my address on a scrap of paper with an eyeliner pencil. At the station, I bundled him into the carriage of the last train returning to his town and waved him off with a tight-laced sigh of relief. *Phew,* my younger self thought. *Damn! What a waste!* thinks my older.

The next week, Stanislaus sent a telegram: "*Toujours, sans de nouvelles de toi, j'en creve.*" "Without news of you, my heart breaks." I liked the idea of receiving a romantic telegram when it was from a safe distance. I wrote a nice chatty letter back telling him that my favourite pop band was Duran Duran.

Four days later, my mother was visiting. We'd just had an evening out eating pizza—always pizza—but as we walked back to my apartment, I sensed someone was following us. I turned and, yes, it was Stanislaus. He'd driven for twelve hours all the way from his home in La Rochelle, France. Still wearing his shabby biker jacket, his dark hair looked as though he hadn't brushed it since the last time we met.

Holding my shoulders, staring down at me intently, he said in French,

"I didn't hear from you. I had to see you," My mother didn't speak French and watched curiously, wondering what was going on. I was flattered but still convinced that he all he wanted was sex. My Catholic education had a lot to answer for.

"You go in, Mum, I'm going to talk with my friend." She went in. We sat in his van.

He leant over to kiss me. I pulled back.

"I have something to tell you." I said. He raised his thick French eyebrows. "I have a boyfriend." I didn't have a boyfriend. I'd never had a boyfriend. His face fell. He suddenly looked tired; it had been such a long drive. "But please come in and stay the night. My mother's here but we can make up a bed."

"No, I'll drive back," he said firmly.

"Tonight? You can't!"

"Yes, I'll go now." He was all dejection. His shoulders slumped.

There wasn't much else to say. I leant towards him and kissed him slowly, sadly. I climbed out of his van and walked back to my apartment, where my mother was waiting. It could have been the most delicious, romantic and exciting thing to have happened to me in my twenty-one years and I blew it. I never saw him again.

But the unforgettable vision of his brother and friend performing to a huge circle in the piazza had given me a new idea. A new possibility.

As soon as my mother had gone back to England, I got to work.

6

A PROPER JOB

*B*ack in my little apartment in Brescia, inspired by the French street performers, I was determined to create my own show. I'd made an English friend called David, who I'd met in a coffee bar near my school. David was twenty-five and had trained as an accountant but then decided to learn Italian and found himself a little office job in Brescia. When I told him that I wanted to put together a street show for the summer holidays, he volunteered to do it with me. I taught him to juggle, and on sunny afternoons on the grass in front of my school we worked out a basic show, featuring a short wooden ladder that he held while I juggled at the top. I asked my mother to make me a little clown costume. She dutifully sent over a cream satin smock, decorated with brightly coloured felt triangles that I wore over a pair of red trousers. She was never good at dress-making, and it was all a bit skew-whiff, but sewn with so much love, I could feel it each time I put it on.

There was no romance with David; he was just a good solid friend, and after five months of being lonely, it was nice to be able to laugh and chat easily in English. Lonely? But what about all those sexy Italian men I was going to meet? What about them? I wasn't fat anymore; walking everywhere in Brescia had whittled me down to a normal size, but somehow, even a sturdy English 'normal' was too big for the Italian men I met. One guy in a nightclub said to me in basic English, "You're nice but you're too big." My older self wants my younger to throw my drink over his expensive designer suit and strut proudly off with a dismissive, 'Go fuck yourself and your skinny arse.' Instead, age twenty-one, blinking back tears, I wandered around the nightclub feeling lost, unattractive and, yup, too big.

David and I pre-paid our inter-rail tickets for July and August. We didn't have a credit card and planned to survive entirely on whatever anyone might put into our hat. How incredible that seems now! No credit card? No access to an overdraft? But not to worry, we had a ladder, a train ticket, two clown costumes and six juggling clubs—what was there to worry about?

And that's what we did for two months, sleeping on trains to save money on hostels, our rucksacks and ladder slung in the overhead rack, our trainers swinging by their laces, gently filling the carriage with a cheesy pong. Our juggling improved, and we made a bit of money on each show, but it was never much. One day, hungry and penniless, David sent me into a bakers to ask for some free bread rolls. The baker shot me and my mother's clown costume a scornful glance, shook his head and turned to the next customer. I slunk out, mortified and red-faced; my middle-class upbringing hadn't trained me to beg.

In my memory, the sun seemed to shine every day as we zig-zagged about Austria, Germany and Switzerland on our inter-rail train ticket. We were just having fun; nothing important was at stake. David was a qualified accountant with a real job, and I was returning to university in October to finish my degree. In September we said goodbye; David returned to Brescia and I went back to Manchester for my final year. A recession was looming, and all of us final-year students jostled to get on graduate training schemes with big corporate firms. That year, British Telecom were looking for especially creative graduates for their new sales and marketing intake.

"If I gave you this plastic cup, what could you do with it?" the interviewer asked me. Ooh, I was good at this.

"I could put it on my nose and be a platypus. I could put it on at a jaunty angle and be a stripper. I could attach it to my bum and be a rabbit. If you had another and a piece of string we could play telephones, I could—"

"Yes, thank you. That's enough for now." He literally had to stop me. Thinking up ideas for what to do with a plastic cup is one thing at which I obviously excel.

I got the job, of course, given the plastic cup creativity criteria. It had a starting salary of £22,000 plus sales bonuses—which in 1991 was a lot of money—a company car and six months of sales training before we started real work. On my first day, a chap from head office looked the group of new fast-track graduates up and down with an especially disapproving glance at my orange floral dress. He told us sternly that we must take the path of least resistance. He told us that we would need a smart dark-blue suit and an expensive briefcase. He shot a withering glance at my tatty orange rucksack. Between the lines of his instructions, I understood that we were to toe the line, obey orders and not rock the invisible corporate boat. It sounded extremely dull.

After six months training, our group was split up and placed in different offices. Most of the other graduates were in London, but I was dropped in an ancient call centre in Romford. This meant that I was back living with my parents thirty minutes away in the quiet, green suburbia of Shenfield, Essex. All my school friends had left and there was really nothing to do; I was not impressed.

The office in Romford was a 1970s concrete building with an energy-sapping quality about it that sucked any good feeling out of you the moment you signed in with the surly doorman.

The men on my new team were fifty-something British Telecom veterans. For thirty years, they had worked their way up through the ranks to reach the respectable position and salary of account managers. Now, here was a fresh 'knows nothing about anything graduate'—a girl even—thrown into their office at the same pay grade as them. It could have turned nasty.

I was given a list of customers to ring.

"Hallo, sir, I'm from BT. I'm glad to tell you that a brand-new phone system for your entire company will work out cheaper than your old one. Shall we arrange a time for me to visit to explain more?" It did work out cheaper—don't ask me how—and I whizzed round to the local industrial factories in my new dark-blue suit, in my shiny red company car, and signed them up. There I was, all fresh and young and smiley. Selling a new, cheaper telephone system was easy.

While my BT graduate friends were nightclubbing and having a great time in London, I had nothing to do in the boring backwaters of Essex except sell telephone systems—which meant that I won the award for the highest sales figures out of the new intake. As a reward, they put me in a brand-new sales team based in Covent Garden, and my London life began.

I loved Covent Garden. During my lunch break, I watched the street performers with nostalgia. I wandered past the theatres, admiring the photographs of the actors. I stood outside the Pineapple dance studios and peered enviously in at a dance class. I felt like Alice in Wonderland locked outside the beautiful garden. But I didn't have the key to the garden door, and in any case, I was the wrong size.

One night, I went to a nightclub in Camden where there was a salsa band and people dancing. I was fascinated. I found a beginner's salsa class, and within a week, I was addicted. When night fell, I would hotfoot it to the salsa nightclubs all over London. Wearing a white frilly top, black tights, black hot pants and high heels, I wiggled in the arms of sexy Cuban Jorge, or street-cool Aladdin from Brixton, who had long dreads, smooth muscles and shouted "*Gepah!*" when the music really kicked. I spun in a sweaty, joyful world of dancers packed onto a tiny dance floor throbbing with rhythm and life. Finally, I was dancing again, and in the pulsing dark of the nightclub, whether you were thin or fat didn't matter a damn.

One night at a salsa club, I saw a guy with the flashiest moves of anyone on the dance floor. His name was Anuar. He was classic Colombian: black satin shirt with diamond sparkle collar, Cuban heels—he was on the short side—shiny black hair, moustache and white, white teeth. I asked for a dance. After a week of seeing each other at the regular dance nights all around London, he asked if I'd like to be his partner for a few dance competitions that were coming up. Yup, that would suit me just fine.

We danced in the clubs almost every night. I had a scarlet dress made for the competitions, spangled with ruby glittering jewels, which flared out when I twirled, flashing my matching red knickers. The shoulders were sewn with expensive heavy gold fringing. Now that I had a generous corporate salary, I could afford it.

Anuar and I won a few small dance competitions and then—*bam!*—we were announced as the winners of the UK championships, in front of a home crowd of Columbians who were all rooting for their flown-in Columbian couple. As our names were called out, the crowd shouted, "No! No! No!" outraged that an English girl had won. I stood on the stage holding my trophy nervously. The judge whispered,

"Do you know the back way out? I'd get a taxi quick if I were you."

Since I wanted be slim for salsa performances, I upped my fitness routine. I biked the thirty minutes from Islington to

Covent Garden to do the 6.30 a.m. circuit class in the gym. Then I lifted weights before arriving in the office still dressed in black dancer sweat pants and trainers. As long as my sales figures were high, my boss didn't care what I wore—I could easily change into a suit for client meetings. After work, I biked back to Islington, then headed out at ten to dance salsa. I was home by 2 a.m. to have a salad supper in the bath, often falling asleep with lettuce leaves floating around me in the tepid water.

I discovered a magical place called Circus Space a couple of streets away from my flat. Back in 1992, Circus Space wasn't the impressive and official National Centre for Circus Arts it is now. Then it was just an old timber yard with rickety steps, leading up to a makeshift café. There was Jake in his bowler hat making tea, and his girlfriend Jo, with a purple Mohican, cooking up a veggie stew. The seats in the café were old packing crates topped with Indian embroidered cushions. You could sit on a crate and have a cup of tea in a chipped mug with a homemade flapjack. Next door was a small studio, one wall covered with mirrors. Next to that was a huge space rigged for trapeze, with trampolines, crash mats and climbing ropes. There were belly-dancing, stilt-walking classes and clown workshops. Tuesday evening was juggling night: thirty jugglers concentrating hard, the air full with clubs and balls. To me, Circus Space felt like a doorway to a magical world.

When I took my first holiday from BT, I booked myself onto a two-week clown course there. Sitting in a circle on the first day, we offered each other our names: Flipflap, Rainbow, Pickins, Zoltowski. I needed a cool name too. I'd always felt the thoroughly nice but normal name my parents had given me wasn't really mine.

On a visit home a week later, I said to my mum and dad,

"I need a name that's me. I need you to give me my proper name."

"Romany," my father said.

Romany, a travelling gypsy dancing in the forest, just like the beautiful girl on my tambourine. Perfect. I told British Telecom that I was now to be called Romany, and to my surprise and their credit, they changed my details without a blink.

7

WHIZ, BANG, KAPUT

*T*hree years after I began work with BT, things began to get weird. I was sitting in my car outside my client's office. I had a business appointment with their data manager to discuss new video conferencing technology, or something. I'd been there for ten minutes. But when I looked out of my car window, my heart beat faster, and it was strangely hard to breathe. I felt as fragile as thin glass. It was time for the meeting, but nothing in me wanted to open the car door. If I stepped outside, a stray gust of wind might shatter me. I imagined myself as a pile of shards on the pavement. The world outside seemed uncontrollable—the air dangerous. I sat for another five minutes. I couldn't move. Now I was late for the meeting.

It didn't matter—I wasn't going anyway.

From the safe world inside my car, I phoned my business contact and told him that traffic was terrible. Could we reschedule? If he had looked out of his window, he would have seen me parked on the pavement below, staring at the windscreen at nothing, waiting for my feeling of panic to subside so I could start the engine and go home.

A few days later in the office, I made a list of everything I needed to do for my clients. It was a long list. I stared at the paper, watching the words swim and muddle. Age twenty-five, I'd been fast-track promoted to be the BT account manager for three major international pharmaceutical companies and was responsible for a whole heap of apparently important stuff. How had it got to this when all I ever wanted was to be like Judy Garland?

The simple answer was that it had happened while I wasn't paying attention to what my soul knew better. When a senior guy in sales had a heart attack caused by stress and died, my BT business mentor recommended me to replace him. My mentor stared at me glassy-eyed over a boozy lunch, took another gulp of red wine and slurred, "I've got just the job for you."

I'd been a people pleaser all my life and I wanted to be the best account manager ever. But since stress had literally killed off my predecessor, everything was in a right old mess. I rolled up my sleeves and got to work, but the workload was far too much for one person. There wasn't any time to go dancing; juggling evenings at Circus Space were a thing of the past. I spent longer and longer days in the office, working against the clock.

At my desk, the phone rang. It was my client from a major international healthcare company that supplied hospitals. He sounded frantic.

"One hundred of our emergency incoming telephone lines are down."

"*What?*"

"One hundred of our emergency incoming lines are down. What the hell is going on?"

I wanted to run. I wanted to run far away and fast. My heart hammered—I felt sick. I didn't know what to do. I called our customer service section.

"Hi, I'm Romany. I'm the account manager for Roche. Their lines are down. What's going on?"

"Oh yeah, there's been a problem." *You don't say.*

"When is it going to be fixed?"

"Well, it's Friday and the guys are clocking off soon, so the lines will be back working on Monday."

Fuck. If it sounds like something written by John Cleese, it wasn't funny. Twenty years later, even now, my heart jumps nervously when the phone rings and that same powerless nervous feeling jangles in the pit of my stomach.

Finally, just before I needed to leave for a meeting in Paris to close a major deal, I physically couldn't open my own hotel door. From the inside.

This might sound crazy, but it's true. I stood in front of the door, intending to go out, staring at the handle. My brain gave the usual instruction to my arm, but my body refused. I sat on the hotel bed and stared at the wall. My mind was empty. In the mirror, I could see my reflection, but I didn't recognise my own face. It was all very strange and not much fun.

After the inter-mind-body competition over the door handle had been resolved, I arrived late to the meeting. I pretended to take notes but actually I was scribbling in Italian—I figured no one could read that over my shoulder—that I was obviously cracking up and needed a holiday.

My team was a hard-nut ambitious group of successful male managers. They usually started with the beers at lunch time, continued drinking after work and personal problems weren't discussed. When my boss asked me how things were going, I would reply brightly,

"Great, thank you. Everything's going great."

I asked for three weeks' leave.

As soon as I took a break, the tidal wave of anxiety I'd been keeping at bay swept in and knocked me way off normal. My 'fight or flight' levels went through the roof and my arms throbbed with nervous tension. I wanted to run but at the same time I couldn't move. Doctors prescribed beta blockers, and when they had no effect, they put me on three times the normal dose of Prozac. I couldn't use the telephone, I couldn't drive or talk to anyone except my parents. If I did manage to get into a car and go somewhere, I couldn't get out again when I arrived, and the idea of meeting anyone made me want to dive straight back under the duvet for a week.

This behaviour might seem odd, but it doesn't seem remotely strange to me. I've had those same feelings, although in a milder way, for the last twenty years. I often get a message on my phone and can't face returning the call. I will call back, but it will take more effort than it would for me to step on stage in front of hundreds of people. Leaving the house is still often tricky. I can measure the well-being of my mental health by whether I can cycle to the local fruit and veg market or not. It's only fifteen minutes by bike, the market is friendly and it's nice to chat to the stall holders who know me. But some days the fridge stares back at me, white and empty, because getting there is just too much. I know—weird. But everyone who has felt the same will understand. Anxiety is a twisty, tenacious parasite. Once it's got its subtle pincers into your thoughts, into the make-up of your body, it can make you behave in all sorts of unusual ways. The idea of calling an agent to promote myself still gives me the same overwhelming feelings of anxiety. So I don't. I wait for them to call me. It's not great for business.

Back to British Telecom. My holiday leave granted, I shut my briefcase on the urgent problems of my clients and went to live with my parents. My world shrank to my childhood room with the green wallpaper dancing with fairies.

Agoraphobia is not fear of open spaces but of anything causing stress. For me, just then, that was everything and everyone.

My parents were bewildered and upset. I'd gone from having a successful career and winning dancing championships to not being able to leave the house or talk to my friends. My father didn't say much, but I knew he was angry—not with me, but with whatever or whoever it was that had caused his precious only daughter to lose the plot.

My sales manager lived in our small town. He came to visit me at home. While I sat silently on the sofa, he chattered on about the team's strong sales figures and business opportunities. He talked cheerfully and sat in an armchair, holding a bone china cup of tea in one hand, the saucer with its delicate sprigs of pink flowers in the other, balancing a plate with a half-eaten fairy cake on his thigh. My father watched him with a strange expression. Suddenly my dad stood up, towering over my boss who stopped talking, surprised.

In the silence, against the elegant backdrop of my mother's posh cream wall-paper and Lladró figurines, my father spoke quietly. "Before you say another word, I have something to say." My boss stared. "What you don't seem to understand is that my daughter started work with you as a happy, capable young woman. Now she can't even use the bloody telephone, let alone sell one. You don't have a clue how to treat your staff. You should be ashamed of yourself, not sit there babbling about business opportunities. We don't give a damn about your sales figures. If you've got nothing better to say, I think you'd better leave."

Ah, that was a great moment—the moment when your dad sticks it to your boss. And your boss has no defence and nothing to say.

My manager continued to stare, open-mouthed and astonished. No one moved. He put his cup, saucer and plate of half-eaten cake carefully on the mahogany side table. The noise of china on wood sounded loud in the silence. He picked up his jacket, excused himself hastily and left.

We all felt a little better after that.

But it wasn't really my manager's fault.

I haven't given you the complete picture. You're missing a piece of the puzzle: the real catalyst, the slowly smouldering fuse, something I've kept secret for thirty-five years. Thirty-five years is a long time to keep a secret, even for a magician.

Maybe because I'll be fifty on my next birthday—maybe it's the thought that my mother died aged fifty-seven—maybe the current of #metoo makes me more aware of the importance of honesty. If by speaking up I can help the thousands of people, mainly women, who struggle with similar issues, it will be an honour. I'm through the worst—this isn't about me anymore.

Shame, sharp as broken glass, whispers urgently, *Don't tell.* Shame whispers again, louder this time: *Don't do this. You'll destroy your life, you'll lose your friends, the respect of your colleagues. You'll be misunderstood and criticised, nothing will ever be the same again.*

I hear that serpent voice, as I have always heard, but I ignore it. Shame whispers again with accurate barbs of well-aimed scorn, *Who do you think you are? Do you really think your life can help anyone? Do you think that anyone is even interested? You'd better shut up now before you ruin everything. I'm warning you, you have no idea of how bad it will be.*

Hello Shame. I know you well. I've listened to your shabby whispers and taken your coward's advice for so many years—too many years. But now? I'm not interested in your opinion anymore. We're done, it's over. If my true story helps one person, just one, whatever I lose will be worth it. And to Fear, who has just jumped up from his comfy seat on the sofa, I say, "How bad can it be? What are they going to do, shoot me?"

Well, in America, Fear replies, *they just might.*

Here goes.

Since I was a little girl, I'd understood that I was the wrong shape. Age five, a shopkeeper said to my mother,
"She's a chubby little girl."
"What does chubby mean?" I asked, curiously.
"Big boned," my mother replied.
From her barely veiled tone of distaste, my little five-year-old self understood that 'big boned' was something to be ashamed of. I felt the first sharp sting of shame. For some reason I didn't understand, there was something about my body that was wrong.

Eight years old, perched on top of a pile of green mats in the school gym cupboard, I stared with distaste at my pink and white mottled thighs. I couldn't come out of the cupboard because the teacher would think I was fat. The tops of my thighs rubbed together when I walk and I hated them. In ballet class, I didn't want to do jumps because I jiggled when I jumped. When my father chucked me affectionately under the chin, I assumed he is pointing out how chubby I was. I hated that word. I furiously batted his hand away.

My mother was tall and slender and made sure she kept that way by weighing herself every morning and cutting down if she weighed a pound over nine stone. I take after my father and am sturdy, with a healthy appetite and a sweet tooth. Mum assumed the responsibility to police my eating. When I got home from school, there would be two Ryvita crisp-breads waiting for me on a plate with a slick of marmalade. My brother, who was two years older and tall and skinny, was allowed homemade chocolate cake and to heap sugar on his cornflakes.

Did you know there are two sides of Ryvita? One side is smooth and designed to make sure you only put on the thinnest smear of butter and the other is bumpy and designed for people who don't give a damn. Of course, I never put butter on Ryvita during my childhood, because we were in the age of Jane Fonda, the grapefruit and the hip and thigh diet. Butter was the devil's spread—forbidden.

I was six when I started to steal food. I woke up in the middle of the night and thought, *chocolate cake.* I tiptoed downstairs, gently—gently down each step, holding my breath, avoiding the stair that creaked. Noiselessly, I smoothed on the dining room light. The dining room had hideous seventies vinyl wallpaper with giant orange flowers on the obligatory brown background, a pine dining table and oatmeal bobbly carpet.

At six, I could jump onto the kitchen work surface easily, open the cupboard and take down the biscuit tin, with its pink and purple flowers, ease the lid up slowly—slowly holding it tight to my chest so that it opened silently. Mmmm, biscuits: Jammy Dodgers, Custard Creams and Ginger Nuts, but my favourite ones were Chocolate Bourbons. I nibbled off the top, then licked the cream slowly in the middle. I sat on the floor with my back to the warm radiator reading an Enid Blyton book. Cosy and warm, I munched through my pile of stolen biscuits, happily lost in the adventures of 'The Famous Five.'

A couple of years later, when I asked for a snack, my mother would say, "If you're hungry, eat an apple." But I craved sugar. Sugar. When her back was turned, I ate teaspoons of white sugar straight from the bowl. My grandmother watched her figure too. I remember asking for a glass of milk while she was in the kitchen. When Mum went to the fridge to pour me a glass, nana asked, "Isn't she too old to be drinking milk? Won't she get fat?"

But I wasn't fat. Looking back at photos of me then, I don't know why I even thought I was. Still, the feeling of being too big grew.

Roll on puberty. Enter Jane Fonda in her leotard: jutting hip bones, lean as fuck. Who could ever get to be that perfect shape?

I tried. Every morning, I got up early before school and did the Jane Fonda fitness video, or the one with the wafer-thin Callanetics lady in her tiny peach-coloured leotard. I watched their perfect tight bodies with envy. I wanted mine to look like that. I meticulously wrote down everything I ate in my Jane Fonda food diary. My diet was the diet of the 1980s: Ryvita, Granny Smith apples, salad and lean skinless chicken breasts. I got a little slimmer but never enough—never as thin as Jane Fonda or peachy-bottomed Miss Callanetics.

On Sunday for tea, there were sandwiches and homemade cakes and roll mop herrings. Mmmm, the smell of cheese toasting on the grill was so tempting. I wanted to eat it all, just as my brother did, but I wanted to look like Jane Fonda more. Treacle sponge pudding and hot custard vs Jane Fonda. My plate featured three dry-as-a-bone Ryvita crackers and two low-fat cheese triangles, a couple of tomatoes and only the smallest slither of cake, which sizzled in my mouth like the devil's food.

I wanted more than anything to be a dancer, and since a dancer needs to be slim, my mother tried to help. She put the family biscuits in a cupboard in the garage with a padlock on the door. She numbered her homemade butterfly cakes in the freezer, writing the number on each bag so that she knew how many there were. My father worked for a burglar alarm company, and my parents routinely set the alarm for the downstairs rooms each night. After finding me in the kitchen making toast, they locked the kitchen door and hid the key.

Age thirteen, being a highly skilled food thief with seven years' experience, I would creep down until I reached the hall cupboard and turn off the alarm. Then I would enter the kitchen, not by the locked door but through the dining room, which had a hatch I could climb through. Softly, softly, I would turn the backdoor key and creep out into the cold garage, bare feet on the gritty concrete floor. I would ease open the freezer, quietly—quietly.

Who cared if the butterfly cakes were numbered? With the focus of a jewel thief, I could remove the wings and with a sharp knife and slice a little coffee butter icing and sponge from each cake before replacing the wings with a bit of lick.

But it wasn't fun any more like it used to be when I was six. Now, I woke up in the night and heard the addict's call with dread. I'd much rather have stayed warm in bed than run that dangerous trip downstairs. One little noise might wake my parents—then the game would be up and the gestapo questioning would start.

"What are you doing downstairs? What have you taken? How many?"

"Three."

"There were six in the packet."

"Five?"

"Who ate the last one? Pixies?"

At seventeen, when I was two stone overweight, I read a book, or maybe it was a magazine article, about eating disorders. I read how some people would eat and then make themselves sick. A normal person would think, *Disgusting. Why would you do that?* I thought, *Genius.*

There I was, seventeen years old; not only could I steal food for England, but I could throw it up afterwards and stay at the same weight. Result: here was the dual life; the binary self. One ate Ryvita and carrots, salads and fruit, the other ate family packs of Diary Milk chocolate, entire packets of biscuits, a whole cake or a loaf at a time.

But now, every mouthful tasted of panic and guilt and shame.

"Please make me thin," I pleaded every night in the dark to a God who wasn't listening, my pillow wet with tears. It's the only thing I prayed for. "Please make me thin."

But I wasn't thin; I was sturdy, solid, robust. *Chubby.* Oh, that word. If that word were a person, I'd stab him deep in the kidneys. Then I'd stab him again and give him a solid kicking for good measure.

By the time I went to university, life was a daily un-merry, merry-go-round: exercise, binge, throw up, sleep, repeat. I tried taking laxatives, but after swallowing an entire packet of raspberry-flavoured ones, I got such extreme stomach pains that I honestly thought I was going to die and never took them again. I did two or three aerobics classes a day, desperately high-kicking, spotty-dog and grapevining. I kept myself busy and as far away from food as possible. At night, I was so hungry, my resolve would fail. By midnight, when everyone else was asleep, I would give up, give in and stuff down the contents of my kitchen cupboard or anyone else's.

After throwing it all back up as quickly as I could before it had the chance to add more unwanted inches to my hips, I went to sleep, exhausted and hating myself more than ever. I set my alarm early so I could get to the shops to replace the biscuits or cereal that I'd stolen from my flatmates before they noticed. It wasn't fun. My throat was raw, my skin grey and my eyes desperate. I wasn't even thin. That's the bitter irony of bulimia; the slim figure you chase is as elusive as the wind. All those aerobic classes that gave me shin splints, all that effort and I was still overweight. I hated myself so much that I could have taken a knife and cut bits off.

The only person who knew my secret was my mum, who told my dad. We didn't talk about it.

Of course, my mother was horrified when she first found out what I was doing. She'd heard suspicious noises in the bathroom, and when I finally came out, she demanded an explanation—and then ordered me to stop.

If only it were that easy. This demon of mine had gathered strength steadily through childhood, and there was no stopping it now. From the moment I woke to the last thing before sleep, a steady stream of thoughts looped in my head: *You're fat, you're useless, you're ugly, you can't even stop eating, you're ruining your life.*

If anyone knew what you do, they would say you were disgusting. You are disgusting!

My mother blamed herself and felt terrible, but she didn't know what to do. She didn't understand my behaviour and she couldn't tell anyone because bulimia was taboo. No one talked about it then; it was only later that Princess Diana was one of the first public figures to admit having it, and when she did, people were shocked and highly critical.

Mum arranged an appointment for us both to see my GP. As if I wasn't even in the room, the doctor said, "Cut her bloody hands off. That'll stop her."

I've forgiven nearly everything and anyone in my life, but I haven't let go of that. I was an overweight seventeen-year-old with low self-esteem, newly caught in a highly addictive, self-abusive behaviour. When my mother and I reached out for professional understanding and help, that doctor was needlessly cruel. I can still see the hard scorn in his eyes, hear the biting tone of his voice, his complete lack of sympathy. That memory gives me a steely resolve to speak up for young women who meet the same lack of compassion and who believe that their behaviour deserves derision, not support. The fact is that bulimia is one of the hardest eating disorders to treat. There isn't a simple solution, believe me. I know, I've tried every type of 'cure' there is.

The student health centre at university offered cognitive behavioural therapy. Sensible stuff, but it didn't help me. There was a group for anorexics at church. They told me that the nasty voice in my head was the devil and offered to pray for me. In their eating disorder help group, the normal-size bulimic girls looked at the larger compulsive eaters with horror and at the pale, listless anorexic nervosa girls with sad pity. The compulsives looked at all the rest with envy, and the waif-thin nervosa girls were too ill and exhausted to care about anyone else.

I went to a women's self-help group and listened to the

women's painful stories of rape and abuse week after week. I didn't speak because with my happy middle-class childhood and loving parents, nothing in my life came close to their suffering. When I started work at BT, my private health insurance paid for two years of weekly sessions of psychotherapy. I was offered hospital in-patient treatment, but that would mean over-exercising would be forbidden, so there was no way I was going to agree to that. I told my gentle, silent therapist about my dreams of theatre and magic and my childhood ambition to be a performer. He said I was living in a fantasy world.

At twenty-five, after trying everything else, in desperation, I found a centre that treated both heroin addicts and eating disorders. I walked in after work, week after week, in my dark-blue line-of-least-resistance suit. I slipped off my high heels and sat on the floor with the other addicts. They put acupuncture needles in our ears and gave us a bowl of porridge. Tasty, but I wasn't sure how that was meant to help. I stared enviously at the pale and listless heroin addicts. *At least they're bloody thin*, I thought. That didn't work either.

There was nothing left to try; my life was a desperate, constant round of starving, eating, throwing up, cycling and dancing for hours and hours each day. Finally, I got to the point where one apple was more than I could stomach without it seeming too much and I would have to throw it up. I had deep tooth-mark scars on the knuckle of my right hand, permanent chipmunk cheeks from swollen glands and even though the constant throwing up gave me nosebleeds and dizzy spells, I couldn't stop. When I looked at my still-plump face in the mirror, my reflection stared back desperate and frightened.

I was twenty-five years old and apparently successful, with my impressive job and salary. Trying to burn more calories, I danced wildly through every night like a frantic skeleton in a weird danse macabre.

"Dance faster!" I would order Anuar, digging my fingernails viciously into his forearms, carving red curves into his brown skin. "Dance faster!"

I was killing myself slowly but surely, and I couldn't do a damn thing about it.

8

LET ME TELL YOU WHERE YOU CAN STICK IT

*I*t wasn't surprising that with all this going on, the machine would overheat and blow a gasket. And it did.

After being signed off on permanent sick leave for stress, I was back at home at my parents' house. Broken and busted. All my springs sprung out. Stuck in a small cage, I could see out but I couldn't get out. It was a strange place to be. I sat on the edge of my single bed in my childhood room and watched the closed door. If I stared at the knots in the wood long enough, they started to shift and move. I examined the groove of the panelling, the walnut-brown, smooth Bakelite doorknob. It had four screws.

Two months passed. One thing was clear. I was stuck here paralysed because, and only because, I'd listened to everyone else's opinion as to what I should do with my life. Everyone—my parents, teachers and those smart corporate recruitment people who came to my university—told us that getting a good education, a top job and owning a house with a mortgage and pension plan was what counts. They were wrong.

Siting on my bed, it became clear to me that I had known best all along. My five-year-old self tip-tapping behind my mother in the supermarket knew, my ten-year-old self high-kicking and reciting poetry in the living room, my fifteen-year-old self dancing joyfully on stage in the Queen's theatre—they could have told me easily that a business career selling telephones and data systems was never going to make my spirit soar.

Inside, I was furious for not listening to myself—furious with everyone else for thinking they knew best. Yes, a career in the arts is a school of hard knocks. Yes, there are more dancers, actors, musicians and artists out there than there are jobs. It's precarious

 to follow a dream; I wouldn't advise anyone to do it unless they will die if they don't. Not following my dream had almost killed me, that's for sure.

In my little childhood room, still watching the closed door, my resolve grew. Soon, when my broken mind had mended, when I had gathered my strength, I would be ready to take up my sword, slash my way through twisted forests, fight fiery dragons and do whatever it took to find my joy.

Now I was determined. *You can stick your corporate job, your generous salary and dark-blue suit of frickin' least resistance where the sun don't shine because I, Jack, ain't interested.*

For the next year, I lived within the restrictive confines of agoraphobia. The super-high dosage of Prozac I was taking (three times the normal amount is commonly prescribed for bulimia) took the edge off, but electricity still ran up and down my arms in a weird, useless sort of way, and my heart raced whenever the telephone rang. If I wanted to meet a friend, they had to collect me from my house and then we could go out together. After six months, I moved back to my house-share in London. With all the free time I had, I wandered around Covent Garden, watching the street performers and feeling a little better as each month passed. I worried that someone from my office might see me and think that I was faking. I wasn't, but that's the thing with mental health, you just can't tell from appearances. With a bubbly personality and quick sense of humour, people assume that I am a happy-go-lucky, positive person. That's nice and it's certainly true more now than it was then, but an outward smile doesn't always reflect the inside. Ever since the crash of that year, I've had to take it gently, keep my pace slow, look after my mind. Once the neurological paths to anxiety have opened, they're impossible to close.

But here is some good news. The good news is that the path away from anxiety is the exact same path to joy. Finding and doing what makes you happy is the way—the only way out. Which is why, a year after cracking up and taking sick leave, I found myself in a long black gown, scarlet lipstick, eyelashes and heels, being tied up and put in a sack in front of a large audience in Austria.

While I was still working in the BT office in Covent Garden, I went to evening classes at the adult education centre near our office. I signed up for a magic class and became great friends with Mick Dow, the magic teacher. He'd told me he was planning to take his magic show to a street performing festival in Austria. He had an escape illusion he wanted to work on and needed a partner. I asked if I could go with him. After a difficult couple of months, I couldn't think of anything better than to be tied up, locked in a box and spring out—*ta-da!*—to astonished applause.

Mick came to stay at my parent's house while we built the props for the street festival. We worked all day in the garage, building a large trunk and thinking up ideas for the show. While Mick showed me how to use a drill and bang nails, I was happy. Or maybe it was the Prozac. Whatever the reason, the door of my cage was open when I was talking magic with Mick. He could tap-dance, make balloon animals, was a brilliant magician and didn't seem to notice that I had lost my marbles.

Our show was ready a couple of months later, and that summer we drove to Austria, heading for the Pflasterspektakel festival in Linz. I still had my company car while on sick leave, and we slept in it every night, pushing the seats back as far as they could go, feet on the dashboard, socks de-fumigating on the bonnet, Mick snoring loudly.

The street festival in Linz is a wondrous thing. It still happens every year. A hundred groups of street performers and musicians from over thirty countries take over the town for one whole week in July. Two hundred thousand visitors—*two hundred thousand!*—watch acrobats, jugglers and acoustic bands perform in each and every corner of the medieval town.

When we arrived after two long days of driving, we headed for the festival headquarters to unload our props. All sorts of odd-looking people were wandering about, mostly performers judging by their creative hair, muscles and tattoos. As I helped Mick unpack and re-build our magic box, I sensed someone watching me. I straightened up and saw a tall, slim, lightly tanned man with long, chestnut brown hair, wearing mid-length tie-dye shorts and an orange vest. He walked over and held out a single flower with a cheeky smile. A dandelion. *Gigolo*, I thought. I've always been suspicious of good-looking men. He introduced himself. His name was Martin. He was German and a juggler.

I blushed, took the flower and then turned my back on him to continue helping Mick re-build our box.

During the festival, each artiste had a set time and place to perform. The schedule for the hundred groups was run with military precision, despite the appearance of spontaneity in the streets. When it was time for our shows, we changed into costume in the headquarters. It was a tight squeeze with so many performers; as I pulled on my tights and hopped about to find my other shoe, three Czech cavemen acrobats were wriggling into their leopard-skin loincloths, the German one-man-band couple were strapping on their cymbals noisily and Rumpelstiltskin from Australia was peering into a mirror held between his knees, trying to fix on his rubber nose.

Mick and I trundled our heavy trunk illusion over the cobbles to our pitch: past the acrobats standing on each other's shoulders in bright blue Lycra; past the oom-pah band in lederhosen and funny green tweed hats. We had a trolley, but it was still a bumpy pull. I had a floor-length black dress with long pointy sleeves, diamonds around my neck and a cascading black hairpiece. I red-rouged my lips and outlined my eyes with heavy black kohl on top of false eyelashes. I looked like Snow White's step-mother. The journey wasn't easy in heels.

When we reached our pitch, we unloaded the magic trunk and started to set up the rest of the show as flamboyantly as possible to attract a crowd, dancing about as we put out the props. Our crowd built, and we performed a few easy rope tricks, then Mick tore a newspaper into small pieces. A breath, a magical gesture and—*hey presto!*—it was back together again. I was still new to magic, and this miracle amazed me every time.

Mick then bound me hand and foot with chains, bundled me into a canvas sack and lifted me into our wooden box. Inside the box, I wriggled out of the sack. No, I can't tell you how. I enjoyed a blissful five minutes of dark and calm as Mick locked the trunk shut with more chains and a large padlock. Two volunteers from the crowd checked the locks.

Inside my box, I listened happily to the crowd responding to Mick and felt smug. I was very pleased with myself. I might be knotted in a sack in a padlocked box in Austria, but I'd escaped the chains of corporate bondage. This might not be Broadway, but it would do for now.

After a dramatic pause, Mick jumped on the lid, winked at the crowd and lifted the heavy red velvet curtain high above his head with both hands. A moment of breath-held suspense and then *surprise!* It was me standing on the box in his place, victorious and free. Mick had vanished. A miracle.

I stood smiling at the huge circle of astonished people, who burst into loud applause. This was my moment. I milked it for every second of the joy it contained. If only my BT boss could have seen me then.

At night, after the shows were done, my new friends gathered in a pub that had a little stage in its basement. We performed for each other all over again, crowded together in a small room that smelt of beer and sausages. On the tiny stage, a group of beautiful blonde Czech girls sang complicated four-part harmonies, a little fat bald man from Bavaria dressed in lederhosen played the flute with his nose, and Mick did some card tricks. I watched, captivated—entranced. This world delighted me. I felt safe. My therapist had told me that the theatrical world I dreamt to be a part of was a fantasy. He was wrong. I felt warm, happy and home.

And then the handsome German juggler who gave me a flower that morning asked if I would like to go for a walk with him in the warm night. *Why not?* I thought.

The town was sleeping as we walked on cobbles through the narrow streets in the moonlight. We chatted easily; his English was perfect. We found ourselves in a small park and sat on the grass under the trees. I watched a cloud go past the bright moon in the night sky. Everything was magical.

Looking at me earnestly, Martin the German juggler said, "I think I love you."

That was the first time anyone had ever said those words to me. I looked down at the grass and pulled out a few stems. Then I pulled out a few more.

Everyone should fall in love the big way at least once. That summer was my once. My mother always said she couldn't imagine the man who would ever fall in love with me. She couldn't have imagined my German juggler. Martin was soft-hearted, generous, idealistic. A slow-speaking dreamer. Long limbed, tanned, athletic. A talented performer. My heart beat fast and my skin tingled whenever I thought about him.

Mick wasn't as impressed.

We did three shows a day for three days, pulling that heavy box between pitches over the cobbles. Once locked inside the trunk, I had to work my way out of the sack, escape from chains and exchange places with Mick in seconds while wearing a full-length tight satin dress with long, flappy sleeves and high heels. The sun was hot—the inside of the box was hotter—and I developed a vivid purple bruise five inches across on my left bum cheek. Don't ask me how. There wasn't much time to spend with Martin. We snatched brief passionate kisses in corners, and when I had those five whole minutes locked in the box, I thought about him dreamily.

When the final shows in Linz were over, most of our performer friends, including Martin, travelled to another festival in an Austrian town called Villach to do it all over again. The town paid travel, food and lodging, and the artists put out their hats at the end of their shows.

Since Martin and I hadn't spent much time alone in Linz, when we got to Villach, he invited me out on our first official date. It might have been a nice romantic evening, if it hadn't been a Sunday night in a remote Austrian town where there was only one restaurant open. We sat in the corner at a table for two while the whole gang of our artist friends lounged in a huge group on the other side of the room, laughing at us and waving. The menu was in German. Martin ordered for me. He mentioned an article on mindfulness where they suggest meditating in silence over your food for five minutes before eating it using your fingers. When our meal arrived, we stared down at our plates in silence. As I contemplated its texture and colour, the beautiful contours of the deep purple sauerkraut swam. The red of the halved plum tomatoes was solid and vibrant. We gave thanks and carefully picked up morsels with our hands. The grease on the breadcrumb-fried schnitzel coated my fingers; Martin reached over and, lifting them to his lips, kissed them gently. A whoop went up from our friends across the room. He quickly dropped my hand, embarrassed.

After three days in Villach, we were all going to yet another festival in a town called Feldkirch. By now, Martin and I were inseparable and woozy in love.

Mick and I performed our street show three times a day again for three days in Feldkirch. There was a competition, with prize money and a performance of the winners in the town square on the final night. Every star must have been in its right place because Martin won first place and Mick and I came third. Under the starry night sky, in a fairy-tale town, we performed in front of the whole town on a huge stage in the main square. We stood together in the finale: me, Mick and Martin in the gleam of the moon and the magical spotlight, everyone cheering and throwing flowers. So happy, so much magic. Perfect.

But perfect doesn't last for long.

9

FLIP, FLAP, FLOP

That summer I fell in love against a backdrop of an amazing technicolour film set. Street shows, apple streusel and bitter coffee in Austrian cafés, Chitty Chitty Bang Bang cobble street-towns, long road-trips through mountain tunnels, funny little Austrian hotels. Crisp air mornings and languorous, hot afternoons when the whole gang of artistes decamped to the nearby lake to flip somersaults and juggle in swimsuits on the grassy bank. Cool freshwater swims in the glass-smooth lake, turning on our backs to gaze at the mountains all around. Back to the streets for more shows every evening. Smiling crowds, hats full of shilling notes, and afterwards late-night feasts on Vienna schnitzel and salty chips in paper. Idyllic in my memory.

When the summer and the festivals were over, it was time to go home. At the station, I detached myself from Martin with a firm promise to meet in Germany in a couple of weeks. Mick and I drove back to England.

Now I had no doubts. I was determined that I was going to earn my living as a performer. I was twenty-six, too old to train as a dancer or even as an actress. I'd missed out on stage school. I'd tried stilt-walking, salsa dancing and street-performing, none of which was going to pay my rent. But I had a plan.

Circus Space had outgrown its ramshackle but lovingly created first home in Camden and become an official circus training school in a former power station in Hoxton. It was about to run its very first National Diploma in Performing Arts course. This was my chance. This was my big chance to train properly and start a new career. At precisely what, I wasn't sure, but I would think about that later. I auditioned, and despite being at least eight years older than everyone else and having scant ability in gymnastics, I was one of twenty new students chosen out of hundreds of hopefuls. The two-year course was to start in October.

Meanwhile, in September, my trade union took my BT management to court, claiming my stress was due to their neglect of care. But my case was thrown out and my sick leave pay cancelled. Work-caused anxiety wasn't taken seriously back then. I gave back the company car a week before the circus course began. I couldn't have been happier.

And of course, now there was Martin. My mother, seeing that I was smitten, asked, "Do you love him?"

"I do, Mum, I think he's the one."

She took a wad of cash out of her knicker drawer. Giving me a chunk, she said, "Well, you'd better go get him then." I did. My visit to Hamburg was as romantic as our time in Austria, and when I left, he promised to come visit me as soon as I was settled on my new course.

On the first day, I sat in the café with the other new circus students drinking coffee. I was twenty-six; the others were between sixteen and eighteen, all different, all circus-cool. Amy had large Chinese symbols, 'courage' and 'tenacity,' tattooed above the nape of her neck on her shaved head. She had piercings in her eyebrows and a steel ball bearing in her tongue, which clicked against her teeth. In class, when the teacher wasn't looking, she practiced sticking a pencil down her throat to train her gag reflex to relax. Amy became the World Guinness Book of Records record holder for sword-swallowing, and as Miss Behave, she blazes an impressive trail around the world with her own successful show.

Emma trained on the trapeze after our classes were over. The calluses on her hands were yellow and thick. She had a bright loopy smile and green streaks in her chestnut hair. She and Joe, a guy in our group, fell in love. They were inseparable, sharing their collection of scruffy, brightly coloured hoodies, sitting close, eating tuna sandwiches made with sliced white bread. After the course, Emma was killed when a trapeze rig fell on top of her. She was only twenty-four.

Luke was skinny and light, with jet-black hair and wiry arms, and was one one of the best jugglers I'd ever seen. When not juggling, his hands were busy with a pack of cards. He spent long hours practicing with Ilka, weaving intricate patterns with their white clubs. Ilka, from Germany, had a shock of purple hair hanging over her eyes and the sides of her head shaved. She was also a passionate juggler, hardworking, abrupt and determined. They went on to create a beautiful inventive act together and performed in variety theatres all over the world. But Luke got lung cancer just before his thirtieth birthday and, never having smoked in his life, suffered a short painful illness and died. Two gone out of twenty.

Every morning, we started with three hours of gymnastics. It had been at least twenty years since I'd done a backwards roll; I'd forgotten how to start. I stood with my back to the royal-blue line of mats and wondered what bit of me I should bend first. We cartwheeled the entire length of a long line of mats then sprinted back to the start and did it all over again. Emile, our Bulgarian coach, wearing his usual white t-shirt that showed off his firm muscles, barked instructions,

"Stretch to ze sky, lengthen ze torso, spring from ze balls of ze feet, from ze balls, allez-oop!"

Then handstand forward rolls, then over to the trampoline to learn somersaults and finally the daily handstand competition to see who could stay upside down the longest. Never me.

Static trapeze next. We climbed up the rope and hung from our knees on a metal bar coated with cotton tape. This, I can tell you, gives you bruises—great big bruises all down the backs of your knees. Blisters too: on the palms of your hands, red raw, as large as pennies. I'd read that real circus artists peed on their hands as the quickest way to get them to form calluses. I peed on mine with great glee and showed everyone proudly.

I worked my butt off to keep up with everyone. As usual, I was watching my weight and struggling. I was still bulimic, still trying every diet, still exercising for hours; it seemed to be the only way. The rest of the students were effortlessly skinny. I appeared to be the wrong size for the circus, too. But apart from that chronic challenge, I was happy. I loved the daily, hard physical training and had the feeling that I was exactly where I wanted to be.

One day, three weeks into the course, I pulled a muscle in my neck while working on somersaults. It was hard work keeping up with my bendy, sixteen-year-old peers. As I cycled home, I could barely hold my head far enough up to keep an eye on the traffic.

Suddenly, I heard a loud crashing noise. In the same moment, I was knocked flying. When I came to, I was lying face down, sprawled flat on the road. The gravel on the ground was rough against my cheek, the white-painted line in the middle of the road felt smooth under my eye. I noticed the different coloured shoes of people crouched round me: light brown suede hush puppies, black boots with worn down heels. *What happened to my bicycle?* Everything hurt.

After a silent moment of shock, I started a sort of shouty wail. A woman's voice said, "Don't cry." Suddenly above my pain, I was furious.

You know what? I shouted at her —in my head —*I've been*

pretty good my whole life at not making a fuss, but now? This is when I get to fucking cry! And I did. Loudly.

The ambulance arrived and they lifted me gently inside. To stop me wailing, the paramedic asked, "What d'you do for a living, luv?"

"I'm a pole dancer." In that moment, I believed it—don't ask me why.

"Hey boys, this one's a pole dancer!" Well, that cheered them all up. "We'll have to come and see you when you're better," he said. The boys nodded enthusiastically.

In the hospital, lying on a bed in a side room with a broken shoulder, plus a broken wrist, a couple of fractured ribs and a banging concussion, I drifted in and out of pain, shivering with shock and cold. The doctors put me in plaster, gave me a plastic bag full of painkillers and called a taxi to drive me home.

That was that. Well, I sprayed my plaster cast gold and stuck on some glittering paste emeralds, but broken is broken. More than the physical pain, I was crushed with disappointment that I had to stop circus training. All my bright dreams smashed. I found out later from witnesses that I'd been hit by a white van coming fast in the opposite direction. He didn't stop. Hit and run. Thanks.

It would have been nice of the driver to wait to see if I were still alive, but he was obviously in a hurry with better things to do.

Anyway, I have my own theory about what really happened. I think he was on a contract. I think he was only following orders.

Huh?

Let me explain.

I've always had an image in my mind of my guardian angel sitting on the sofa waiting for me to give him instructions. He's a big burly angel, a bit of a bruiser, and the sofa is rather small. He's been sitting there, bored out of his brain when he hears the voice of a faint thought. Mine.

Hello? Is anybody there? My faint thought-voice asks. *If anyone is there, I'd just like to say that this corporate job thing isn't working out for me. I'd like to do something I love. I'd like to do something worthwhile. I'd like to be of use. And if there were some sequins and spotlights and feathers that would be great.*

Really? my angel asks, startled.

Really!

Angels don't muck about. Falling off his sofa in surprise, he gets to work. *Boom!* He spins the wheel at Telecom: stress and pressure increase. I spin off and find my way to the course at Circus Space, which is more or less in the right direction. But I'm never going to be any good at even climbing onto the trapeze, let alone flying on it. As usual I'm the wrong shape, but more than that, it's just not my thing. *Boff!* A nice little bike accident. Let's make sure she doesn't continue with circus; we'll break both sides of her body to make double sure she can't move much, just enough to practice a little prestidigitation. No dancing either, no circus training; she can sit still and learn magic. She doesn't know it yet, but magic is her destiny and path to her joy. Sequins and spotlights? No problem, wait right there.

10

BROKEN

*B*roken. Well and truly. Everything hurt—really hurt. I could just about walk. For three months, I could do little else but sit and practice the magic tricks I'd learn from Mick's class at the adult education centre. I bought more books on magic and studied them all day, every day, fascinated. I hired a private magic teacher. He would make something miraculously appear or vanish and then, while I was still reeling in wonder, ask, "Would you like to learn that?"

"*Wow!* Would I?" I practiced enthusiastically and couldn't wait for the next lesson. Four months after the accident, I went back to my course at Circus Space again. I practiced magic in my free time, and Martin and I took turns visiting each other every month.

In March, five months after the crash, while I was staying the weekend with Martin in Germany, the phone rang late at night. It was my dad.

"Mum's in hospital. She's got a brain tumour." Everything narrowed into sharp focus.

I flew home early the next morning. In the hospital, my mother lay sleeping. When she opened her eyes and saw me, she smiled. Then she remembered that I'd been in Germany and looked anxious.

"Oh, I didn't want you to come back. I didn't want you to worry." As if anything else could have been more important.

The doctor called my father, brother and me into his office. He told us that my mother had a fast-growing, inoperable brain tumour and six months to live. There was a chance that chemo and radiation might give her another couple of months, but it was unlikely.

There's not much you can say to that. We looked at each other in silence. My heart felt as if it had expanded in my chest, leaving my lungs less space for air.

I didn't think twice. I rang Circus Space to say that I was leaving the course. The most important thing now was to spend this precious time with my mother.

As anyone who has spent months with their dying loved ones knows: this time is sad and intense and blessed all at the same time. Blessed in the sense that if you focus on someone else, focus on making their life easier, ironically it can make you feel better. If you've got to save someone else from their burning bridge, you stop worrying about your own. During the few difficult months of chemo and radiotherapy, I sat by her bed, quietly practicing card and coin moves.

While my mother's health deteriorated, I paid a quick visit to Martin in Germany. We had been invited to a bonfire party in a little country village near Hamburg. A bright-yellow truck with one of those big scoops on the front was going in the direction of the party. We thought it would be fun to travel in the scoop. Not being overly bothered by health and safety, the driver agreed. We climbed up, ignoring the scratch of the dried mud at the bottom and snuggled in, all pleased with ourselves, looking out the top occasionally to wave at passing cars.

The truck stopped at the bonfire party and the driver got out to get a beer. We watched the fire, sitting high in our scoop under the stars.

"Will you marry me?" Martin asked.

Back then I was romantic and idealistic and still believed in happy ever after. Sitting in a yellow scoop with the bonfire below and bright shining stars above, I said, "Yes."

Yes, yes, yes.

11

AMAZING GRACE

When I approached my mother's bed in the hospice where she had been for the last few months, something was different. She had been sleeping for weeks now, lost in morphine. But that day, there was a feeling of lightness around her bed—something like those white clouds you see in a film version of heaven. Invisible but present all the same.

"You're in a state of grace today, aren't you?" I said. She didn't reply, as she hadn't in weeks. I didn't know if she'd heard me. I hoped she had.

The lady in the bed opposite was called Louise. She was only thirty, but also had terminal cancer. Louise was usually bright and bubbly and showed me the big lumps of multiple tumours all over her body. Some days she was not so cheerful and drew the dull green curtains around her bed.

A week before, hearing that I was an entertainer, she asked if I could bring in a costume she could wear to surprise her friends in the day room. I brought in my cream satin Pierrot costume with a ruffled frill around the neck and three large, blue sequin-covered buttons on the front. It had a matching conical hat with a dark-blue pompom on the top and a few tiny brass bells on the rim.

I was worried about my mother. I didn't feel like dressing

Louise in my costume that day, but I put on a smile, eased the cream silk smock over her head, pulled the elastic of the pointy hat under her chin and set her pom-pom straight. Pushing her in a wheelchair, we set off to the day room. Halfway there, I felt an imperative tug at my core to return to my mum. I left Louise at the day room and rushed back.

A nurse stood by her bed.

"This is probably it," she said.

The invisible white clouds around my mother seemed more tangible—there was grace here. I stood holding her hand, just us, my beautiful, gentle mother and me. She breathed more deeply, each breath longer. I felt only grateful; my heart swelled with love.

"Thank you," I whispered. "Thank you."

Soft gold descended around us. Gently, gently, she breathed one slow last breath. I could feel the great help around me—the beauty. I never imagined how full of grace this moment would be. Tears coursed down my face.

After my mother had passed and I sat by the bed, my father rushed in. He hadn't left my mother's side for months but had been persuaded that day to take a break and go for a swim in the local pool. A nurse had already told him the news. He asked me furiously, "What did you do?"

"Do?"

"Didn't you try to stop her?"

Which is why I think she chose me to be with her, willing her on, celebrating her passage, instead of her beloved husband, who couldn't bear to let her go.

I was twenty-seven when she died. My memory of my mother is of a gentle, often funny, self-diminishing woman, devoted to me and my happiness. Her husband and two children were the most precious thing in her life. Yes, the food thing all went badly wrong, but apart from that she loved me and did everything she could to help me. The thought that my unhappiness gave her ten years of anguish makes me incredibly sad. I would have got well for her if I could have. My biggest regret is that I never got to talk to her woman to woman, to find out more about her life. I was so busy trying to survive that I didn't have any extra attention for her. She would have loved to see me now, with a nice home of my own, Bongo the dog and gorgeous Johnny Walkabout. She would have loved to see my show or come as my guest on a cruise. I could have taken her to see Arctic penguins, Komodo dragons and Maasai warriors. I would have loved to have shown her my world.

12

STARTING OVER

After I crashed and burnt with BT, after I'd been smashed by the hit-and-run driver, after my mother's six-month illness and death, I needed to start over. I hired a van and packed it full, ready to begin a new life in Hamburg with Martin.

I didn't have a job or an income or any friends, and I didn't speak German. But Hamburg is a beautiful town. I had a bicycle, a boyfriend whom I adored and nothing to do but to work on my magic.

I was desperate to learn new tricks and visited the local magic club in Hamburg. One magician showed me a few slips of plain paper. As he blew on them, they turned to real money. As I almost dribbled with desire to know the secret, he put the notes back in his pocket and winked. *Bastard*. Magicians don't share their secrets easily. I didn't go back.

The Fédération Internationale des Sociétés Magiques (FISM) is an international magic convention held every three years in different countries, attended by thousands of magicians from all over the world. There were lectures and nightly shows, a huge colourful dealer hall selling magic of all descriptions, and for a whole week, the local bars were crammed full to the early hours with magicians fooling each other with complicated card tricks.

To my huge excitement, I discovered that that summer FISM was being held in Dresden, Germany. I asked if I could work as an interpreter in return for a free pass. My French and Italian were adequate, although my German was still basic. Someone agreed and I drove down. I didn't have enough money for a hotel, so I slept in my car, parked on the double yellow lines outside the convention centre, my glove compartment full of screwed-up parking tickets. I took a shower at the local swimming pool and cleaned my teeth in McDonald's.

At the convention, the organisers gave me and the rest of the support team a name tag, a blue waistcoat and a specific duty. My job was to stand outside the lecture rooms, keep an eye on the queue, then open the doors to let the magicians in at the right time, but as soon as I opened the doors, I ripped off my blue waistcoat and raced to sit gleefully in the middle seat of the front row.

I was a sponge, fresh to this fascinating world of stage magic, greedily drinking it all in. The best magicians in the world were there: Cellini, John Carney, David Williamson, Eugene Burger. Each had a nugget of gold to share. David Williamson, a giant comic genius, said something so important I've never forgotten it.

"Imagine if Michael Jackson or Meryl Streep were to perform just one trick. Imagine how they would polish it to the limit of its possibility. Take one trick. Make it your greatest gift to the audience. Then, and only then, are you ready to perform."

This was the year I met the late Eugene Burger, with his long white beard and deep voice full of wisdom and gravel. He was an inspired thinker about performance and one of the most admired and loved teachers of magic in the world. In his lecture, he said, "If you go to see Dolly Parton in concert, she doesn't just sing songs about the good times; she sings about times of yearning, of betrayal. She takes us on a rollercoaster of emotions. As magicians, we have the power to do that too." He insisted on the importance of a script. "How can we adjust pauses, pace or timing, if we have no script? How can we make our magic meaningful? How can we get our audience hooked emotionally?" According to Eugene, "The magician teaches us that we are the magicians of our own lives, not the victim of circumstance but a seeker who can learn and wield the secrets of the universe."

I started working on a script the very next week. I haggled over each word, lifting and shaping each sentence like a jeweller with precious silver.

FISM that year was hot. Every day was breathless. The huge convention theatre was dark and cool. From ten in the morning until late afternoon there was an international stage competition. One ten-minute act after another. I played truant again from my blue waistcoat duties and sat in the dark cool theatre. Most acts were dreadful. Middle-aged men dancing in Lycra, tubby wives squeezed into boxes—only the rare act was extraordinary. What I saw wasn't magic but desperate dreams of glory.

One man was a magic "phantom of the opera." Cloaked and masked, he strutted about the stage. As the soundtrack soared, he pulled a huge silver candelabra from under a cloth, complete with eight burning candles. He'd spent a fortune on these props. He'd dreamt of this ambitious act for ten years and practiced in his garage for two. He'd rehearsed it in his living room night after night for the last two months, driving his wife nuts. He'd imagined the winner's trophy on his mantelpiece. But he'd never taken an acting or movement lesson in his life and bumbled about the stage awkwardly. The huge appearing candelabra was impressive, but the rest of his act was amateur and would never be booked.

I watched and heeded the warning.

On the final night, there was a big party for the thousands of magicians. Since the gathering was ninety-five percent male, there were only a few couples on the dance floor dancing to the swing band. I'd discarded my blue waistcoat, put on a summer dress, and suddenly, I was in great demand.

"I want to do a stage act," I said to the star of that night's gala show as he whirled me round the dance floor, making me laugh.

"Why would you want to do that?" he replied, "didn't you see all those people in the stage competition? It's impossible to get a good act."

"You have."

"That's true," he agreed and whirled me around some more.

13

HELMUT & NORA

*B*ack home in Hamburg, my passion for magic re-fired, I wrote a new magic act. I was so excited—I could see it all in my imagination. I filled notebooks full of sketches and ideas.

Imagine this.

Swirling Venetian mist fills the stage. To the side, there is an elegant antique table, set with an old-fashioned silver tea service on a lace cloth. The backdrop is a Venetian palace, a wide stone staircase in the centre, rich tapestries hanging on either side. As the last chime of midnight fades away and the lights come up, we see the ghost of a beautiful, dark-haired courtesan standing centre stage in an ethereal gown of cobweb grey silk. Raising her gaze to look at the audience with a faint smile, she silently stretches out a graceful arm and plucks a crystal ball from thin air, balancing it easily on the back of her hand. She gently blows on it; suddenly the ball is full of clear, sparkling water. A goldfish glitters inside.

Another breath—ball, water and goldfish are gone.

She makes another circular motion with her arm and a long green-blue peacock feather appears. She balances it easily on the tip of one finger. Then, smiling, puts it for an instant on her nose and takes her hand away—no old milk bottles here. With a toss of her head, she flicks it gracefully into the air. It flies upwards for a moment, and as it falls back into her outstretched hand, suddenly it has the weight and glitter of a thick emerald necklace. She holds it up, turning it in the light, flashing deep-green, and then she fastens it around her white neck.

She walks over to the table and picks up the silver teapot, takes off the lid and turns the pot upside down. It's empty. The music changes to a lilting waltz played by a gypsy violin. Moving gracefully to the music, she reaches into the air. Silver coins appear from her fingers, glinting in the spotlight. She drops them one by one into the teapot with a clinking sound. Taking a china cup from the table, she makes a pouring gesture with the pot, but only white smoke falls from the spout—the coins have melted into nothing. She smiles, shrugs, then replaces the teapot and cup back on the table.

A gold lamé cloth lies shimmering on the floor. Bending down, she draws it up slowly—slowly—holding it with both hands, letting it linger sensually against the curves of her body. Closing her eyes, she breathes in, raises the cloth above her head, and as she lets the breath out, drops the cloth to the floor. The ethereal figure in grey has vanished. Instead, the courtesan blazes suddenly in a vivid scarlet satin gown; the emeralds around her neck are now glittering rubies. The audience break into loud applause.

A large picture frame is balanced on an ornate brass stand in the middle of the stage. The frame is covered with a black cloth, brass legs showing beneath. With a gentle tug at the bottom corner, she pulls the cloth away. Where a picture should be in the golden frame, there is only a black empty background. More layers of mist hang above the floor, lit with blue light. The audience watch in silence, wondering.

Stepping forward, she holds the cloth at arm's length between herself and the audience. It hides her whole body; only a glimpse of the scarlet gown can be seen beneath the bottom of the cloth. The mist thickens and swirls as the stage lights dim. The music swells. A loud crack of thunder, a flash of lightening, the cloth drops. Where she stood in her red gown only seconds earlier, there is nothing. No one.

The audience gasps.

A split second later, there is the sound of another astonished en-masse intake of breath. In the golden picture frame where a minute before the canvas was black, there is a portrait of the courtesan in that same scarlet gown, gazing serenely out, an enigmatic Mona Lisa smile on her lips. The audience erupts into a loud and enthusiastic applause. Blackout.

Exciting huh? I thought so. I couldn't wait to get started.

I bought a crystal ball. Well, it was made of acrylic, really. Acrylic balls shouldn't be left in the sun, even indoors. They act like a magnifying glass and will generate a spark guaranteed to burn your house down. I managed to incinerate a whole basket of juggling balls before discovering clouds of black acrid smoke and how to use a fire extinguisher. Crystal or acrylic, it never became a magical ball full of sparkling water anyway.

I bought two goldfish from the pet shop. I wanted a classic round goldfish bowl, but Germans are unusually concerned for the mental health of their goldfish and you can only buy rectangular fish tanks. Apparently, swimming in a constant circle makes them depressed. I know how they feel.

I dutifully bought a small rectangular tank and christened my fish Helmut and Nora. I don't remember why. But I couldn't face putting them through the indignities of what had to be done to make them appear anywhere other than their bowl. Helmut and Nora lived out peaceful lives nibbling fish food, gazing serenely out of their glass world, untroubled by the glare of a theatrical spotlight, never knowing what excitement and probable trauma they had missed.

I managed to pull silver coins out the air and drop them with a satisfying clatter in my mother's antique silver teapot, but the smoke from the smoke tablets stank, and the heat they emitted when ignited burnt my fingers through the bottom of the teapot.

I practiced balancing a peacock feather on the tip of my finger. I could manage a whole five minutes. I could definitely flick it into the air and catch it again. But I couldn't manage to get my grandmother's paste emeralds out from my pocket and into the air at the same time. I tried. Nope. I tried. Nope. I tried again. And again. Nope. *Bloody hell.*

Keep windows open when attempting to make dry ice. I'm saving you a whole world of trouble here. (Dry ice is the theatrical method to give the effect of mist on stage). Martin and I almost asphyxiated ourselves as we attempted to replicate Venetian swirling mists. As the CO_2 gas we used to make the dry ice emptied our apartment of oxygen, we grew increasingly lightheaded, and it was only when, for some unexplained reason, a box fell off a shelf with a loud crash that we realised we'd gone all woozy and opening a window might be a good idea.

I made a cobweb-grey Venetian gown and hemmed a length of golden lamé for the quick-change cloth. A local seamstress made me a red satin ball gown. Months of work. But I didn't manage to change into it on a breath. Or even without a breath. I've found out since that quick-change is the closely guarded and extremely complicated secret of Russian experts and that it was never likely that I could have worked it out myself. I bought a golden picture frame and found a brass stand for it in a junk shop. I asked magicians in Hamburg how I could disappear from the centre of the stage and make a portrait appear. If anyone knew, they weren't telling.

No one—no one, can say I didn't try.

Meanwhile, the phone rang. It was a booking for Martin's juggling show, and so off we went. Now thirty-three, he'd been performing his solo street show for fifteen years and it was impressive to watch.

Martin watched the empty Hamburg town square with an experienced eye. Choosing a spot, he made an event of arriving, even though no one was about. Wearing a flamboyant sky-blue floor-length coat over black trousers with a burnt-orange waistcoat sparkling with tiny mirrors and a tall orange hat of soft felt, he had an embroidered Indian bag slung over his shoulder with the tops of five white juggling clubs sticking out. It's not every day that a tall man with long hair in such a flamboyant outfit appears from nowhere wheeling a five-foot high unicycle. Laying the unicycle centre stage, he unpacked his bag, giving ceremonial attention to each prop. He placed the five white clubs in a semi-circle in front of the unicycle, then seven bright yellow balls in a wider arc outside those. Finally, he fished out a sky-blue diabolo—the toy that looks like a strange cotton reel with a narrow centre—from the bottom of the bag and laid that next to the unicycle.

As he put out each prop, he sang a little song to himself. People started to drift over, a couple here, a group of friends there. Martin gave them a conspiratorial glance and half a smile. In his pocket, he had a small bag of chalk. Choosing green chalk today, he drew a perimeter line between the widest circle of his yellow balls and the few people that had stopped to watch. Putting a gentle hand on their shoulders, he moved the watchers up to the chalk line. Intrigued, they stood on the line obediently.

More people drifted over as they noticed that something was happening. The square in front of the town hall was a crossing between two shopping districts and the perfect place to catch people away from the distraction and noise of the shops. Now that there was an obvious place to stand, more people gathered on the green chalk line, and soon the front row was full. Women put down their shopping bags; their husbands placed their feet apart, arms folded or hands in pockets, glad of a break from the shops.

Picking up the diabolo, Martin whipped it up and down on the string between the sticks he held in each hand.

"This is a magic diabolo; its singing can only be heard by the pure of heart," Martin loudly announced as he spun it faster and faster. The crowd quietened to listen and then smiled when they hear the diabolo hum. The circle of watchers grew; more passers-by curiously walked forward to join the audience. After the diabolo, he picked up the balls: three at first in pleasing patterns, then five, then seven. The crowd was impressed. Then three clubs, then five. People nodded their heads in recognition that this guy knew what he was doing.

"Would you like to see the high unicycle or hear a poem?' Martin asked when the applause had died down.

"Poem! Poem!" they called out, smiling. They thought it would be funny, or better still, rude.

"Poem?" Martin asked. "Are you sure?'

The crowd nodded, smiling.

"Okay then." Martin laid down the unicycle, straightened his bright multicoloured tie and stood, feet wide, shoulders back, grounded. He waited for silence. The crowd watched.

"'The Children's Hymn' by Bertolt Brecht," he announced. They hadn't expected this. This wasn't a funny poem.

Spare no effort, spare no passion, thoughtfulness and grace expand,
So that Germany may flourish like every other well-loved land.
That other people need not fear us like they would a raging pack
And towards us as towards others, as we
reach out that they reach back
And not superior nor inferior of other lands are we to be
From the Rhine out to the Oder, from the Alps up to the Sea

And as we make our country better, we
love her dearly, think her grand
And she will seem so dear to us as other people's lands to them.[1]

Most in his crowd were aged above fifty, some even older. They would have lived through Germany's defeat and post-war shame. Martin recited the poem, his open face earnest and passionate. As I watched his audience. I saw them pull back their shoulders and stand a little straighter—tears falling silently down some faces. A woman fished in her pocket for a tissue. By the final line, the silence was complete. Something had changed in the world. There is a pause before people quietly started to clap. Martin stood, acknowledging the moment.

"And now, for the high unicycle!" he shouted, grabbing the bike. Leaping into the air, his sky-blue coat flying in the wind, he jumped onto the saddle, lifted his tall orange hat and opened his arms wide. The audience, shocked out of their reverie, laughed and applauded again.

I was jealous. The only thing I wanted, still, always, was to have a show—my show. As months passed, I moped about our one-bedroom flat, getting precisely nowhere with magic; as I got more miserable, the frequency and violence of my bulimia increased. Ironically, it had improved while I was totally focused on looking after my mum. But now, lost in grief, in a new town where I didn't speak the language, with no work and no friends, it took back its vicious control. Not being able to eat without throwing up was exhausting and bleak.

Martin desperately wanted to help, but he didn't know how. He tried. But no one can help an addict when they won't release

---

[1] Translated from the German by Martin Dronsfield

their hold on their destructive behaviour themselves. I wanted my fix more than I wanted to be free. I wanted the release bulimia gave me from my constant craving for comfort in the form of sugary food, even if it drained energy from my mind and body and left me empty day after day. I held tight to my addiction as an integral part of who I was. *Love me—love this poisoned hook.*

One afternoon, as I stared miserably out the window, the Half Lady act downloaded into my thoughts. I quickly described the scene in my notebook: a woman talking to camera, the film crew watching. I could see her clearly, half a woman 'sat' on a table. Under the table, there was nothing: no legs, no feet. I could see it all precisely: the elegant room, the chandelier, the clock on the wall. I could see her gown, the glass of red wine on the table with the lipstick smear, the faint trace of white powder against the mahogany wood, her brittle smile and clenched jaw. I knew her well; I knew her daily battle, her hope that if she ignores her desperation and shame for long enough they might never have been true.

It's not hard to imagine what inspired me to write that piece. Art mimics life. That half-lady was me, minus the wine, drugs and white coats, thank God. Bulimia was—is—a wire around my throat. It loosens when things are going well but tightens when they're not. In Hamburg, I often felt paralysed. I couldn't think straight, leave the house or do anything more than sit and stare at the wall, miserable and powerless. One night, I was suddenly so scared that bulimia might literally kill me, I called my old magic teacher, my friend Mick.

"I think I'm killing myself."

"Nah, you're alright." He didn't understand. How could he? I hadn't told him about the eating disorder; I hadn't told anyone. I knew the isolation, frustration and fear of the half lady. I knew there was a whole world of bright lights and friends and fun out there waiting for me, but each time I tried to get there, I broke the way.

14

BRIGHT QUEEN

"*I* think we should go to Findhorn in Scotland to hear Caroline Myss," Martin suggested one afternoon.

"Who?"

He held up an article in a magazine written by Caroline Myss, the author of *Why People Don't Heal and How They Can*. I'd never heard of her.

"Scotland? I'd rather go to Italy."

"Read this."

I'd only read half the article when I felt beyond certain that I absolutely had to go see her. I'll explain more about her later. For now, all you need to know is this:

In the Bible, there's a story[2] about a woman who had been ill for twelve years, who believed that if she could touch Jesus' cloak she would be healed. At that time, her particular condition made her an outcast. Like me. She hid in the crowd, and when no one was looking, she touched the hem of his cloak. Jesus stopped and looked around.

"Who touched me?" he asked. His disciples looked at him as if he were nuts.

---

[2] Mark 5:25-34: A woman has been bleeding for twelve years.

"There are people everywhere; what do you mean who touched you?"

"Someone touched me," Jesus insisted. Looking around, he saw the woman, now weeping, hiding her face in her hands, crouched on the floor. He helped her to her feet. "Your faith has healed you," he said to her. And it had.

When I read that article about Caroline Myss, I felt that if I could only hear her speak, touch the hem of her cloak, I would find the way to untwist this wire around my neck.

"Let's go."

The Findhorn Foundation is an official UNESCO recognised eco-village in the village of Findhorn in Scotland. Founded in the seventies, it's now home to two hundred permanent residents and hosts a continual program of workshops. It has a completely cosmic history, which I have no trouble believing because I believe in many things, but it might sound odd to you. Briefly, a couple called Eileen and Peter Caddy were down on their luck, living in a caravan park in Findhorn with their children. Eileen had a very close relationship with God, so when God gave her practical instructions on how to grow food in their garden, she wrote it all down and passed it to Peter, who put it into action. Soon, their vegetables not only grew to extraordinary super-size dimensions, but even their roses and other flowers flourished so abundantly that the National Soil Association visited to investigate and the BBC made a documentary. More people interested in working with Devas—nature spirits—came up to help work the land, and soon a little community was established. Twenty years or so later, it's a beautiful eco-village. You can go and see it for yourself if you don't believe me. Take a puffa jacket and wear thick socks; it gets breezy up in there. Eileen was awarded an MBE by the Queen in 2004. If the Queen believed in the giant cabbages, then it must all be true.

Martin and I signed up for a week's conference with Caroline

Myss. We flew from Hamburg to Aberdeen and hitchhiked the rest of the way, waiting by the roadside in the soft Scottish rain with some caramel woolly haired long-horned Highland cows for company. Monday morning, excited and eager, we were waiting outside the Universal Hall, Findhorn's central hub and conference centre. The front of the building was made of glass spun between thick cedar vertical beams, etched with swirling curves of colourful stained glass. It looked like it was built by angels. The solid front doors with two huge stained-glass wings cut into the wood were shut.

When the doors open, we were swept with everyone else into an airy, pentagonal hall designed like a small amphitheatre. More stained-glass windows streamed bright colour into the space. A young man played a large wooden harp in the centre of the hall. The quiet, gentle music washed through the air as we took our places.

When the room was full, buzzing with the expectations of five hundred people, Caroline Myss stepped forward.

Caroline is neither quiet nor gentle. She's funny and sharp and sarcastic. I've been following her inspired teaching for more than twenty years now. I owe her my life. She's right up at the top of the list of my most admired, brilliant, inspirational people. She's a chain-smoking, coffee-drinking Chicago journalist, or she was. In her early thirties, she found that she could 'see' people's individual state of health just by knowing their name and age—which was, by her own admission, completely weird. When a Harvard-trained neurosurgeon who was investigating the accuracy of medical intuitivism tested her remotely with his own patients, he found that she was usually ninety-five percent accurate in her diagnosis, despite having no medical training whatsoever. Yes, I know that might sound hard to believe. But do you understand how your smart phone works? No. Exactly. But you don't disbelieve that it does work. Bear with me.

At Findhorn, I was enjoying its kooky atmosphere, tasty vegetarian communal meals and fresh Scottish air. I was brim full of hope.

Caroline was a brilliant speaker: energetic and precise. She had a lot she wanted to get through—five days were not enough, each session was intense. We grabbed a cappuccino during the break—snatched a quick lunch, taking just enough time for our brains to settle between sessions. We headed back in to absorb more information. Everyone was sitting on the edge of their seats. The atmosphere was electric.

I was desperate to know how to escape the destructive hold of my eating disorder. But five hundred other people there had their own questions, their own struggles. Everyone was eager and enthusiastic. We had five days together; the workshop would finish before lunch on Friday. Thursday came and went. Although I was enjoying the week and fascinated by her lectures, my own question was still unanswered.

Friday morning. It was another fascinating session, but its topic was nothing specific to me. Caroline spoke faster and faster as the minutes ticked away; she wanted to communicate every ounce of information she had.

And then. I can't remember what she was talking about. But whatever it was, I disagreed so strongly that my hand shot up. There were five hundred people listening intently to the last hour of her talk; it wasn't a good time to ask questions. Caroline stopped mid-flow. She looked at me directly and raised her eyebrows. I blurted out my point of view. She ignored it. Instead she asked.

"What's your name?"

"Romany."

"May I do a reading?" she asked.

I gulped.

"Yes."

The room was silent. I could feel my heart hammering fast.

"How old are you?"

"Thirty."

"Who are your heroines?" I took a quick moment to think and then replied.

"Sylvia Plath, Marilyn Monroe, Emily Bronte, Antigone, Judy Garland."

"All talented women that died tragically young or addicted," she remarked drily.

I gulped again.

"Your archetypes are queen, alchemist, magician, artist. You're using the power of the black queen. I bet you just love a grand entrance."

How could she have possibly known that I do indeed love a dramatic entrance? How could she have picked out magician and alchemist from just looking at me? If this was a magic act, it was a damn good one.

"You can't swallow," she said. My hand flew to my throat.

In front of five hundred strangers, I said quietly.

"I'm bulimic." The words burnt my mouth. Shame sat in my seat and breathed my air.

Silence. Caroline nodded, staring back at me with kind but serious eyes.

"You need to get out of black; it's killing you. You need to leave the black queen behind. You have to tell your truth; you have to be your bright self. And you, are you with her?" she asked, looking at Martin, "Yes? You're in for a rocky ride; you'd better watch out."

It was true that I'd been wearing nothing but black for the last ten years; it's slimming and makes you invisible. I had no idea what she meant about Martin. Looking back, she was right.

She finished the session and we went outside. I was both grateful and astonished at getting a personal reading in the last hour but mortified to have confessed my shameful secret. I kept my eyes on the ground.

"Here, take this." An older woman held out her own cerise woollen scarf, "It's my favourite." She smiled, her eyes kind.

Wrapping her warm scarf gently around my neck, she gave it a little tug to keep it in place. "I heard what you said," she added, patting it again. "I hope this helps." It was such a precious gift. More precious than she could have known. I raised my hands to my throat, feeling the soft wool. It felt like new magical armour. I wear a scarf of the same colour around my throat to this day, almost twenty years later. I have a drawer full of them. When I put one on, I feel safer, stronger. I don't really understand why. Caroline could probably tell me.

Too overwhelmed to eat lunch, I walked back to our tent, thinking hard. Caroline had said, "You have to leave the black queen behind." Mirror, mirror on the wall, who's the fairest of them all? I knew the black queen well. Head-girl, fast-track graduate job, BT top sales winner, salsa champion. I hadn't sent a huntsman into the forest to carve anyone's heart out, but I'd certainly cast an imperious eye over my competition and used that controlling ego-centered energy to discipline myself to be top-dog.

Confused, I called my friend Betty. Betty is a witch—the good type—and the wisest, kindest woman I know.

"Betty, if I'm not the black queen, who am I?"

"There are two sides to every archetype," she replied, "the bright and the shadow. You're neither one nor the other. You choose which side you want to act from. Who is the bright queen to you?" Without hesitation, I answered,

"Glinda the good witch, from The Wizard of Oz."

"Fine. Then be her."

This was a revelation—a vital turning point. I decided in that moment that I was going to be as much like Glinda the good witch as I could. I was going to try at least. It seemed to be the only lifeline I had left.

I did change. Slowly, slowly, regulating each action to turn it around from snappish, selfish and controlling, to a softer, kinder personality. It didn't come naturally, and when my guard was down or I was overtired, that sharp, critical black queen snapped straight back into thought again—but not action at least, I had her under control. Most of the time.

When I got home, I knew I needed to change more than from dark to bright queen. I knew this was the time to change my life in order to save my life.

Caroline talked about the expectations and traditions of our tribe and how much we are individually affected by them. I was born into an English Christian working-class family. This class works hard and obeys the rules; its driving aspiration is to own a better house, earn a higher salary and get one's children into university. I'd tried my best to fit into this structure. It had done me no favours at all.

The first thing I did on leaving Findhorn was to change my surname by deed poll. I cast it off as if I were shedding a toxic skin. To me, my surname symbolised the rules and expectations of my tribe. I didn't want any of it. I completed the papers in the solicitor's office, signing my old name for the last time and then the new. The solicitor insisted that legally I needed a first and second name so I made Romany Romany my official name. As I signed, I was consciously creating my own world in which I wrote my own story, lived by my own rules and took my chances. My father was less than impressed when I told him what I'd done. I didn't care. I wasn't waiting for anyone's advice or validation any more. I gave the black queen magic costume and all my black clothes to a charity shop. Since my wardrobe was now empty, I then grabbed my credit card, hit the shops and bought armfuls of new clothes in bright vibrant colours.

After that, I felt much, much better.

15

ESCAPE FROM HAMBURG

*B*ack in Hamburg, Martin and I had a brilliant idea. We would do a duo knife throwing and fire-juggling show! Why hadn't we thought of it before! We chose a classic vaudeville number in which a knife thrower throws knives at a member of the audience who is blindfolded and tied to a board. The volunteer holds a balloon in each hand and has another between their legs. When the knife thrower throws the knives, they stick into the wood and pop the balloons.

What really happens, what the guy doesn't realise, is that the knives aren't thrown at all. Martin does throw them at the board at the start of the show, but after the volunteer has been chosen and blindfolded, Martin passes the knives to me and I stick them into the wood, popping the balloons with no risk to the volunteer or anyone else. Hilarious. Well, the poor man strapped to a board, apparently getting knives thrown at him by idiots, probably doesn't think so.

We made a board, bought some throwing knives and Martin practiced in the living room. We added a comic dance, a light storyline and some juggling. When I stood on Martin's shoulders, he complained that I was too heavy: method acting at its best. I pretended to be outraged and appealed to the women in the audience, announcing, "I stand here for women's rights. I shall throw the knives!"

The blindfolded guy on the board is now really scared. He's seen Martin throw the knives accurately in the first half of the show, but he has no reason to think that I can throw them too. Since no one is going to actually throw the knives, he's completely safe, but he doesn't know that. The audience seemed to find that funny. Add some whip-cracking and a finale with me jumping onto Martin's shoulders to juggle fire clubs—it was a decent little show. We called ourselves the Cobble Comedy Company, with a nod to both the cobbled streets in Linz where we first met and the supremely cobbled together quality of our act.

That summer we tried it out at a local German beach resort. Camping by the beach, we swam and cycled and played crazy golf during the day, then performed the show three times a night in the square for the holiday makers. Crowds formed a circle as we set out our props. Kids sat cross-legged on the floor, slurping ice creams, rows of happy on-holiday adults behind them. At the end of the show, we each held out a hat, smiling at the audience as they filled them with notes and coins. Afterwards, we had a candlelit supper of pizza in a restaurant paid for with a pile of fresh, happily given cash. There is nothing better in the world.

Satisfied, tired and full, we cuddled up in our little tent by the sea and did the same thing all over again the next day. And the next. Six weeks of several shows a night. A night off if it rained. I was supremely happy. Once again, as in Austria, I was doing what I loved, with a man I loved. I was tanned, slim and content, no eating disorder in sight.

If that seems strange, let me explain. When I'm really happy, for example during that wonderful first summer with Martin, everything seems easy. Easy to eat, easy to like my reflection in the mirror, easy to let go of control. Bulimia cannot function in the bright light of joy. Happiness takes its power. That's why, these days, if I'm clever, I do things that make me happy, spending time with Bongo my dog, creating magic, running with friends, sticking bright rhinestones onto costumes, baking bread, dancing. When I forget, when I let my happiness guard down, bulimia comes sneaking back through the cracks, malicious and sly.

When the summer began to turn, it was time to go home. But the thought of a miserable, lonely winter in Hamburg was too horrible to think about.

"Can't we go away? Can't we keep on doing the show?" I urged Martin.

Why not? We had no kids, no debts. We had saved the money from the shows in the summer and it would be easy to sub-rent our flat and just take off.

So we did.

We organised our four-month trip so that we would spend time in four places: South Africa, Australia, New Zealand and Hawaii. We didn't know much about South Africa; it seemed a mysterious place. We wrote to *Kaskade*, the international juggling magazine, out of ignorance and before Google, to ask whether people spoke English in South Africa. Garth, a juggler from Johannesburg, replied. He offered to pick us up from the airport, take us to his home where we could have our own room, bathroom and use of his second car. He would also introduce us to his agent so we could get some work—and yes, they did speak English.

Good as his word, Garth greeted us smiling at the airport. He took us to his agent on the way home and showed us the street-performing pitch in the Johannesburg Waterfront shopping resort. The next night, we played our new show for passing shoppers. It wasn't that good still, but we kept at it, performing a couple of shows every day, slowly improving. After two weeks, we went on to Cape Town to perform at the Waterfront shopping area there.

In 1997, South Africa was deep in the middle of the Truth and Reconciliation Commission set up by Bishop Desmond Tutu, following the abolition of apartheid in 1994. Criminals could request amnesty from both civil and criminal prosecution if they confessed their crimes to court. Every day, the newspapers were full of horrendous stories. HIV and AIDS had also swept the country, and thousands of children were now orphans or infected with HIV.

Martin and I wanted to do something to help. We contacted a charity called Lifeline, explained that we were street performers and would like to offer a free show in a township.

"What colour are you?" the voice on the other end of the phone asked.

"White."

"It's too dangerous. No."

"But we would really like to."

The charity offered to pick us up and drive us with a social worker to a township. Khayelitsha was, and still is, one of the poorest shanty towns on the outskirts of Cape Town. People live in ramshackle tin shacks so close together that the danger of fire and disease spreading is constant. Originally, in the mid 1980s, Khayelitsha was established as an 'apartheid dumping ground.' Terrible gang violence, particularly rape and drug crime, became commonplace, made worse by extreme poverty and over seventy percent unemployment. The epidemic of AIDS and HIV made everything much, much worse.

Our first show was at a 'Coloured' school. Wikipedia defines 'Coloured' as *an ethnic label for people of mixed ethnic origin who possess ancestry from Europe, Asia, and various Khoisan and Bantu ethnic groups of southern Africa.*

Martin and I weren't expecting the smartly dressed, bright-eyed kids that greeted us in the first classroom. At my school, my posh convent school that is, we did everything we could to look as scruffy as possible. We screwed our socks down, paraded with our coats unbuttoned, knotted our ties half way up. These kids were pristine.

Seeing our surprise, the teacher explained, "These children have nothing, they live in shacks. Many of their parents are dead and they live with neighbours and other families. We teach them that they can at least take pride in their own appearance and in their uniform, so that's what they do."

The children sat on chairs in a circle in the playground to watch our show. The kids spoke Xhosa, the language with the fascinating clicks, not English. But everyone understands magic. As I pulled silver coins from their ears, their eyes widened and mouths dropped open in amazement. A silk scarf vanished and another turned into an egg; three pieces of rope became one long piece. The kids gasped and laughed. They were the best audience I'd ever had.

Martin brought out his giant unicycle and perched on the saddle, high up above the kids, pretended he was about to fall off. He shouted, bent over double, peddling towards the kids at high speed before saving himself at the last moment. The children screamed and jumped up from their chairs, laughing. We juggled, I stood on Martin's shoulders; finally, we juggled the fire torches and the kids screamed some more.

Afterwards, we went into each classroom to meet the children and teachers. The teachers seemed desperate to tell us about their work, to tell anyone who would listen. Their stories were heart-breaking. Many of these children had been raped, many had lost their parents to HIV or violence and all were living in poverty with little opportunity for the future. There was no funding and no support.

From there, we were driven to a larger 'Black' school where the pupils were already expecting us. Sitting on red plastic chairs in the hot playground, a thousand kids waited patiently. Rows and rows of smartly turned-out children wearing royal-blue jumpers, with beautiful dark black skin and excited eyes, smiled at us. We repeated what we did at the last school, and again the kids laughed and screamed as Martin almost fell off his unicycle into the audience.

The head teacher thanked us in English, then told the kids in Xhosa to return to their class. In one movement, the entire school stood up, placed their chairs on their heads and turned to go. That scene stays with me, etched deep in my memory: the faces of those beautiful children, red chairs on heads, bright blue jumpers, wide-eyed, watching us over their shoulders as they turned their backs and returned to class. Those children will be in their thirties now. I wonder what their lives are like today.

We visited individual classrooms again and heard the same heart-wrenching stories from their teachers. At our next stop, at the rape counselling centre, we listened to even more desperate cases. I felt terrible guilt on behalf of my white race.

Khayelitsha was a difficult place to live then, and it is even worse now. I look around at my comfortable house filled with everything I could wish for: my garden bright with flowers, food in the fridge and too many clothes in the wardrobe. Life isn't fair. I shut my eyes and ask the kind goddesses, the divine wind and every angel to take comfort, to take relief, to take joy to Khayelitsha.

Nam myoho renge kyo.
May all beings know peace.
May ALL beings know peace.

16

CHALK & CONFETTI

After South Africa, we planned to arrive in Perth in late November and then fly to Melbourne for Christmas.

Perth. We hadn't expected such heat. We should have. Australia in December—of course it would be hot. Everyone carried on their daily business regardless. No sleepy afternoon siestas for Perth, no pulling down of shutters until the cool of the evening. Businessmen strode about in dark pinstripe suits and polished shoes; nine-to-five busy days continued under the relentless heat of the sun as if it were a mild English day in May.

We slept through the first day in a youth hostel after the eleven-hour flight. The next morning, we had to earn some cash to buy our first meal. Perth is a modern city with wide streets and smooth pavements. We quickly found a pedestrian area, put on our music, drew a chalk circle to mark the front line of the audience and ran around cheerily putting out the knife-throwing board, whip, throwing knives, juggling clubs and fire torches. We skipped about in our costumes under the full glare of the noon sun, Martin in black trousers, red shirt and gold embroidered Moroccan waistcoat and me wearing my black frilly shorts, opaque black tights, a gold top with red and gold frilled sleeves and sunblock on my nose. When everything was ready, we stood together facing the crowd, squinting in the bright sunlight, feeling the sweat running down our backs. So hungry. So hot. A man stepped into the circle. He wore a light blue shirt, grey peaked cap with a silver badge and had a baton and handcuffs hanging from his belt. He wasn't smiling.

"You can't do that here," he said curtly. He pointed to the chalk line. "That's graffiti." He looked at the confetti Martin had thrown. "That's littering in a public place. Clean it up."

We started to protest but he held up one hand, "Clean it up or I'll give you a fifty dollar fine right here."

We turned off the music and packed up in silence. The policeman stood in the middle of our circle, watching us as the crowd drifted away. A curious few stayed. There was a small portacabin nearby advertising double glazing. A woman came out carrying a small bowl of water and a little sponge. She smiled at me kindly.

"Here you go love; you can clean the chalk off with this." I was jet-lagged, hungry and hot. Seeing her sympathetic face, I started to cry. Keeping my head low, I shuffled forward on my knees around the circle, scrubbing at the line, tears dripping onto the mess of chalk and water. Martin was on his knees too, picking up each tiny piece of confetti scattered by the hot wind. Half-way round, I looked up and noticed the policeman had gone. I took the bowl back to the woman and thanked her again. She fished out a tissue and wiped the mascara smudges from my cheeks. We trailed miserably back to the youth hostel even hungrier, still with no money. I stole someone's cheese and pickle sandwiches from the hostel's communal fridge and shared them with Martin. We ate them in glum, guilty silence. If you ever had your sandwiches pinched from a youth hostel in Perth, it was me. Sorry.

The next day, we went out again. This time we managed to start and finish a show. We went for breakfast. It was a great breakfast. Each mouthful tasted of relief. We did a couple of shows a day after that, still with no problems, and after a week of seeing nothing more of Perth than its hot city centre, we flew to Melbourne. Since we were living hand to mouth doing street shows, we didn't have the time or money to see anything that is fabulous about Australia. We spent our days pretending to throw knives at people and juggling with fire torches. We were sort of having fun. Scratch that. We weren't having fun. It was hot, hard work and we were just making enough money to pay our way— just. Looking back, I remember that time as being difficult. But only because doing a newish street show in an unfamiliar town *is* difficult. We weren't making much money, we weren't playing wonderful joyful shows, but underneath it all we were happy because we were on an adventure together, still following a bright dream of making an audience happy, and that was much, much better than anything else.

But still.

Christmas Day was the final straw. We had offered the local charity to do a free show for the local pensioners' Christmas lunch. In a large hall walled with temporary boards advertising remedies for indigestion and arthritis, in the middle of a sea of beige cardigans and coloured paper hats, we were introduced and received a curious applause. We began our opening dance. At first the pensioners clapped along with our music, but a minute in, as soon as their meal was served, they stopped to focus on their prawn cocktail starter. As we threw juggling clubs, all we could see were the tops of grey heads bobbing as they chewed. After the turkey, roast potatoes and puréed sprouts, they looked up, puzzled, probably wondering why one of their party had been blindfolded and was being threatened by a young lady welding a knife. When the Christmas pudding and brandy butter arrived, heads dropped again until the last spoonful was gone. We rushed through the show, playing to a complete lack of interest and no applause at all.

Just after, as we stood at the back of the hall, gratefully drinking some water, the next entertainer bounded on, dressed in a jolly red jumper with a white fluffy reindeer on the front.

"Come along everyone, I'm dreaming of a white Christmas! All together now!"

Oh, they liked that much better. As the music played and cracked voices crooned, we slunk out more miserable than ever.

"Shall we use our credit card?" one of us said, I can't remember who.

"Oh God, yes!" We went for a slap-up three-course dinner and paid for it with plastic. As the Visa advert says: priceless.

When we arrived at our next stop in New Zealand, we had our credit card out and we weren't afraid to use it. New Zealand has a scant population of four and a half million, a third of which live in Auckland, with the rest scattered around the two islands. We performed a few shows in Auckland, then asked around where we should go next to play our show.

"Go to Rotorua. There are lots of people in Rotorua," helpful people said.

There aren't lots of people in Rotorua. There's hardly anyone in Rotorua. There are so few people in Rotorua that you think they must be hiding behind trees. They're not. I ran over to a tree and looked behind it just to check. I really did. Nope, no one there. Plus, anyone who is there will be walking in the beautiful forests, mountain biking or bathing in the sulphurous mud spas smelling of rotten eggs that Rotorua is famous for. We stood in the main square and looked about at no one.

Wondering what to do with ourselves in this pleasant but deserted town, we wandered about and came across a circle of beautiful wooden house trucks on the village green. Each one had stained-glass windows, a little metal chimney and cast-iron steps leading to the front door. Pink and red geraniums bloomed brightly in colourful pots on the corners of the steps. One truck, painted pale yellow, had a chalkboard sign advertising coffee and homemade cake. Half the truck's side panel was propped open as a roof; underneath were two pale-green wrought-iron tables with chairs, each one a different pastel colour. Through the side opening, on a counter, a three-layered Victoria sponge cake sat in a glass dome-covered cake stand. Against the wall on a shelf was a professional Gaggia coffee machine and a row of pastel mugs.

A little white Jack Russell with one brown ear and a patch of brown on his back was sleeping under a table. She sprang up barking when we approached but allowed herself to be petted when we held out our hands for her to sniff. A tall man with brown dreadlocks grizzled with grey, the sides of his head shaved, a sleeve of tattoos on both arms, poked his head out of the opening. We must have looked hot and weary carrying all our gear, including the knife-throwing board and a heavy flight case of sound equipment, because he came out smiling and said with a New Zealand twang, "Hey guys, you look like you've been travelling. Take a seat. What can I get you? Coffee's on the house."

Such hospitality. We ordered coffee and a slice of the Victoria sponge. When we'd hungrily gobbled that, we ordered another. Our host sat down with us, chatting and asking questions. His wife appeared with their toddler, and soon more people came out from their afternoon siestas in their house trucks to join us. Rosie, the little Jack Russell, went back to sleep under her table. This group, who had all built their own house trucks, met up every weekend in different towns to create a tiny village fair. They parked their trucks in a circle around the green and set out stalls selling homemade soap, handmade clothes and beeswax candles.

A guy dressed in black leather from top to toe with his sturdy arms covered in Maori tattoos introduced himself as Dave. He was a blacksmith and travelled with his own mini-forge so that people could watch him making candlesticks and cast-iron doorknobs and buy them to take home. He never removed his mirror sunglasses. The rest of his face was covered with a dark beard and thick eyebrows, and his many silver piercings glinted when they caught the sun. In the middle of the afternoon, in front of a small gathering of people—which New Zealand might call a crowd—he gave an ear-splitting loud display of whip cracking, six whips at a time, three in each hand. We were impressed. Everyone was impressed. He offered to teach us and to make us our own whips, but it wasn't looking like we were going to make any money in New Zealand and we explained that we couldn't afford to buy them.

"Wait here," he said. He returned after ten minutes, "I've cleared it with the boss." We had no idea that there even was a boss. "She says," —ah, the boss is a she, good—"that if you'd like to meet us at weekends, you can pitch your tent behind the circle and do two shows on the green each afternoon. You can put out your hat and we'll make sure you have enough to eat."

Wonderful! We'd found a perfect community of creative new friends, little family audiences and a constant supply of homemade cake, good food and strong coffee. For the rest of our time in New Zealand, we met them each weekend, did four shows on the village green, practiced whip cracking with Dave the blacksmith and chatted long into the warm starry nights. It seems dreamlike to me now, we were so free. We went where the wind blew, our show on our backs like vagabond snails.

On our last night, after a delicious supper of bean stew and cornbread, Dave said, "We've got something to show you." Intrigued, we piled into a car and went in convoy with more cars out into the dark countryside. We stopped; everyone got out. It was a clear warm night with a full moon. Just there, a narrow track led into a thick forest. We followed along and soon heard the sound of water. I could see a river running through the trees with a strange mist hovering above. When we reached the bank, the group started taking off their clothes. The first of our group, butt naked, delicately edged his way over twigs and small stones into the shallows.

"Ahh," he said, as if he had got into a lovely hot bath, which he had. The river, like all the natural water in New Zealand, was volcanically heated. The rest of the group followed him in. Martin and I whipped off our clothes too and plonked ourselves down in the water. I squished my bum into the small gravelly stones on the bottom so that the water came up to my neck and gazed up at the moon half-covered by clouds. *Ahhh.*

We all sat there for an hour or two, lightly chatting in the hot bubbling water under the stars.

"I'll have to turn off the hot water tap," my brain said. Then it remembered that there was no tap—that all this, the hot river, the starry full-moon night, our new friends, all of this fantastic adventure, was gloriously, amazingly and wonderfully free.

"Thank you," I said to the God in the stars. "Thank you."

17

BURNT MILK

Hawaii was our final stop. We were going to stay at Club Volcano for their annual week-long juggling convention. Club Volcano is the home of an international group of jugglers who built a small permanent community on a patch of land near the beach. For years before I met him, Martin had earned money all summer doing street shows and then spent it on a winter in this paradise of mangoes, bananas and guava trees. He hadn't had a penny to his name when I met him, but no one can say he hadn't had a damn good life.

The jugglers at the convention were amongst the best in the world. I watched in awe as volleys of clubs soared easily into the air in complex patterns.

We weren't planning to perform here, and after working hard for three months solid, this was the perfect time and place to rest. We camped for free on the beach, and when the bright early sun made the tent too hot to sleep, we splashed awake in the clear turquoise ocean. We picked papaya fruit from the trees for breakfast and swam with technicolour fish. There was a café on the beach serving strong Kona coffee, and we spent the days juggling and practicing our new whip-cracking skills. It was much, much better than boring old Hamburg.

One day, Martin suggested I take a traditional Hawaiian *lomi lomi* massage with a healer he knew. I didn't know what to expect but booked a session anyway. We drove up the twisting dust track to her house, which was perched overlooking tall mango trees, the lush forest on both sides of the road peppered with deep-orange hibiscus flowers. A tall, slim woman with long dark hair introduced herself as Anne-Marie and invited me to sit on a wicker chair on her porch. Martin hugged her and drove off, promising to come back in an hour or so.

"What is it you want to heal?" she asked directly. With such a direct question from someone I didn't know and would probably never see again, my answer came out clear and concise.

"I have an eating disorder I can't shake. It ruins everything."

"Fine. Sit here." She motioned to a wooden step on the veranda. She sat close beside me. "Close your eyes."

She placed her hands on my head and gently massaged my temples. I felt myself relax more deeply as Anne-Marie slid her hands to my shoulders and eased out the knots.

"Where does it hurt?" she asked, her voice soft.

"Here." I put both hands to my throat.

"Look inside. What does it look like?" I was so relaxed that this question didn't sound strange. In my mind, I looked curiously at the inside of my oesophagus.

"It's covered with black. Like when you've burnt the milk and you can't scrape it off the bottom of the pan." I knew about burnt milk. Six months in Germany boiling milk in an enamel saucepan for Martin's *milchkaffee* each morning; it burnt every time, so annoying. Why we didn't buy a non-stick pan I don't know.

"Let's go up," she said. "Let's go up through the roof, into the blue sky. Feel the warm sun. Let's go up further beyond the clouds, beyond."

I floated effortlessly up, flying on her words: through the

clouds, through the last layers of the warm sun, up, up into the darkness. "What do you see?"

Stretching out beyond my line of vision I could see liquid black, deep beyond imagination. On it some way off, there was a tiny flame resting on the surface of the tar, as if its wick were pulling from the black. It was very small, and the black was infinitely deep. Instinctively, I knew that the black was pain. I knew the vast black was the feeling of being lost, separated. The black was the turning in on oneself and closing eyes because it hurt too much.

Somehow, I knew that the tiny flame, burning as brightly as it could, was my best effort to counteract the darkness. I was giving it my all, but it wasn't enough. I was tiny and inconsequential in the balance. I felt the pull of the bottomless black liquid; it would have been easy to give up, give in, lose myself. The black was caked inside my oesophagus, thin layer upon layer. I couldn't scrape it off. I couldn't swallow the pain—it stuck in my throat.

"Look." The healer whispered, a voice in my ear. "Look."

With my eyes still tightly shut, my inner vision more real than the day outside my eyes, I looked.

The same endless black, and my tiny, urgent but tired persistent flame. Then, from nothing, a whole infinite layer of tiny flames, identical to mine, shimmered into view. Flickering, glittering, as far as the eye could see. I knew what they were. In that moment, I saw everything in perfect balance. I saw that I wasn't alone, struggling hopelessly to balance the infinite pain of the world, but that there were a million, trillion, countless souls doing the exact same. I suddenly understood the quote from the mystic Julien of Norwich that I'd learnt at school. *It was necessary that there should be sin; but all shall be well, and all shall be well, and all manner of thing shall be well.'* There is pain, there is confusion and there is the perfect balance of light. Tears fell down my face.

"Come on," Anne-Marie said gently, "it's time for your massage."

For the rest of our time in Hawaii, knowing that we would soon return to Europe where the fish are less than tropical and papaya doesn't grow on trees, we made the most of living outdoors, hiking and swimming. We kayaked to watch whales and swam with dolphins from black volcanic beaches. We hiked up the steepest set of stone steps in the world and down a tumbling trail into the lush Waimanu Valley, where we sat under cold crystal-clear waterfalls and camped on the deserted beach.

Finally, on our last weekend, we went to Kilauea National Park, where you could watch a still-active volcano that glowed prehistoric orange in the night. At five o'clock on a chilly morning, we walked towards the orange glow. A sign said, "Warning, dangerous, do not go any further." Martin insisted that it was only for the tourists. I was skeptical. And weren't we tourists? When we reached another official sign that read, "Warning: Last year sixteen people died when ground here gave way, do NOT go any further," I sat down on the jagged grey lava floor and declared that I wouldn't marry him if he went on. He went on. I sulkily joined him, warily testing each step, terrified that I was going to fall through to the molten core of the earth at any moment.

All of which is a fairly accurate metaphor for married life I would say.

Speaking of which.

18

LEAPING THE BROOM

$\mathcal{I}$t was Spring again in Europe when we returned to our apartment in Hamburg. After four months of honing our juggling knife-throwing show around the world, we could charge proper fees for street performing gigs up and down the country. When we weren't working, as spring blossomed into early summer, we went on long bike rides out to the beautiful farmlands, whizzing past fields of cherry trees covered by nets to keep the birds away. I was much happier in Hamburg now that I was finally performing and had learnt some German.

We'd been engaged a whole year and planned to get married in Linz in July, at the street festival where we first met.

It turned out to be a huge wedding. We hadn't planned it to be so big—we didn't think anyone would want to travel to Austria, so we sent invitations to everyone we knew. I mean *everyone*. I even invited my trade union rep from British Telecom. When two hundred and fifty people accepted our invitation, we were a little overwhelmed. My union rep brought his four children. The story of two street performers from different countries who fell in love at their festival and returned to get married was great publicity and the organiser of the Linz festival gave us the town hall for our reception for free, and threw in a massive wedding cake.

We used the grounds of a medieval castle overlooking the Danube for the ceremony. Once everyone had climbed the steep cobbled lane from the main square and arrived at the gardens, Martin's mother, Ursul taught everyone a simple Jewish circle dance. Step clap, step clap, walk two three clap, and repeat. Many of the guests were self-conscious, but the laughter and mistakes broke the ice, and by the time Martin and I arrived, our friends and family from Germany and England were all mixed together, dancing in a huge circle, all smiles. No one mentioned the war.

Mick, my first magic teacher and first street-show partner, was my bridesmaid. He arrived wearing corduroy shorts, an old black tailcoat and wrinkled ankle socks. When my confused father asked him to explain his outfit, Mick replied that he'd been wearing these same clothes when Martin and I met. My beautiful Italian friend Loredana was a bridesmaid too, but it was Mick that everyone wondered about. Our great friend Betty was our pagan priestess celebrant. We wrote our own vows. We promised to stay together 'as long as love shall last.' We called in the energies of the four directions: fire, earth, water and air. I gave Miss Muriel, my old dancing teacher, a reading for air; my father a reading for earth. Two of Martin's friends were water and fire. There was a lot of puzzled eyebrow-raising from some born-again Christian friends, and my Catholic aunt was scandalised. I felt bad that I had left Jesus out. I asked Betty to mention him. She dutifully and succinctly announced, "Romany would like to mention Jesus." More puzzled looks.

In the centre of the huge circle of our friends, Betty and her husband, Ian, wrapped our wrists with cerise hand-spun silk and laid a broom made of birch on the grass for us to jump over.

"And now," Betty announced to the crowd, "the bride and groom will jump the broom to begin their new lives together." I drew back the skirt of my golden wedding gown. A loud gasp went up. Jezebel! My shoes were crimson red brocade with clunky high platform heels. Holding tight to Martin's hand, I leapt over the broom in my red shoes into the new life I'd chosen on my own terms.

The ceremony over, a samba band, daubed in mud and naked except for a few well-placed rags, danced our whole crowd down narrow streets to a courtyard where champagne and television cameras were waiting. Our wedding not only made the news, but was featured on TV every couple of hours for a whole week. The TV company even paid for our champagne and canapés, for two hundred and fifty guests. That was handy because we didn't have a bean.

After lunch, we performed our show in front of even more cameras and the biggest crowd we had ever gathered. I stripped out of my wedding dress down to my usual street costume that I had on underneath, jumped on my new husband's shoulders and juggled fire. As you do.

Just two weeks after the wedding, I was sitting on a plane to San Francisco. Alone. Don't panic; I'll explain.

19

MYSTERY SCHOOL

I'd read an article in a magic magazine about a magician called Jeff McBride. For no reason I could explain, when I read it, the hairs on my arms stood to attention and wiggled. I wrote, *"Go meet Jeff McBride!"* in imperative red ink and block capitals on the front page of my notebook.

Apparently, he was a big name in the magic world. This is how Wikipedia describes him: *"Jeff McBride is a foremost innovator and among magic's most exciting performers. McBride combines mask, martial arts, kabuki theatre, world class sleight-of-hand, myths & stories from around the world, grand illusion—and more—to create electrifying performances that thrill a wide range of audiences."*

Despite being as broke as two street performers could be after a four-month hand-to-mouth tour plus an epic wedding, I somehow did all but steal the funds necessary to fly to San Francisco and pay the fee for "Mystery School" created by McBride and a few other visionary magicians.

I had no idea what Mystery School could be. I just knew I had to go.

I packed the scant magic I'd learnt so far into a rucksack, together with the top half of the Venetian courtesan costume of my dream magic act. There was no way the voluminous crinoline skirt was going to fit as well. I landed in San Francisco and took a bus to Santa Barbara. Once there, I wandered around, wondering where I was going to sleep. These days, armed with several credit cards and money in the bank, I like to 'arrive expected and arrive welcome' with a note addressed to adventure saying, 'Not today, thank you.' But my thirty-year-old self didn't have anywhere to stay that night and wasn't overly worried.

The Mystery School didn't start until the next day. In the park, a juggler was practicing under the shade of a leafy tree. I told him that I was a juggler too and, assuming the worldwide brotherhood of jugglers, asked if he had a spare room for one night. He wasn't sure. He phoned his wife. His wife was sure—they didn't. Instead, he offered me the use of his lock-up garage on the outskirts of town. Great. We drove over and he creaked open the up-and-over door.

It was a garage just like you'd expect—full of crap. Bikes, boxes, dusty shelves with nowhere to actually sleep. He moved a few things around ineffectually and, not being able to make the state of his garage any more hospitable, excused himself and beetled back to his wife.

I scrunched up a few old curtains on the floor to make a bed, then shut the up-and-over door. I made myself comfortable in my velvet nest, closed my eyes and drifted off to sleep. I was tired after my long flight. When I woke in total darkness, I realised that I didn't know where the light switch was.

I was desperate for a pee. I didn't dare open the door in case I couldn't close it again, so I felt my way to the sink that I remembered was in the corner, bumping my toes on mysterious objects in the way. Exploring its contents with my hands, I found a large empty mug. Crouching down in the dark, I peed in it, congratulating myself for my accuracy. I know what you're thinking, but what else was I to do?

I bumped my way back to my nest of curtains and tried to get back to sleep.

A sound—a scrabbling sound of little claws. Rats! I love animals, but I didn't fancy being nibbled at while I slept. I felt my way over the piles of boxes and bumped up against what had to be a table. It wasn't big enough to lie on full-length, but it would have to do.

Lying scrunched up on the table top, I drifted back into sleep, but the loud revving of motorbikes rattled me awake. Hells Angels? Marauding gangs of evil bikers? Vampire bikers? They must have been joy-riding in circles around the garages; it went on for hours. I was cold, hungry and more than a bit scared. Suddenly my mother was there.

"Don't worry, I'm not leaving you until the sun comes up," she said.

Typical of my loyal mother to come all this way to a grimy lock-up in Santa Barbara to soothe my fears and guard me from the rats. I hoped she hadn't noticed me peeing in the mug.

As soon as it was light, hardly having slept but at least still un-nibbled, I peeled myself off the table and opened the up-and-over door, breathing in the clean, fresh morning air. Hauling my rucksack, I walked into town, passing white stucco houses with red roofs with a glimpse of the bright blue ocean down the roads between. I felt excited and free. I'd survived the night and was back on an adventure.

Coffee. A café had just opened. I ordered pastries and strong black coffee while the Mexican cleaner mopped the red tile floor. I said good morning in my best beginner's Spanish. She stared at me blankly and didn't reply. Back on the road, the early sunshine was warm and bright. Following the directions in my welcome letter, I walked for an hour or so down a remote lane heading away from the town until I found a Catholic retreat centre almost hidden in a little copse of trees. A sun-sparkling river ran over a jumble of moss-covered rocks just behind.

In the entrance hallway of the centre, sitting at a desk, a woman with a pile of paperwork in front of her looked up. She was wearing a plain green t-shirt with blue jeans and had shoulder-length brown hair hanging down either side of her face from a centre parting. She didn't look mysterious in the least.

"I've come for the Mystery School."

"You're too early," she replied curtly. "It isn't open yet."

Jet-lagged, short on sleep and just having walked for two hours in the heat with a heavy rucksack full of magic, I was on the verge of tears when I heard someone say,

"You can hang in my room." A tall angel appeared out of nowhere, gave me his key and promptly vanished. *He must be a proper magician.*

I fell into a deep sleep on his bed. When he joggled me awake, it was lunch time and he led me to the canteen, where eighty-odd other magicians were noisily greeting each other like long-lost friends and helping themselves to the buffet.

And then?

What happened after that?

Well, I can't tell you everything. It's a secret, a mystery.

What I can say is that we had lectures on stage magic, movement, and creating character. There was drumming, writing classes and even a mask-making workshop. I made a golden Venetian mask with gold spray and plastic jewels. Spray can in hand, fingers sticky with glue and glitter; I remembered my corporate days and breathed a sigh of relief. I might have fulfilled their plastic cup creativity criteria, but they certainly hadn't met mine.

For the rest of the week, for the first time in my experience of magic, I felt welcome and included. Unlike the secretive Hamburg magicians, the group here was happy to share information. Want to change a silk scarf into a rabbit? Look in Rice's *Encyclopedia of Silk*, volume two, chapter three. Want to make a large bowl of water appear from nowhere? Look in *Mahatma* magic magazine, or better still, I'll show you how right now.

Each night something different happened. One evening, we were asked to wear the masks we had made. When darkness fell and vibrated with the whirring hum of crickets, I wandered about in my golden mask, astonished by odd theatrical installations popping up in unexpected places. I saw a cowled monk with a long white beard sitting quietly under the trees, surrounded by piled-up old books and candles dripping wax. A small group of students stood watching him curiously. As I joined them, he looked at us and asked, in the deepest of voices, "If you were invisible and could do anything, anything at all—tell me, what is it that you would you do?" From his unmistakable voice I knew the monk was Eugene Burger, the magician and teacher that had inspired and supported my magic for twenty years. Behind my golden mask, I replied in my thoughts, *I would whisper in each ear of every person through all time, "All is well; you are loved more than you can know."*

The night I was really excited about was the works-in-progress session. I was about to perform my new Venetian courtesan magic act for the very first time to an audience of real magicians.

Since I couldn't fit the crinoline skirt in my rucksack, I'd bought two hula hoops from a toyshop in Santa Barbara, covered them with newspaper and hung them with string from an elastic waistband to make a makeshift skirt. I wore the normal top half of my gown and made a natty little newspaper hat to match. Full of nerves, I waited outside in the garden. When it was my turn, I stood on the stage, looking out over the audience. My new friends smiled back.

"Before I start, I have to tell you something." I began. My audience nodded expectantly. "The thing is, you'll have to imagine the magic I describe, because I can't actually do it yet." They nodded again, assuming I was being modest.

"Mist swirls about the stage," I explained. "A clock strikes midnight. Bong, bong, bong." There were a few titters from the crowd, but I continued seriously. "Bong, bong, bong. On the stroke of twelve, I appear, slowly, out of thin air. Here I come." A few more giggles. "I pluck a crystal ball out of the ether." Stretching out my hand, I made a plucking movement. If the assembled magi were expecting to see an actual ball appear, they were disappointed.

"Blowing on it softly, my magic ball transforms into a bowl of clear, sparkling water with a goldfish glittering inside." The giggles got louder as the magicians realised that when I said I couldn't actually do any of the magic, I'd meant it.

I ignored them and continued, describing one magical effect after another until the audience were wiping their eyes, howling with laughter.

"And as suddenly as I appeared, I am gone. All that is left of me is my beautiful portrait on the golden stand in the centre of the stage."

That wasn't there, either. Just me. And I was still there too.

The crowd was hysterical. I made my exit with grave Venetian dignity and waited outside. I didn't understand. Why were they laughing?

Jeff McBride bounded out to find me and said, "That was really good!"

"But why were they laughing?"

"Because you're funny," he said and bounded off.

20

SNOW QUEEN

$\mathcal{B}$ack in Hamburg, the excitement of our wedding and the fun of finding a new community of friendly magicians at Mystery School threatened to evaporate in the prospect of another winter. I still hadn't made many friends in Hamburg, I didn't have any magic work, and my eating disorder was gaining the upper hand. I was almost completely healthy during our world tour and even better while I was enjoying myself at Mystery School. But once home and lonely again—back it came. As a measure of unhappiness, bulimia is unforgivingly accurate.

One long, quiet weekend alone while Martin was away, I passed the time reading *Women Who Run with the Wolves* by Clarissa Pinkola Estés, a fabulous book of fairy tales and their symbolic meaning. When I read *The Red Shoes* and her explanation about women who are seduced by the golden lure of marriage into giving up their dream, I felt as if I had been hit on the head with a hammer. By joining Martin in Germany, I had landed in a place where somehow, I found it impossible to thrive. Yes, we were in love; yes, we had a nice flat in a beautiful town, but I couldn't seem to move towards my dream of having my own show and, once more, I was in a cage with that wire tightening around my neck.

I was so shocked by this realisation that I didn't bother to sugar-coat my words. Before Martin was hardly through the door, I burst out bluntly, "I've had enough. I've tried but I'm not happy here. I'm going back to England. You can come with me or not, but I'm going back."

And bless his generous, kind-hearted German woolly socks, he came.

We rented a tiny bedsit in Shepherds Bush in the house of some friends of my parents. We had one room and a minuscule kitchen. By the time we squashed in the knife-throwing board, unicycle, costumes and the rest of our props, there was only two square feet of empty floor space left. Financially, we were totally dependent on any gigs I could get.

My old magic teacher kindly gave me a weekly Sunday lunchtime job performing strolling magic in a family restaurant. Although all my glorious ideas for stage acts had come to nothing, I wasn't too shabby at close-up magic with cards and coins. Since I had killed off the black queen and given her costume away, I needed a new image. What could be better than a magic Carmen Miranda? Don't answer that.

With a chain of brightly coloured plastic fruit slung from one shoulder to the other over my gold wedding dress, plus a matching turban decorated with a bunch of plastic bananas, I performed card and coin tricks from table to table. I was doing my best and deadly serious as I wandered about covered in plastic fruit. People started to laugh the moment I started a trick. I just couldn't understand it.

As Christmas approached, one agent sent me for an interview with a party planner. Corporate business was booming in London, and the grand Christmas office party was very much alive.

"We're looking for something slightly different this year," said the perfectly coiffured blonde with sharp highlights. She'd run her event company efficiently for years and knew exactly what she wanted. Her team had built a huge marquee in a disused car park in central London. Each night leading up to Christmas, they hosted luxury parties for a thousand office revellers, complete with dodgems, casino and an Abba tribute band.

"We've had lots of magicians in the past doing card tricks, but now we're looking for something different. Our theme this year is 'Winter Wonderland.'"

My father often warned me. *Think before you speak.* I should have listened. Instead, when I heard the words 'Winter Wonderland' and 'different,' my brain fired straight into over-excited response mode.

"I could be a Snow Queen!"

The organiser raised her perfect eyebrows, but nodded encouragingly.

"I could make balls of fire appear from my hands—*POW!*—" I mimed the action, eager and animated. "I could turn flames into cascades of golden streamers. I'll conjure a blue silk scarf out of the air, then—*POOF!*—Nothing in my hands but a tiny bluebird with white tail feathers. I'll squeeze ice-cubes into a sparkling diamond necklace. I'll have a beautiful ice-blue silk gown and a gleaming silver crown hung with real quartz crystal!"

Wow! How could they refuse? Much better than a boring old magician in a smelly tuxedo.

"Thank you. We'll discuss it at our planning meeting next Tuesday and let you know."

That was May. I didn't hear back and assumed they'd forgotten. In late October, I got a call.

"We would like the Snow Queen, please. You'll be doing twenty-three nights starting December the first."

Oh, bloody hell.

So far, I could make a Heinz ketchup bottle vanish, turn three pieces of rope into one long one and do a couple of coin tricks.

Balls of fire? Ice-cubes into a diamond necklace? Glorious ice-blue gown *and* a crystal crown?

These days, I've learnt my lesson from those early years. I won't promise you an act I can't do, no matter how far in advance you book or how much you pay. The scars of the Snow Queen are burnt deep upon my soul.

Daunted but optimistic, I set to work. I had two whole months, surely that had to be enough? A friend recommended another friend who had just finished her fashion degree. I commissioned her to make the gown. No, I hadn't seen her work. I found a metal worker to make the crown. I ordered ambitious promises from the magic shop: fireballs from hand, appearing gold and silver streamers and blue silk scarfs. I bought a sequinned bird with white tail feathers and metres of ice-blue silk, shot through with silver thread.

The fashion graduate took my measurements and armfuls of fabric. I gave the metal worker a hefty deposit to buy crystals for the crown—everything was set in motion. I spent my day trying to create the magic I'd promised the event company. The task was impossible, but I didn't know that yet. I got up early and worked until late, researching and experimenting. Nothing worked. As weeks passed, I ignored the quiet persistent voice reminding me that time was slipping by and still I couldn't do any of the magic.

I met with my costume maker once, twice, three times. Each time, she assured me that everything was in hand, but I only ever saw the very basic shaping of a gown. Her deadline was mid-November, two weeks before my first night. Once I had the costume, I would have two weeks to design and make the pockets for the fireballs and ice cubes. I enrolled the family that owned our bedsit to help. Their job was to roll and re-roll the gold and silver streamers after I practiced throwing them. Carole, Jerome and their kids absent-mindedly wound spools of streamers while watching TV—heaps of gold and silver by their feet, gleaming in the blue glow of the screen.

Two weeks before the opening night, I drove over to collect the gown. My costume maker opened the door, her face red and blotchy. Inside, piles of cut ice-blue silk covered the floor.

"I couldn't do it," she sobbed, "I'm really sorry, but I just couldn't do it."

Panic opened in my chest, my throat narrowed. Outwardly composed, I said brightly, "That's all right, don't worry." I gave her shoulders a rub, half my brain congratulating the other half on keeping so calm.

Gathering up armfuls of useless remnants of blue silk, I left. Outside, the air drained from the world. I couldn't breathe. My contract began in two weeks, and like Cinderella, I had nothing to wear and no magic powers. I appeared to be having an asthma attack. From the dark alley by my car, I called the metal worker. Between dry sobs I gasped, "Is the crown ready?"

"Yup, come round." In his industrial workshop, crowded with tools and metal shavings, the crown sat proudly on a stand, a beautiful tangle of twisted metal at least a foot tall, polished steel dripping with shining lead crystal. At least something was ready.

Back home that night, I didn't know what to do—my first professional magic contract was teetering on the edge of disaster. At times like these, it's handy to believe in 'real' magic. I knelt at my altar, lit some candles and desperately asked the angels for help.

There is a quote attributed to Saint Augustine: *"Pray as if everything depends on God. Work as if everything depends on you."*

I got to work.

I had no dress-making skills to speak of, but our entire winter earnings were at stake. The next day, I bought metres of new fabric and sewed late into the early hours making the costume up as I went along. In our cramped bed-sit, Martin slept soundly, his head a couple of feet from the whirring sewing machine. I followed my intuition, performing one small action after another. Out of nothing, the ice-blue crinoline skirt with secret pockets and a corset glittering with Swarovski crystals began to take shape. Flying against time, I used a glue gun for most of the sewing—my fingers blistered with hot glue burns.

Since making the costume took priority, I'd abandoned work on the magic I'd promised and, in any case, it was all far beyond my ability.

With assistance from helpful whispering angels, the gown was ready a week before the first night, literally held together with glue and a prayer. I couldn't quite believe it myself. I looked at the reflection in my mirror and saw a regal snow queen in an ice-blue gossamer gown sparkling with diamonds, crowned with a gleaming crystal crown.

I'd planned ahead and organised a walk-about gig in a shopping centre so that I could use it as a dress rehearsal. In full Snow Queen costume, I glided through the pseudo marble halls, but within a few minutes of wearing my crystal crown, my neck went into spasm and I hastily returned to the dressing-room. It was far too heavy to wear.

Even without the crown, I was obviously a natural snow queen. Entertainers were required to wander about the main shopping halls among the shoppers but forbidden to enter the shops themselves. I've never been one for obeying rules, so I wandered into a fashion store.

"Do you think this is me?" I demanded loudly in my best snow queen voice, holding up an ice-blue cashmere jumper.

"Come on, Miss," a gruff voice at my elbow said, "out with

you now." The store had called security. I did enjoy being forcibly ejected by two puzzled security guards.

On the first night of the corporate Winter Wonderland party, I swished through tipsy bankers in my regal gown with flamboyant bravado. Abandoning the too-heavy crystal crown, I'd made another hat out of a cereal box, white fake fur and a couple of metal coat hangers.

"I thought you were going to make fireballs turn to showers of golden streamers and turn ice-cubes into diamonds? And what happened to the bluebirds?" the organiser remarked coldly while I took a break.

"Wasn't allowed," I replied, equally cool. "Fire regulations."

Phew.

21

FOLLOW ME

So, there we were, Martin and I, bumbling along, trying to establish ourselves as performers in England. The proverb says, "*When poverty comes in the front door, love flies out the window.*" It was hard to keep up any romance while counting every penny, squashed in a tiny bedsit and having no money for fun.

And then.

Martin was thirty-three, super fit and healthy, although he'd been suffering from slight acid reflux. He took some indigestion remedy, and when that didn't help, he saw the doctor who gave him some more. After a month, he was referred for a scan. We were summoned to see a surgeon.

"You have a tumour the size of a grapefruit between your heart, lungs and spine," the surgeon said. "If it grows any larger and touches any of those organs, it will be fatal. We have to operate within the next couple of weeks."

A week later, still in shock, I was booked to go to an Angels, Faeries and Nature Spirits conference in Findhorn. These things are tax deductible if you're a magician. I asked my roommate, who was on the psychic side, if she had any insight as to why Martin should have developed this tumour. Not knowing Martin in the least, she offered that he could be carrying a stone near his heart created by sorrow.

I reported this back to Martin and he agreed. His brother had died in a windsurfing accident when he was eighteen and Martin only sixteen. As the sole remaining son of his divorced mother, Martin had wanted to support her and hadn't cried once. Years ago, in an art therapy class, he had sketched a large grey stone by his heart that he felt was the unexpressed sorrow he carried for his brother. Now it was a real stone that needed to be cut out before it killed him. When we returned to the surgeon, Martin refused to be operated on, saying, "I grew that tumour, so I'm going to shrink it."

The surgeon was apoplectic and washed his hands of any responsibility. That summer, Martin threw himself into grief. He wept at his brother's grave. His grandmother had recently died too. She was a nasty, vindictive woman and the whole family was relieved. When Martin bawled long and loud at the funeral, everyone stared at him in amazement. He wept for everyone and everything and went back for a scan in the autumn. No change; it hadn't grown but it hadn't shrunk either. The surgeon set a date to operate.

At 3 a.m. in our bedsit, I got up for a pee. For some reason, instead of going back to bed, I sat on the step outside our room, listening to the hush of the house.

"You have to leave Martin," a quiet voice said. I was surprised to hear that voice in the stillness of the night. But it wasn't the first time.

Do I mean it wasn't the first time I'd heard the voice? Or the first time it told me to leave Martin?

Both.

The first time that quiet voice told me to leave Martin was in a loo in Portugal with white stucco walls, cerise bougainvillea covering the door. We'd only been married for two years.

God often speaks to me in the toilet. Or in the shower. He likes small spaces with water. That might sound barmy. If so, I need to give you a little background so you'll understand.

I went to a Catholic convent school and my family went to Mass every Sunday. I sang along loudly with all the hymns. I liked the hymns. Eight years old, I used to saunter home from school warbling,

All that I am, all that I do,
All that I'll ever have I offer now to you.

I was a bit wary of the one that went,

Come Lord Jesus come,
Come take my hands, take them for your work.

I thought He might zip down with a big surgeon's knife and chop them off.

Later, fourteen years old, at lunchtimes in my convent school, I would chat to my mate the Virgin Mary in the tiny chapel. After making a soggy sign of the cross with water from the stoop by the door, I would take a waxy new candle from the iron rack of candles that flickered and dripped wax onto the tinfoil-covered tray and light it from one that was already burning, thinking up a wish. I wiggled it into a holder, then found a pew. Kneeling on the embroidered hassocks, I said to Mary, *Hello, it's me. How are you?*

Sometimes I went to the chapel in the morning before school as well as lunchtimes. It was dark and peaceful, still smelling of incense from the early mass. If I held two fingers up and crossed them, the Virgin Mary and I were like that. I chatted to her constantly in my head. She didn't say much, but she was a good listener.

Later, in my first year at university, I happened to share a flat with a born-again Christian and a mature student who'd been a missionary. Sitting on my narrow bed one night, they asked, "Do you know Jesus? Do you think you're going to heaven?" I stared at them with pity. Didn't they understand that as a Catholic, I had a gold VIP first-in-line, straight-in-at-the-gate ticket through the pearly gates? Everyone knows that the Catholics with a capital C are the best. As Protestants, they were way down on the guest list.

Then, when I started my first job in London, I shared a house in Clapham with four born-again Christians. Before dinner, they said grace and I chipped in with a Hail Mary. While I prayed, they looked at me daggers. Born-agains don't like Mary. Idolatry apparently. You would have thought we'd all be on the same side, but the born-again housemates and I had a bubbling-under-the-surface rivalry going on.

One night, in the early hours, I was suddenly awake. Maybe the born-agains had put something in my tea—maybe they did have a hotline to God after all. I sat bolt upright, feeling an odd tingling sensation of liquid golden light coursing through my veins. I felt curiously and gloriously full of enormous gratitude and love. I got out of bed, fell on my knees and wept. I don't care if that is a cliché. It's probably a cliché because that's what people do when they are woken up in the early hours and filled with Light.

"I'm a Christian! I'm a Christian!" I shouted to them as soon as I heard them getting up for work. Great rejoicing from my housemates. Born-agains—one, Catholics—nil.

"You're a Christian? What were you before?" my mother remarked dryly. "I thought Catholics *were* Christians."

All that week, hymns and bubbling joy streamed through my thoughts. I joined the Holy Trinity Brompton church and enthusiastically got stuck into worship sessions and Bible study groups. I even got the gift of tongues. Which was a bit weird, I admit.

I'll tell you about it, although it's meant to be a secret.

A large group of us were on a weekend away specifically to receive the gift of tongues. On the first evening, the pastor asked us to pray. We prayed. People around me started to burble with strange noises. It sounded like a cross between Hebrew and gobbledygook.

I tried opening and shutting my mouth. I waggled my tongue

a bit but nothing came out. I was desperately disappointed. Everyone else was joyfully gabbling away and hugging. I seemed to be the only one who hadn't got it. I left quietly and shut myself in the ladies' loo to cry.

When I finally blew my nose and came out, there was a delicious young man with dark curly hair standing in the corridor. Seeing my tear-stained face, he asked why I was upset.

"Everyone else got the gift of tongues and I didn't." I sniffed.

"Come with me." He called a few of his mates and they trooped outside into the garden and up a ladder into a tree house. Yes, a tree house.

"We're going to pray with you. Just relax and try making a few noises. It will come."

The boys prayed. Rather self-consciously, I tried out a few burbles—and then, I too was gabbling in a strange tongue which felt oddly safe and comforting.

"See? It's easy."

I liked my new gift of speaking in tongues. The pastor explained that we could use it to pray purely, a direct line between our higher self and God, without crappy bits of ego getting in the way. Instead of praying, "I'd like a brand-new car and a boyfriend and a smart flat," my higher self would be tooting praises and praying for my real good, whatever that is. I thought it sounded rather sensible.

My new found born-again Christianity was going well—up to a point. At the church, there were lots of good-looking boys. They were rich too, since it was Knightsbridge. Trouble was, they'd all been told they had to ask and receive divine permission before asking a girl out. God obviously hadn't given anyone permission to ask me out. No sex before marriage, either. All very boring. The most exciting social thing my Bible study group did was bowling. I bloody hate bowling.

What I preferred was salsa dancing. I zapped straight from

Sunday evening church to La Finca, a noisy, writhing Latin nightclub in Islington. One minute I was singing hallelujahs praising God, and the next I was pressed up against a wall, enthusiastically snogging a sweaty Columbian guy. Fantastic.

My housemates didn't agree. Nor did my Bible study group. Everything I liked was 'wrong.' According to them, juggling was almost witchcraft and stilt-walking the activity of the devil. My housemate who got up early for work and had the room next to the bathroom didn't seem to love me quite so much when I had a shower after salsa in the early hours and the noise of the immersion heater woke her up.

Jesus said, "It's time to move."

He didn't really. I figured that one out myself. I found a flat in Camden with a housemate who hadn't the slightest interest in God. I severed all ties with the born-agains, kept on good terms with God, Mary and my new housemate, and everything was cool.

So now that you know that it wasn't unusual for me to have a nice chat with God, you won't find it so odd when I say that God often speaks to me in the toilet. Or the shower. I repeat because it's true: He likes small spaces with water.

The first time the voice told me to leave Martin, we were in Porto at a street festival performing our comedy knife-throwing show. In the evenings, we sat around long tables with the other artistes, plates piled high with fresh grilled sardines, warm bread and red ripe tomatoes. I'd nipped off for a pee.

I was minding my own business in the loo, when God said, "You have to leave Martin."

"*What?*"

"You have to leave Martin."

"I can't, I love him. Why?"

No answer.

Odd. We were struggling with being broke but were still in love and happy. I filed the incident away as a weird blip of my imagination and carried on as normal.

Now, a year later, in our bedsit in Shepherds Bush, at 3 a.m., the same quiet voice had the same clear message.

Maybe, I thought, *he's going to die with this tumour and that's why I'm going to leave him.*

I don't want you to think that I was taking all this calmly. I was bewildered and upset. And *very* pissed off with God.

The other thing you need to know is that I was brought up with stories of Jesus asking his disciples to leave their families to follow him. We sang hymns about it.

Follow me, follow me, leave your home and family,
Leave your fishing nets and boats upon the shore.
Leave the seed that you have sown, leave the crops you have grown,
Leave the people you have known and follow me.

I'd always told God that I wanted to do His will. I'd said it over and over. But leaving Martin was not what I wanted at all.

I apologise here for the use of the term 'God.' I will be changing it soon to 'Spirit,' 'Goddess,' 'All That There Is,' and other funkier names. They all refer to the Divine, whichever flavour you're comfortable with. That night, sobbing silently on the step outside my bedsit, I was still in my 'God' phase.

After a bit, there was nothing more to be heard, and I went back to bed. I didn't tell a soul: not Martin, no one.

It was urgent now to find somewhere else to live so that Martin could have a comfortable place to recuperate after his operation. We hadn't any time to waste, and after an entire weekend of house hunting, we used my BT emergency nest egg that I'd put in a five-year investment plan to put down a deposit on a tiny little two-bedroom house in Newhaven near Brighton.

While Martin was in hospital having the tumour removed, I moved us in.

The operation went smoothly, and after five months of recuperation, Martin was back to full health, albeit with a vicious ten-inch scar behind his left shoulder blade. That summer, we went back to perform our comedy knife-throwing juggling street show in Linz. Everything seemed to be looking up.

Everything except for that quiet instruction that whispered at the back of my mind.

22

A DIVA IS BORN

In our tiny, two-bedroom house in the backwater town of Newhaven, just outside Brighton, we painted the walls a deep pink, hung gold organza at the windows and looped fairy lights everywhere. We made a tiny theatre in the living room, hung black velvet over the walls and put up spotlights. You could fit fifteen people in if you 'squooze' them very tightly. I heard an expert say that you should perform your act one hundred times before you even consider it practiced. But where do you perform a new act? In your living room of course.

Over two years, we did shows for about six hundred people—fifteen at a time. Once the audience had got a little tipsy in the kitchen, I would appear in full feathers and diamonds, then theatrically invite them to the theatre. The neighbours had never seen anything like it.

Although professionally we were performing our comedy juggling show and I was doing frequent gigs of small walkabout close-up magic, my dream of having a wonderful stage act was as important and apparently as far out of reach as ever. In my boxing class, I slammed the red punch bag as hard as I could, muttering, "I am a world star of magic! I am a world star of magic!" On every bike ride over the hills, I shouted to the wind, "I am a world star of magic!" I set up a buddy system with a writer friend. We gave ourselves goals, she to write, me to work on my act. I worked through every creative exercise in *The Artist's Way* by Julia Cameron. Nothing was more important to me than to have this act. Nothing.

Well, nothing except my determination to have the right-shaped body to perform it. I hired a personal trainer and filled the fridge with skinless chicken breasts. I ran and boxed and biked. As a friend pointed out, if I had spent as much time practising magic as I did exercising, my dream act would have been ready years ago. On top of that, many of my days were completely lost to bulimia, and I was often too tired and dispirited to do much more than fall into long afternoons of oblivious sleep.

These days, I feel sad that I wasted so much time and risked my health for such an apparently petty concern. For nearly forty years, my daily waking thought has been, *I'm too big*. My mind has been one-third focused on eating, not-eating or feeling that I've failed to have the discipline to achieve the figure I'd like. In my defence, I work daily, hourly, to turn this chronic way of thinking around. Sometimes I win, sometimes I don't. I'm fit and healthy, but every day I think that if I let my guard down and eat some lovely toast for breakfast or—heaven forbid—a whole pizza for dinner, an extra ten pounds will rapidly appear on my frame and my career will vanish. That's not just my imagination; the moment I do less exercise and stop watching what I eat, the pounds swiftly pile back on. I've just got one of those physiques. Like it or not, showbiz demands that its workers are slim. Watch any film, go see any show: the heroines are slender. That's just how it is. If you had to find a Hollywood star to play me in a film of my life, they'd have to fatten up first.

I hired a theatrical director called Sarah Brignall to help me with my act. She trained at the Jacques Lecoq clown school in Paris and was a comedy actress herself. She asked me to bring what I had of my act.

I had a head full of dreams and a notebook full of ideas, but as always, even after five years of trying, I couldn't do any of the magic I'd dreamt up. At our first meeting, embarrassed, I confessed.

"Tell me what you would do if you could," she suggested.

As before at Mystery School, I described my dream act. It was even more elaborate now. Now there were bright golden balls appearing out of thin air, a crystal-clear fountain bubbling suddenly from a table. Fluttering white doves flew from white silk scarves, and a bowl of fire transformed into a glittering pile of cascading jewels. I recited a poem with corresponding actions and, at the end, I vanished and appeared—you guessed it—as a portrait in a golden picture frame.

Sarah laughed so much that she almost fell off her sofa.

"That's your act! That's it! You've got it all already!"

I was getting rather huffy that everyone found it so hilarious when I tried to do magic. But each week, as I explained my more ambitious plans and acted them out, we both fell about laughing. I mean we literally fell on the floor gasping for breath. One session, I showed Sarah how I planned to levitate. I can't tell you precise details or The Magic Circle will throw me out. All you need to know is that I had the strongest magnets to be found on the planet attached to the bottom of one shoe. I was near a table with metal hinges, and as I raised one leg, my shoe snapped onto the hinge, swiping my other leg from underneath. In an instant, I hit the floor. Sarah collapsed in hysterics again. When I tried to explain the miracle that should have happened, she laughed even more. I joined her and spent another five minutes lost in helpless giggles with my foot firmly attached to the underside of a table.

It felt good to see five years of frustration turn into comedy. After six months of weekly three-hour sessions, the character that I've been playing now for fifteen years, the Diva of Magic, was born.

The Diva of Magic is a grand theatrical star. In the act Sarah and I devised, something has gone very wrong. The Diva enters stage right, dressed in a skirt and cape made out of newspaper, a purple Brazilian feather headdress on her head. She clears her throat and announces, "How marvellous to be with you tonight after flying in from my sell-out show in Las Vegas! However—there has been a terrible tragedy." She pauses to compose herself. "At the airport, some of my flight cases containing my stage set, costumes and props were thought suspicious by security and destroyed in a controlled explosion."

This was a month after 9/11. I was actually chatting on the phone to Sarah with the television on when we both watched the planes fly into the twin towers.

"My loyal team rushed in to prevent the blast that would destroy my props, and poor Vera, poor, poor Vera, my wardrobe mistress and dear friend, is no more. Simon on sound, has survived—just. I'm sure he'll do very well with his remaining arm and use of his left eye."

She glances up towards the sound and lighting booth.

"Even worse, my whole troupe of Brazilian dancers, including lovely, lovely Leroy, were stopped by immigration, and as I speak, are on their way back to Brazil."

She takes a deep breath.

"But the show must go on! So come with me! Use your imagination and create in your mind the splendid costumes and stage sets that were! We start the act with my elegant descent from the diamond encrusted staircase." She pauses and peers into the wings. "Trevor, bring out my diamond encrusted staircase." Trevor, a thick-set grumpy stagehand walks out slowly, carrying an aluminium step ladder badly disguised with a few bits of silver tinsel. He sets it centre stage and holds it while she climbs to the top carefully. She looks towards the sound desk and gives a discrete nod. Silence.

"Thank you, Simon." Still nothing.

"Simon, I do understand that you are injured, but I did give you a stick. Put it between your teeth and push the buttons with that!"

Simon has a terrible ringing in his ears. He's replaced the missing golden ball needed for the next section of the show with an orange ballcock from the third ladies' loo on the right, but everyone is just going to have to imagine the magical fountain. The doves are dead. Simon is not having a good day.

Finally, he finds a track and music rings out. But it's not the music for her grand entrance on the staircase but for the Brazilian extravaganza.

"That's the Brazilians, Simon!"

Simon is past caring. Glaring at him, she whips off her feather headdress and replaces it with a gold plastic fruit covered Carmen Miranda turban.

"This is my Brazilian extravaganza!" she tells the audience. "Imagine palm trees here." She points stage right, "and palm trees there," stage left. "Fifty beautiful Brazilian dancing girls are behind me, all wearing itsy-bitsy bikinis and Carmen Miranda hats."

She dances with the samba music to the front of the stage. "I'm in the middle, because I'm the star!"

She loves being the star. She was born to be a star. "And here are the Brazilian boys, thirty-two of them, wearing nothing but golden body paint and tight leather loincloths. Lovely Leroy spins in and takes hold of my ankle—butch, beautiful Bruno the other. They lift and I rise, suspended on their rippling muscles." She lifts her arms in the air like a ballerina, stands on one leg and begins to turn around slowly. The audience begin to wonder whether she might be quite mad. "I rotate like Celine Dion, the girls dancing underneath me, their feathers tickling my—oooh—oooh! And down."

With both feet back on the floor, she continues, "My beautiful Brazilians take a bow and the audience goes wild." The audience does not go wild. A little out of breath, she removes her Carmen Miranda hat and hands it to Trevor in the wings, returning with a bright orange ballcock in her hand.

"Over here, from nowhere, an abundant fountain rises." She motions with her hands, gazing rapt at the mystical waters rising in her imagination. "The water is pure, sparkling, reflecting all the colourful lights. The lights bounce off the water in a cascade of vibrant rainbows. A golden ball, beautiful and delicate, set with fantastic jewels, rubies and diamonds rises on the water." Holding the ballcock out to the audience, she adds, "Ladies, please avoid using the third loo in from the right. It won't flush without this." She walks forward. "And now, a poem of love, to the audience." She throws the ballcock above her head and recites:

I shall not die an un-lived life.
I shall not live in fear of falling or of catching fire.[3]

As she catches it, the golden ball splits in two, bright flame springing up from the opening.

Except, being a ballcock, it doesn't split in two and there isn't any fire. She mimes shutting the two halves of the ball, and when she opens them again, they are full of fresh, fragrant flowers. Still only being a ballcock, there are no flowers.

I choose to inhabit my days,
To allow my living to open me.

She throws both arms wide and two white doves fly from her outstretched hands. Tonight, only a few feathers flutter sadly down.

---

[3] "I shall not die an un-lived life" by Dawna Markova

"Poor Muffy and Fluffy," she mutters sadly, more to herself than to the audience. Pulling herself together, she looks out to the audience once more. "But oh, you have to see my grand finale. You're going to love my grand finale!" She walks upstage.

"Imagine dry ice everywhere, up to the knee, no expense spared," she gestures expansively about the stage. "I walk through the mists of time in a golden gown, sparkling with jewels, into the spotlight, into the glorious light. Everywhere is dark, but I am in the spotlight—and the wind-machine. Two splendid white stallions canter in from the wings. They parade around me in a circle and then—off they go."

There are no stallions, not even a little horse.

"Flame springs from my empty hands, then turns in a flash to a cascade of white silk."

This time, real flames do appear from her hands and magically change into a large square of white silk. This was one thing I could actually do. "I raise the silk cloth higher and higher as I rise into the light. Suddenly the cloth flutters to the floor and—" She runs to the wings, returning seconds later with a large black cloth bag. She climbs in and closes the top. "I've disappeared! There's nothing here! You can't see me. I'm lost in the mists of time."

But the audience can see her, the dry ice machine has packed up, and there are no mists of time.

"This is how they do it in Vegas," the black bag explains in a whisper. It looks up towards the sound desk. "Angel music please, Simon."

The ringing in Simon's ears is getting worse, his injured hand is throbbing and he's beginning to get a migraine. Instead of the angelic choir, whether by mistake or spite, he plays the opening Brazilian samba.

"That's the Brazilians again!" She tries to see what he's doing up there in the sound booth but everything is dark through the fabric. "Angels, Simon, *bloody, ruddy angels!*"

Simon finally finds the right track, the angels burst into the "Hallelujah Chorus" and she busts out of the bag in a glorious red satin ball gown, golden confetti raining down from the skies, *Ta da!* This time, ball gown, confetti and applause are real.

I nervously took the act up to the Happy Clappy Hour try-out spot in Fulham.

The Happy Clappy Hour was a free variety show where the audience gave performers a safe space to perform new acts. I paced back and forth in the dressing room dressed in newspaper, purple feather headdress on my head, orange ballcock in hand, terrified.

I needn't have worried. By the time I was jumping about in the black bag telling them about how I'd vanished in the mists of time, the audience had tears of laughter running down their face and the applause at the end was loud and genuine.

I sat in my car afterwards astonished. *Astonished.* I can make people laugh? Not just smile but really laugh? Incredible.

That was all the encouragement I needed. I booked myself onto a masterclass in Amsterdam two months later with my magic teachers Jeff McBride and Eugene Burger so that I could show them the act and get their feedback. I couldn't wait.

In Amsterdam, our small group of fifteen students sat in a horseshoe of desks facing the stage, notebooks and pens in hand. When it was my turn to perform, my friends watched in wide-eyed puzzled silence. *Silence.* No one laughed, no one smiled, no one seemed to understand that it was funny. In their defence, they were Dutch, which is almost German.

When I finished, there was a faint sputter of applause. I stood on stage, breathing hard in my rumpled red ball gown. My friends stared down at their notebooks, embarrassed.

"Wow!" said Jeff, bounding onto the stage. "That was different, huh?"

As Jeff critiqued the act, I fixed my eyes on the floor. As soon as he had finished, I excused myself to the ladies' room. Sobbing, I tore off my costume. When I could breathe normally again, I washed my face and returned to class, but as I pretended to listen to the next lecture, I couldn't stop tears streaming down my face, dripping inky splodges onto my notes.

Looking back, I wish I could have told that 'me' sobbing in the bathroom, embarrassed and disappointed, not to take everything so seriously—that it would all work out fine.

It did all work out fine. But we haven't got there yet.

What's next?

Ah, the Fire.

The Fire's a good bit.

23

FIRE & MAGIC

*T*he next day at the Amsterdam masterclass, I'd more or less bounced back. It wasn't my fault if my Dutch friends didn't understand English humour.

And even if no one understood my magic act, it was good to have a break in the Amsterdam spring sunshine after the long winter of Martin's operation and convalescence. I sauntered along cobbled streets by the canals and wandered through the tulip market, enjoying the fresh vibrant colours: bright pinks and orange and red.

Last night at the bar, Jeff had said, "You should come to Firedance. You'll like it."

He didn't explain more except to say that Firedance was a festival near Santa Cruz, California, with a fire and dancing and a forest. What's not to like? It sounded like fun. The festival was in four months' time in August. When I got home, I booked a return flight to San Francisco.

My amateur-magician friend, Lloyd, who I met at Mystery School, picked me up at the airport in his shiny black Lexus and drove me to the scout camp at the top of the mountains above Santa Cruz. We twisted up winding, dusty roads, up, up to where the fir trees were thick and the air was clear.

A sun-faded, fraying banner announcing Camp Cutter in scout green flapped from a fir on one side of the road to the other. As we curved in and parked, we were met by clouds of dust and mosquitos. Lloyd valiantly helped me pitch my tiny tent under the trees, then dived back into his now not-so-shiny car and zoomed off, wheels spinning in the dust. He promised to return the next day after he had finished some urgent tax business. He didn't. The busy mosquitoes were hungry and I quickly applied industrial strength insect repellent all over. Within hours, my plastic sports watch had dissolved. God knows what it did to the rest of me.

Just as I was organising my little tent in the patch of forest I'd chosen, a huge black SUV pulled up. The doors opened and a woman got out. She was tall, slim and tanned, with long dark auburn hair. Two good-looking young men followed her. They had tattoos, tight T-shirts over muscles, combat trousers and heavy boots. Quickly, they unpacked her car and set out her camp. Her tent was enormous, with a double inflatable mattress, full-length mirror, ethnic hangings and a rug. I wouldn't have been surprised to see a fridge, home gym and a Jacuzzi. They filled a clothes-rail full and set up a dressing-table with bowls full of jewellery and scarves. I heard them calling her Samina. *Ah*, I thought, *this is how Samina camps.*

Samina was a queen. I'd never seen anyone like her before. When she danced around the fire, dressed in nothing but a crimson scarf jingling with gold coins around her waist, her firm, tanned breasts bare, I challenge anyone not to stare in awe. She was a goddess—a sexy, sassy she-warrior. I found her intriguing, fascinating. I could barely squeeze into my tiny tent—Samina had not one but two gorgeous men in hers. Samina became my new role model. I quickly devised a phrase—not "What would Jesus do?" like the born-agains would ask, but "What would Samina do?" I watched her from a distance, too in awe to say hello.

As the first day darkened into evening, I went in search of

the main dining room, enticed by the welcome smells of cooking. Camp Cutter had a large wooden dining hall with a well-equipped kitchen catering three meals a day for the two hundred people during the festival. There were proper toilets and showers with lights and mirrors. It was all very civilised, except for the mosquitoes.

After dinner, people drifted back to their tents for a pre-fire snooze. Jet-lagged after my long journey, I fell into a deep sleep in my tiny tent. Deep in my dreams, I heard a long drawn-out howl. I wasn't sure whether the sound was part of my dream or real. There it was again. Three times. On the third howl, I opened my eyes. Everything was black. For a moment, I had no idea where I was or why it was so dark, but then I remembered. Someone was blowing a conch, calling everyone to the fire.

Next door, lights went on in Samina's enclosure—surely, she couldn't have electricity? My watch showed 11.45 p.m. Within minutes, in the dark, I was fully dressed. Watching the shadows through the walls of Samina's giant tent, I could see that her preparations were far more elaborate. I left her to it.

In the darkness, I could make out groups of people walking in the same direction on the main well-trodden path through the forest. I followed them curiously. After a while, bamboo citronella torches lit the path. By an iron arch where the trees gave way to a clearing, a line of people waited. The silhouette of the queue looked strange. Getting closer, I realised that people were wearing headdresses, cloaks and an odd collection of hats. A bear's head seemed to be floating in mid-air. *Odd.* Clothes-wise, everyone had gone to town: lots of chiffon, glitter, face-paint, even horns. I wished I'd brought horns.

Under the iron arch gate, a smiling, vibrant brunette dressed head to foot in white, a cloth wrapped around her hair with a diamond at the centre of her forehead, held a black crow's wing above her head. She beat the wing over each person as they passed through the arch, wafting smoke from the mother of pearl inlaid shell in her hand. The smell reminded me of Christmas. I inhaled again. *Ah, sage!*

When it was my turn, she smiled at me warmly and raised her eyebrows slightly. When I nodded, I wasn't sure what for, she murmured, "By air and fire, cast out all that is harmful, take in all that is good and healing, by the power of the Mother of Life, The Great Goddess, so mote it be!" and wafted the perfumed smoke over my head and down to my feet. It was just like the Catholics all over again—but different.

Through the iron arch, the path led into a large ring of dark firs around a circle of flat ground, swept clear of twigs and fallen branches. In the centre there was a pile of firewood, still unlit, and a larger pile of cut wood by the outer edge of trees. A circle perimeter of bamboo citronella torches lit the space, filling the air with a citrusy, woody scent. Spanning out from the fire pit, five or six concentric rings the width of running tracks were drawn with lines of white flour. Outside these rings, still within the circle of torches, ten drummers sat quietly in a group behind their djembe drums. Behind them, larger drums rested on stands, and a table was piled with tambourines, rattles and shakers. On the opposite side of the circle to the drummers, there was another long table piled high with food: stacks of muffins and bowls of fruit, even a platter of fresh strawberries. Around the whole area, a circle boundary of faded Tibetan prayer flags moved gently in the night breeze.

I walked down to the main arena in the centre of the circle of trees, placing my feet softly on the ground. I felt as if I were walking into an empty church, the air still thick with prayer and incense from the last Mass. People moved quietly. Some walked slowly, heads down, beating a faint rhythm with a rattle in their hands; others stood in the space between the boundary fire torches and the outside ring of flour, contemplating the unlit fire. I stood with them, watching.

When the circle around the outer rings of the fire pit was almost full, the energy grew expectant. Samina stepped forward. No wonder she had taken so long to get ready. Like the brunette at the iron smudge gate, she too was dressed from head to toe in white. Her toga clung to her curves, and her tanned arms glittered with gold bracelets. She held a sturdy branch above her head with both hands, the muscles of her upper arms taut. It burnt with a bright flame at one end. In the silence, in a strong confident voice, she sang,

> *Behold there is magic all around us*
> *Behold there is magic all around us*
> *Awaken, rejoice and sing!*

Everyone was listening, watching, waiting. She raised her voice again,

> *I am the fire around you, I am the spark of life within you*
> *I am the flame burning through you, I am all that I am.*

She lowered her branch to the logs in the fire pit. We watched as the fire ignited. Three more people stepped forward from each quarter of the circle. They too held burning branches and sang into the silence, summoning air, water and earth. Each one threw their burning branch into the flames. A chorus of voices around me repeated,

> *Behold there is magic all around us. Awaken, rejoice and sing!*[4]

On the last word, the silence broke dramatically—the drummers let loose and the whole scene erupted into noise and movement. People rushed forward, dancing, clapping their hands and jumping around the fire. How could I have imagined this? Every one of my senses was caught by the throbbing drums, the jumbled scent of citronella, sage and incense, the vibrant colours of swirling dancers. I tasted wood smoke on my lips. I wanted to

---

4   Words and music by Abigail Spinner McBride

join in but I felt too self-conscious—too English. I stayed where I was, feet rooted to the ground.

After fifteen minutes, when the edge of the pent-up burst of opening energy had dulled, Jeff's wife Spinner walked in to change the rhythm. A regal high priestess, shimmering in a red chiffon sari edged with gold, a bindi glittering on her forehead, she stretched out her bare arms to the fire. Raising her clear voice, she sang in a slow six-eight rhythm,

I am the fire and the union of opposites. I am the mystery.
I am calling you in your dreams. I am bringing you home to me.

Pulled forward at last into the music, I stepped onto the outside track, walking at first, but within minutes I relaxed into the rhythm, my thoughts bound and swept up in the looping, melodious chant. I moved through the concentric rings, each one nearer the fire. I accelerated until I was running full speed round the nearest track to the fire, eyes fixed on the flames, looking through, heart open.

The world fell away.

Everything was here. All now. Just me and God in the fire.

For hours and hours, I danced, staring into the flames, lost in the beat of the drums and the fierce heat. I prayed to the God of the fire: *Take my small self, my fear, my shame, my disappointment. Take my cracked dreams. Take my trudging in dull circles. Take all that divides me from you. Let me be of use. Break me. Melt me. Mould me. Fill me, top full with gold. Let me have my show.*

Under the stars, to the beat of the drums, other voices rose in melody, footsteps paced time, round and around and around. The singing, drumming and dancing swirled through the night until dawn.

Towards dawn, there was a change in energy, a rising first sniff of morning, a hint of daybreak. Everyone was eager to see the sun, to watch the breaking of darkness, to welcome the comforting light. Quiet excitement mounted; you'd have thought we'd never had a morning before. A tall man with a caduceus tattoo across his shoulders and a top hat with golden wings appeared half-way up the rocky hillside at the back of the fire circle, holding a large round mirror. He held the mirror high in the air, catching the reflection of the new sun. Abruptly the drumming stopped.

A voice called, *"Golden rays pierce our hearts, like arrows of light, dispelling illusion, releasing the night."*

Another voice: *"Solar alchemy, filling each cell of our bodies, transforming, transmuting lead into purest gold."*

A third: *"As above, so below, the sun sees itself in the fire. In each other, we see God."*

We all fell to our knees.

I, like everyone else, was speechless with gratitude and wonder because morning had come to bless us with air and light and life.

In the early hours of the morning of the second day, an older woman wearing a lilac kaftan with long grey hair streaked through with purple walked forward into the dancing area. Dancers paused, drums fell silent. She had a crutch, and I noticed her leg below her right knee was missing. Balanced on the crutch under her armpit, she squared up to the crowd, who watched her curiously. A single drum began a slow steady rhythm. She raised a brass bowl high in the air and called out in a loud confident voice, "Gather close. Think of your heart's desire. Hold your wish strong in your heart and in your mind. Come and drink. As you drink, the seeds of magic will start to grow." People queued to drink from the bowl, which was refilled over and over.

I didn't join the queue for wish-granting wine because I was busy comforting a dreadlocked drummer who was sobbing against my shoulder. I had been minding my own business, taking a break from the fire, when a guy looking ridiculously like an American version of Martin, even wearing tie-dye shorts and a vest, walked away from the huge barrel-like drum he'd been pounding and stood next to me.

He observed the fire silently, watching the people make a queue for the wine. I was musing about what I was going to wish for, waiting for the queue to subside. Out of the corner of my eye, I noticed him crouch down on the ground on one knee, supporting himself with one hand, while he covered his eyes with the other. His shoulders shook. I was wondering whether I should leave him to it or say something, when he straightened up, tears streaming down his face.

"Can I have a hug?" He sniffed. Now he was sobbing on my shoulder. I still had one eye on the queue and would have liked to have made a wish, but it seemed rude to throw him off. I watched as the brass bowl was put away and the dancing resumed with extra vigour. With my tie-dye drummer still sobbing on my shoulder, I wondered what I would have wished for.

A few days later, I was still miffed that I had missed out on the magic wish-granting wine. But while I was waiting my turn at the shower block, the same woman with grey and purple hair asked me to help her shower. Her name was Earil. With only one leg, it was difficult for her. As I patted her down with a towel, I told her that I had missed her wine ritual but thought, given another opportunity, I might wish for courage.

"Ha," she snorted, "that's how I lost my leg."

That told me. Careful what you wish for.

Spinner, the regal high priestess, Samina, the sexy she-warrior, and Earil, the wishing ceremony high priestess, were not the only fascinating characters by the fire. One striking woman had long blonde dreadlocks, golden skin and a strong athletic body. Wearing a white diaphanous toga, she writhed in ecstasy in front of the drummers. Caught up in her beauty, in the sparking energy she spun, the musicians leant forward and drummed faster just for her. She glowed with confidence and charisma. I was busy throwing my chronic feelings of being lumpy and bumpy into the fire as fast as they came up, but it was never fast enough. Despite enjoying the week so much, my chronic feeling of being too big was always present. I wanted to look like the hippy chicks with their flat chests and bikini-strap vests. That blonde girl with the dreads was clearly supremely happy in her own skin. *That's how I'm going to be,* I thought.

When the night darkened and the stars were bright, Jeff McBride, my magic teacher, transformed into Magnus, arch mage of the fire. Dressed in black, gold sequins running through his shirt, he held two large golden fans, which he cracked open and shut, beating time with the drums. He pulled real balls of fire out of the air and threw them down into the flames, which roared up in a burst of golden sparks. He ignited blue lights on his fingertips and enchanted a silver ball to float in mid-air. In his black top hat with gold mercurial wings, brandishing his caduceus staff, he used every trick in his repertoire to heighten—or is it deepen?—the mystery of the fire, whipping up the energy when it dipped, revitalising the magic of the whole arena.

On the first night, tired after dancing for hours, I took a stroll in the cool night air and came across the Cosmic Coffee Cruiser deep in the forest. Some bright spark had had the brilliant idea to weld the top half of a vintage VW camper to another whole VW, making a double-decker coffee shop on wheels, parked in a clearing in the forest. Inside, tall lean Cosmic Steve was doing a great trade on his gleaming Gaggia coffee machine, steaming up a double cappuccino with chocolate sprinkles, a soya latte with hazelnut syrup, or a kicking triple espresso.

This crowd was my kind of gang. Most were professional performers, musicians, poets, dancers or magicians. They sang, they danced—when they drummed, they rocked—when they spun magic, it was real. By sheer chance, I'd stumbled upon a faery ring: an enchanted circle of magical performers dancing around the fire in the mountain forest moonlight.

On the morning of the second fire, an hour after the sun had risen again, surprising and glorious out of the dark, I was sitting on a straw bale on the edge of the fire circle, the straw pricking the bare backs of my legs. I gazed empty-minded and content at the scene around me. People were wearily picking up their possessions, chatting easily as they headed off for breakfast. Over the other side from where I was sitting, there was a clump of tall fir trees. A quiet voice, the one I've come to recognise as Spirit, God, my inner wisdom, said softly, *Go over there.*

I walked over to the trees. One of the wide trunks was damaged and hollowed out. Soft pine needles made a springy carpet on the floor. Curious, I looked closer and saw that in the hollow of the damaged tree, someone had left a stack of drawing paper. There was a children's paint set, a tiny pot of gold paint and some paintbrushes standing in a jar of cloudy water. I sat on my knees and bowed my head. The space within the trees felt sacred, peaceful. I knelt there in the silence, listening to the breeze, listening to the quiet hum of everything.

Put the mark of gold on your forehead, said the voice.

"Huh?" I was puzzled.

Put a dab of gold paint on your forehead.

I stuck my finger in the tiny pot of gold paint and dabbed it on the space between my eyebrows. It felt right. I laid my head on the pine-needle floor and closed my eyes. I think I must have dosed off because I came to with a little jump. When I opened my eyes, everything was normal again. The air felt prosaic, the space ordinary—there was no need to stay any longer, it was time for breakfast. I was hungry, but curious. What did the gold mark mean?

I hurried off to find Jeff; he would know. He was sitting on a fallen tree trunk by the edge of the fire circle. He had one sock on and was rubbing the ball of his other foot.

"Jeff?" I said.

"Uh huh?" He sounded tired.

"I just got told to put some gold paint on my forehead." I showed him the mark.

"And?"

"What does it mean?" I asked.

"What do you think it means?" he replied with a quizzical smile.

I thought for a moment.

"That I'm a magician?"

"Right," he said, putting on his other sock. He winked at me, got up and left.

"Oh." I stayed where I was, thinking. It seemed that I had just been conscripted into service, officially marked, ordained.

"Okay," I said to no one, "fine by me."

And off I went to breakfast.

24

THE THIRD CALL

*J*eff had been right, I did like Firedance. After I'd got over my initial townie's mistrust of the forest, I sauntered along dark paths between trees, feeling safe and secure, the stars clear and bright in the night sky. Safe that was, except for the pigs. "*Pigged!* I've been pigged!" was a frequent cry in the dark. The wild pigs living in the forest loved to snack on whatever delicious treats they could find, despite clear instructions to campers not to leave food in tents. When a pig has had a midnight feast in your forest boudoir and a little sit down on your sleeping bag, the aftermath is not pretty.

After dancing through each night, I snoozed in the hot afternoons in the official snuggle tent. The snuggle tent was a large pentagonal canopy made out of burnt-orange Moroccan-embroidered cloth, sparkling with tiny mirrors and hung with silver lanterns. Set in the shade under trees, it was both cool and cosy at the same time. Thick sheepskin rugs and dozens of jewel-coloured cushions blanketed the floor. You could sleep all day, read a book or even snuggle up with someone if you fancied. Once, having a little snoozette, I was woken by softly chiming hand cymbals and the flicker of moving lights. When I opened my eyes, three young women in glittering belly-dance chiffon swam into focus. They danced graciously, holding small painted glasses with tea lights flickering inside.

When you say you danced all night, aren't you exaggerating? Just a little?

Nope. I had work to do. I'd paid a lot of money for my flight and travelled half way round the world to be there. Plus, I had a strange feeling that this fire festival was an essential part of my journey towards my dream act.

In the hours between night and morning of the third and final fire, I took a short break. I walked slowly along the path through the trees towards my tent. I watched the brown-grey forest floor softly absorb the dappled early morning light. In the silence, I heard that unmistakable, soft, quiet voice again.

Leave Martin. Sell your house. Go to Las Vegas.

The voice was in my thoughts—not outside, but not my thought. A precise instruction. A voice without sound but absolutely clear. This was the third time. The first, in that pretty loo in Portugal, the second on the step outside my bedroom in Shepherds Bush, and now here, in the middle of the Santa Cruz forest.

I loved Martin. I couldn't bear to think how much he would suffer if I left him. How much I would suffer. If I did this, I was going to tear his heart open and mine too. Selling the house, going to Las Vegas was easy—with Martin. But leave him? Impossible.

In the silence of the forest, it was clear that I had a choice. It didn't matter to the world which path I took. If I carried on muddling through in the same way I'd been doing, everyone would get along just fine. But I had been asking for something specific on every birthday wish, on each blow on a dandelion seed head. I'd been praying, *Let me create a beautiful show woven through with bright colour. Let me create a show to soothe weary hearts. Let me live with joy.* I'd been dancing round the fire, spinning like a dervish, telling the God in the flames over and over, *This is what I want to do with my life. Show me how.*

In fairy tales, things happen in threes. Once, twice I'd ignored the voice, reasoned it away with common sense. That morning, I had the feeling that if I ignored it a third time, someone up there would go back to the staff room, take off his overalls, make a nice cup of tea with a chocolate digestive biscuit and say to his colleagues, "There's just no helping some people." And I'd never hear that patient, quiet, loving voice again.

I went back to my tent and sat on the floor in the doorway, thinking.

I sat there for a long time.

"Okay."

No reply. I waited another couple of minutes.

Nope. Nothing. Nada.

Typical. He'd probably gone off for another cup of tea.

My decision made, there wasn't much else to do. It was five in the morning; there was still an hour of the fire before sunrise. I went back to the arena where a few people were still dancing and snuggled up in a quiet spot alone under a tree. I was new at Firedance; my friends now were strangers to me then. They didn't know me, or Martin. I didn't mention the voice or my decision to anyone. Wrapped up in a blanket to keep out the morning damp, I wept for the confusion and the hurt I was going to cause, for breaking my promises, for leaving Martin to travel on without me. I wept for the fun we would miss, for the children we would never have, for our growing old together. I wept silently, unnoticed, my heart missing him already.

The three nights of fire were danced out and done. The festival was officially finished. Once the core team had dismantled the main arena, snuggle tent and other installations, I travelled with about thirty people to another forest campsite nearer Santa Cruz for two days of 'afterglow' and relaxation. In the morning, after a blissful uninterrupted night's sleep, people were organising car rides for a trip into Santa Cruz. I wanted to go too—I fancied a taste of civilisation after this last week of forest life. What I really wanted was a Java Juice: carrot, beetroot and ginger. But a persistent thought looped through my brain: *You need to write a letter to Martin. You need to do a ritual.* Hmmm, I wasn't sure about that. I was sure I'd rather go shopping.

During Firedance, lots of people had got a new tattoo. Abraham, a really gifted tattooist from New York, worked solidly through the week in his makeshift studio in the forest. While he worked, people had their friends hold sacred space, drumming or singing as the needle buzzed. Inspired by this, I thought, *I'll get a drummer to drum while I write the letter to Martin.* The first person I found was Starhawk. He looked like the rest of the guys: long brown hair, a couple of tattoos, hippy trousers, leather thong sandals.

"Hey Starhawk, would you hold sacred space for me and drum while I do a ritual?" For a Catholic girl from Essex, I'd picked up this pagan lingo fast.

"I'm not much of a drummer," he replied. "I'll bring my guitar, though. I'll ask Earil too."

Earil was that woman with purple hair, wishing wine and one leg, a no-nonsense, straight-talking, belly-laughing, powerful high priestess. I couldn't have chosen anyone better, but I was a little daunted.

The rest of the group drove off in high spirits to enjoy all the worldly delights that Santa Cruz had to offer. The forest was quiet again. I'd chosen the perfect place for my ritual: a ring of trees, sun shining through, delicate foliage dappling the light. Starhawk and Earil walked towards me, Starhawk carrying a fold-up chair with his guitar slung over his shoulder, Earil wearing a flowing purple kaftan. She had a large mother of pearl shell with sticks of incense in one hand and a long brown pheasant feather in the other. When I explained that I wanted their help to create sacred space while I wrote an important letter to my husband, they listened quietly. If this sounds all kinds of odd to you, it does to me too. It also seems extraordinarily callous to end a perfectly decent marriage with a 'Dear John' note on a scrap piece of paper. And for why? Because of a thought, because of a voice in a sleep-deprived state at a festival? Ridiculous. But it wasn't ridiculous. I had prayed from my soul, and now I was intent on obeying the guidance I heard.

Feeling nervous, I sat on a fallen tree trunk and fished out a small notepad and pen from my bag. Starhawk sat on the ground and softly strummed a gentle melody on his guitar. Earil sat on the fold-up chair and lit the incense, wafting fragrant smoke over us with her feather.

I took a deep breath and started to write.

"Dear Martin. I love you. I love you but I'm leaving to follow my dream." Such a crap cliché. My left hand clenched, nails digging sharp into my palm. I was about to smash everything. I kept writing. I said how much I loved him, how sorry I was, and that my decision was final, that I was going to Vegas, alone.

So dramatic! Was it all necessary? At the time, it felt as if it were the only way. These days I live my life with more compromise. I'll surrender this if I can have that. But maybe, sometimes, going for broke is the only way.

Two pages filled, I stopped writing. My tears had smudged the ink. Earil raised her voice and said loudly,

"And the wind wipes away the tears." As the words left her lips, an actual wind blew. I'm not kidding. Before that moment, there hadn't been as much as a breeze. My tears stopped; they were literally blown away. One half of my brain was astonished. *Did you see that? Did you see that actual wind come out of nowhere?* And the other half, the half that knows magic, smugly replied, *Well, if you will invite a purple-haired high priestess to help you do a ritual, what do you expect?*

We were done. It felt done. Earil fished out three large chocolate chip cookies from a pocket and we ate them in silence, floating back down to earth.

25

BREAKING

A week later, at the start of September, I was back in England. Two days after getting home, that note was still in my pocket. It smouldered there, silently ticking. Finally, in our narrow hall—maybe I was hoping the walls would contain the blast—I took it out. Such a small piece of paper. How can you destroy a whole love story with such a small piece of paper? Once I'd given it to him, nothing would ever be the same again.

"I have to give you something I need you to read," I said with a downturn of voice to avoid any assumption that it could be anything nice. Martin took the note, unfolded it slowly, read the tear-splattered words and looked at me, his face bewildered.

"But we're going to be together forever," he said. The corners of his mouth turned down; he looked desperately shocked. Seeing my sad but determined face, he started to cry.

I tried to explain that I had heard a voice, but none of it made any sense. How could it? All I could do was to repeat that I was leaving. It was terrible. Worse than that. To say that Martin was shaken, heart-wounded, devastated, doesn't touch the raw hurt of it. He argued, but although I wanted to say it was all a stupid mistake, a stupid festival thing, sleep deprivation, I knew my decision was made and my path was set.

I had four months to pack up the house before leaving for Las Vegas. Four months to deal with the real business of heartbreak. Packing boxes was the easy part.

In those four months, in our little house with the love-heart red fairy lights hanging in the window, the walls painted pink and orange, all I could think, all I could feel, was how much I loved Martin—how my heart felt when we were together. When we sat either end of the sofa, feet entwined, I didn't know where I ended and where he began. Now, far from the fire, far from the forest and magic, I didn't give a damn about any voice or any stupid dream of showbusiness.

Too late. The deal was struck, the price agreed, the magic set in motion.

That October, Martin went to a conflict resolution workshop in Germany where he started a romance with the American female facilitator. He was officially single and probably on a big-time rebound after the shock of my announcement.

While he was away, realising how much I loved him, I gave up on my plan to leave. When he got home, I begged him to stay, but he was already thinking about another woman. It seemed to me that when I lacked the resolve and courage to carry my resolution through, he helped me out by finishing the deed.

It happens all the time in fairy tales. You promise your first-born son to the nasty man with the odd name who agrees to get you out of a fix. You forget for a while and all is well—until your son is born and that nasty man comes to collect his fee. You try to protect him but it's no use; he will be taken. And so it was with me. I had asked for my show; guidance had been provided. When I tried to go back on the deal, instead of a clean break, the knife was twisted by my struggle.

That was when my heart really broke.

I remember it even now. I had a constant vicious pain in my chest, then the knife turned and the pain jabbed deeper. I couldn't sleep—often it was hard to breathe. I sobbed through the night. Everything was in sharp jagged pieces and it was my own fault. Martin moved into the spare room and chatted through the night to his new American love on the phone. I lay awake, trying not to listen. His cheerful voice, chatting away, sliced a fresh hurt minute by minute. He wasn't to blame. I had cut the cord; he was free. It hurt like a burn.

The rest of November and December were months of more breaking. We put the house on the market, sold the furniture and gave our books and kitchenware to charity. I boot-faired my old costumes and props, the glorious snow queen crystal crown sold for a meagre ten pounds.

Martin left a week before Christmas. A few days before he went, we lit a fire in the grate and set candles all around. At our wedding, our wrists were bound together with silken cords before we jumped over the broomstick. This time we bound our wrists again with a bit of string from the kitchen drawer. On a page of lined paper, we wrote down everything we were looking forward to: kids, travel, new shows, growing old together. We threw the list into the fire, watched the paper curl and burn, erasing the words. We cut the string and threw that into the fire too. We fetched the wedding broomstick down from the attic and broke it into grate size pieces and fed those to the fire. Having undone our vows, we made a new one. We made a solemn promise that we would always be family. It was a terribly sad afternoon, the rain grey and cold against the curtainless windows.

With all the fairy lights gone, my props and costumes sold, the walls now painted a neutral cream, the house was pale and empty. The only furniture left was two wooden chairs. Night after night,

I made up a fire and sat staring into the flames, the other empty chair silently accusing me of the stupid, careless thing I'd done.

It wasn't my best Christmas.

But don't worry. We're going to Vegas.

26

LOVING LAS VEGAS

$\mathcal{I}$n my show these days, when I tell the audience that a voice told me to leave my job, sell my house and go to Las Vegas, it sounds light-hearted, a bit of fun, an adventure. I don't mention the bit about leaving Martin.

"Where exactly on the Strip were you performing? Which show were you in?" people ask me eagerly.

But I wasn't in a show. I didn't have a professional act. What I brought to Vegas in February, age thirty-three, was only the beginnings of the comedy magic act performed in my living room and at open mic nights in the backrooms of pubs. I'd tried out so many ideas but they'd all fallen flat on their ambitious noses. When I booked my flight to spend three months in Las Vegas, I'd assumed I'd be studying magic with Jeff McBride, although I hadn't actually organised anything. But on the night I arrived, he told me that he was leaving for a three-month tour of Japan. I couldn't hide my disappointment. Taking pity on me, he asked, "Do you want to put on your own show in my theatre for one night when I get back?"

"Yes," I gulped. I knew it was the correct answer.

"Great," he smiled.

Oh, bloody hell. Now I'd done it, my own show in Vegas in three months' time. I got to work.

I love Las Vegas. Who doesn't? Well, plenty of people don't. But I do.

Vegas is tacky, fake and noisy, full of slot machines and endless blinking lights. It has a replica Eiffel tower and a pretend Venice with pretend Italian-singing gondoliers. It has huge elegant hotels and fireworks and fountains and is crowded with the best shows, most talented performers and creative magicians. Vegas is the place to give up sensible self-control, dull greys and boring dark blues. In this town that never sleeps, you're invited to shake loose, throw caution to the wind and indulge in whatever takes your fancy: gambling, drinking, New York cheesecake? Vegas welcomes you with open arms. Come, play! Forget the rules! What rules?

Admittedly by Vegas standards, I'm on the boring side. I don't drink alcohol, haven't much use for a lap dance, and no interest in gambling. But I loved driving down the strip, drinking in all the lights and sights and sounds, thinking how lucky I was to be there. I went poking about and discovered glorious corners. One night I found a ballroom full of twinkle-toed Mexicans and a twenty-seven-piece salsa band. I'd seen a poster advertising a salsa night in the ballroom of the Sahara Hotel. Curiously, I waited on my own in the queue behind a red plush rope, all round me the rapid-fire chatter of Latinos on a night out, flashy shirts, short skirts and lots of gold.

Once the heavy-set bouncers pulled the velvet barrier aside, I chose a table, ordered a Coke and looked over the vast room. At the far end of the polished dance floor, there was a wide stage with a closed dark-blue curtain edged with luxurious gold fringing. Only five minutes more to wait. I fiddled with the straw in my Coke, feeling self-conscious sitting alone at my table.

At nine, the curtain swept open dramatically and revealed brass trombones, trumpets and horns gleaming in the spotlights, a gold Mylar backdrop shimmering behind. Music burst out, and I counted twenty Colombian musicians in sharp white suits, three strutting male lead vocals, each with collar-length, black, shiny hair, and four diminutive but sassy backing singers in tiny silver dresses, scarlet lipstick and vertiginous heels. *Wow!* I wanted to say. *Look at this! And it's free!* But there was no one to tell. I curled my toes in excitement and did a little inner squeak of pleasure.

The music was loud and vibrant and enticing. I knew all the songs. I spent a good half hour watching the dancers and picked out a guy who was dancing with lots of different women rather than just his wife. With false bravado, I tapped him on the shoulder and asked him to dance. He looked dubious. A white English girl dance salsa? He took me cautiously in his arms. We swayed. Ah, she can move; he could feel it. Before the end of the second bar we were off, all turns and twirls and fancy footwork.

I danced every Friday night after that, with Mexican strangers who courteously escorted me back to my table before returning to their wives. I joined the twenty-four-hour gym and was offered fat-burning pills and a shag by the personal trainer. Is that a standard thing in Vegas? I refrained from shagging the trainer, the fat burning pills didn't work, and my Friday night dances in the Sahara were the limit of my Vegas hedonism.

Back at the fire in Camp Cutter, I'd written a wish on a piece of paper that I would find a real home in Vegas. The cosmic angels of interplanetary accommodation were most obliging and introduced me through a series of coincidences to Patti and Badger, who are the nicest couple ever. They adopted me as family and offered me their large spare room with a double-mirrored wardrobe, which was perfect for magic practice. Badger is a professional stagehand with an obsession for tie-dye, and Patti is a midwife. They had three dogs and a cat who thought she was a dog. Perfect.

I had three short months to pull something together to perform in Jeff's theatre in front of a crowd of not only friends but Vegas professional magicians.

A goal is a dream with a deadline, Jeff teaches. It's true. There's nothing like putting the fear of bejeezus into someone to get them to pull that rabbit out of the hat.

My unglamorous, un-rock 'n' roll lifestyle in Vegas went something like this: I got up early and went to the gym. As always, I wanted to lose ten pounds for the show. I tried a Pilates class, but as soon as I walked in, I knew I was in the wrong place. Waiting in prime position at the front of the mirrored studio, Vegas ex-dancers of a certain age lay on their mats, lazily stretching one long leg behind their heads. Hair pulled back in tight buns, they glared at me haughtily with frozen faces and permanently raised eyebrows. I retreated hastily with my mat still tightly rolled under my arm.

The spin classes were welcoming but terrifyingly professional. The class was full of men dressed in real cycling clothes, cycling shoes and water bottles in their specially designed back pockets. We panted up fictitious hills with Led Zeppelin and zoomed down equally fictitious slopes with Alice Cooper blaring out of the speakers, our Lycra-clad legs spinning like pistons.

"Push it, push it, work those legs, squeeze those glutes!" cried our intrepid cycle leader, who wore a helmet even on his stationary bike. "And up, and down, and up, and down. Now spin!" Ninety minutes later we almost fell off our bikes, red-faced and gasping, legs weak as water.

The kick-boxing classes were like nothing I'd ever seen. Sixty hard-core fitness addicts stood in lines facing the mirror, ready for battle. The Brazilian kick-boxing teacher, a handsome ex-pro, was all muscle and tanned sinew. In the front row, a line of thin blonde groupies waited ready for battle. Not one had a spare ounce of fat; their plastic breasts stood pert to attention.

"Ready?" The teacher took off his training hoodie, revealing his perfect bronzed and sculpted torso.

"Ready!" chorused the groupies, jumping up and down, blonde ponytails bouncing. I hid myself at the back with the other curvy brunettes but had to leave after twenty minutes feeling sick. But nothing puts my back up as much as a thin blonde with attitude. Game on. During the next three months, I inched slowly forward with dogged determination, row by row, until I was just behind the high-kicking groupies. I found it especially motivating to imagine that I was kicking one or two of their skinny butts. By my last week in Vegas, I could kick as high and as ferociously as any blonde. That class lifted my arse and no mistake.

For the rest of the day, I worked in my bedroom, writing and rewriting scripts for tricks and practicing magic in front of a video camera. That was it. Every day.

The show was scheduled in three months. I wasn't lonely, I was living with lovely Patti and Badger and their dogs and cat. Apart from having to refuse Badger's joyful carnivorous offer of barbecued ribs and mountains of home-baked sugary cookies, I relaxed into the good feeling that I'd done the right thing to come to Vegas.

My show in Jeff's theatre was less than a week away. I'd invited everyone I knew. Jeff was going to be back from his tour and had promised to open for me. Jeff's friends, big magic stars from shows on the strip, were coming: Mac King, Kevin James—maybe David Copperfield would pop by. I was terrified.

On the day of the show, I pulled up to the theatre in my rental car packed full with props and costumes. I locked the car and walked into the empty space. I needed to put out a hundred or so of the chairs stacked against the wall and organise a table in the foyer to take the tickets. This was happening. This was real. I took a deep breath. *Okay, let's do this.*

Back at the car, I reached into my pockets for the car keys. Nothing. Not in that pocket, not in the other, not on the ground. I ran back into the theatre, scanning the empty floor. Nothing in the dressing room, nothing in the foyer. I checked my pockets again, still empty. All my props were locked inside the car. No key, no show. Thirty minutes of panicked breath-held frenetic searching later, I found them in my handbag, exactly where I'd put them.

Now really panicking, short on time, I rushed about setting out the chairs, realising that I should have organised a team to help. I should have been preparing my act calmly backstage, instead of running around setting out soft drinks and answering last-minute phone calls to explain where the theatre was.

Finally, the chairs were out, the audience was in, chatting among themselves happily. Backstage, I realised that I had nowhere on my costume to hook the microphone pack. The only person backstage was Jeff, the Vegas magic megastar.

"Can you hook this on my knickers?" I asked, embarrassed. As he fixed the pack on my G-string, I apologised again, red-faced. "I'm so sorry."

"Are you kidding?" He laughed. "I'm enjoying myself."

I did the show. I did my best. I forgot an entire ten-minute chunk of the middle, and the confetti explosion failed to go off, but at the end, my friends and their friends stood clapping and cheering. Jeff bounded backstage smiling,

"Wow! That was great! Did you hear them all laughing?" Then he bounced off again.

As I changed back into my normal clothes, my Vegas crowd were waiting for me in the foyer. But in the dressing room, I was hit by a tsunami of shame. Shame looked back at me from the mirror as I took off my eyelashes and scoffed, *All that work and you're still crap. When Jeff said, 'That it was great,' he didn't mean you were any good. He meant the sort of 'great' you say to your five-year-old when they come home with a messy painting that you put on the fridge door.*

I stayed in my dressing room, taking my time to pack, feeling more dejected by the minute. I couldn't face anyone. Patti stuck her head round the door. Lovely warm Patti.

"Everyone's waiting. We've got something for you." She took my hand, and as I stepped into the foyer, I saw a huge chocolate cake with *Congratulations Romany* piped in white icing. I looked around at happy smiling faces.

Make them smile, God had said to me in a shower in Austria.

Okay, I thought. *They're smiling. They're happy. That's all I need to do.*

After everyone had left, I packed my props and drove home. On the way, I pulled over. In three days' time I would be flying back to England. Sitting in the car, I had another little chat with God.

"Should I apply for a green card visa and live in Las Vegas?" I asked.

Silence. No reply. He was probably out. "Why not?" I answered myself. Decision made, I drove happily back to Patti and Badger's to pack my things and go in search of a visa.

27

MAGIC ELEPHANTS & WILD PIGS

*B*ack in England, I had nowhere to live after selling my house. My good friend Nicky, who is a talented musician and sings like Ella Fitzgerald, offered me her spare room.

The room was so small that with my props and a single futon inside, the door only opened enough for me to barely squeeze in and out. I practiced magic diligently, daily, hopefully. Just me and the mirror. I hung red love-heart fairy-lights in the window and a man knocked politely on the door one night to ask if this was, by any chance, a brothel.

Now that I planned to move to the States, I needed a green card or an 'alien of extraordinary ability' visa. Who thinks up these names? I didn't have a clue how I was going to get one. What I did know was that I wanted to get back to Firedance. I needed to spin more magic, to speed up momentum. Four months after leaving Las Vegas, a year after the voice told me to leave Martin, I was back at the same Camp Cutter scout camp above Santa Cruz. This time I borrowed a bigger tent.

The Vegas Firedance gang, who were now my friends, were all there: Patti and Badger, Samina, Spinner and Earil. This time I'd got the right clothes with lots of sequins and floaty chiffon—damn, forgot the horns—and as usual, I spent the nights sprinting round the fire as fast as I could. The track nearest to the fire was the fast track, known as the mercury ring. It's the place for speed, for intense intention and fervent prayer; there were only a few regulars that could keep up the pace for long. One was my magic teacher, Jeff, and then there was me and this guy who looked like an elfin woodland warrior without the pointy ears. He had long titian hair tied back in a plait and a thin leather headband around his forehead. Tall and slim, with lean, long muscles, his arms were tattooed with delicate swirls and Celtic symbols. His chest was bare and he wore those odd-looking trouser-skirt things that tie up at the back. He'd obviously trained in martial arts because in the early hours of the morning, when the energy was soft and the dancing more gentle, he practiced graceful swoops and turns with a long sword a little way off from the dance circle.

"Who's that guy?" I asked my girlfriends.

"Patrick Pigeon Hawk."

"What's he like?"

"Yeah, cool."

"Single?"

The information from the girls was that he was single, lived in San Francisco and was 'nice.' That would do. I kept my eye on him.

About 4 a.m. each morning, there was a silly hour around the fire. It could be sleep deprivation, low blood sugar, who knows, but it's definitely a giggly time for mucking about. It was just about then, as the only two still dancing the mercury track that we sorta bumped. Being the silly hour, we didn't apologise, dust ourselves off and return to our solitary paths, instead we did it again. We bumped and then started doing a contact improvisation dance with each other. Contact improvisation? Google describes it as: *a partner dance form based on the physical principles of touch, momentum, shared weight, and most quintessentially—following a shared point of contact. This dance practice explores the skills of falling, rolling, counterbalance, lifting using minimal effort.* So now you know. I did quite a lot of contact improvisation at Circus Space, and this Pigeon Hawk guy seemed to know it too. We rolled and spun and got all juicy and physical without saying a word. Delicious.

Then the sun came up and everyone went for breakfast. We did too. But not together. We hadn't actually spoken. It wasn't until the next night and the next fire that we faced each other again across the flames. The same thing happened, only this time an even stronger current of magnetic force flowed between us. We bumped and danced all over again.

Like the year before, the wild pigs were having a great time ransacking tents and feasting on any snacks inside. Cries of *"Pigged!* We've been pigged!" rang out frequently. About five in the morning, someone ran into the arena shouting that a whole herd of pigs had trampled a bunch of tents. Patrick and I rushed to help but there wasn't much to be done except to put the tents back up and clear away the rubbish. These particular pigs were surprisingly gifted at snaffling the grub but leaving the wrappers.

"Fancy a cup of tea?" Patrick asked. He probably didn't say those exact words, being from San Francisco, and I don't remember any tea. I do remember the sweet comfort of him pulling me down onto the blankets of a narrow single bed in a back room of the building. We snuggled up, warm and close and fell asleep.

That morning, which was really just a couple of hours later, we did talk. The girls were right—he was nice. Trouble was that the festival was ending and he was leaving that day. He was hitching a ride with some friends to San Francisco where he lived in an eco-village further out in the country. Doesn't it always seem to be the way that Mr. Wonderful appears on the very last night of the trip or just as you're about to get off the train? I decided that this Mr. Wonderful was not going to get away so easily. Since I didn't have any firm plans for the next couple of days before my flight home, I invited myself onto his ride and we bumped along in the open back of a dusty truck all the way down to San Francisco, cushioned by piles of Moroccan rugs.

Tao, the driver of the truck, his wife Jasper, and the few other friends travelling with them lived in San Francisco and invited me and Patrick to stay over. Every Californian has a hot tub in the back yard, and that night after supper, they filled it with hot bubbling water. Everyone stripped off and jumped in. Being English, I got in quickly while no one was looking and sat self-consciously facing outwards in the tub watching the stars with my bits bobbing in the bubbles.

Back in the house, dry and wrapped up on the sofa in warm blankets, we drowsily listened to our friend Julie Woods play guitar. She hadn't bothered putting her clothes back on. Chocolate-brown shaved head, beautiful, supremely at ease in her own skin and nothing else, she sang, and sang, wrapping her deep soulful melodies around our contented little gang.

Before I continue with this story of Patrick Pigeon Hawk, I need to confess that I've omitted one important detail. Which I will now un-omit. I swear that every word is true.

There I was spinning around the flames on the third night at my second summer Firedance. I was praying not only for a show but for a way to stay in the States. As I danced, a precise and colourful vision of Ganesha, the Hindu elephant God, suddenly appeared before me. I was a little surprised.

"Don't worry," said the elephant, "it's all going to work out fine."

It's important to say that I am not given to visions—I'd never had one before. I've never had one since. And no, I hadn't been smoking anything. I didn't know anything about Ganesha. I didn't know that he's known as the God that removes all obstacles. I certainly didn't have a visual image of him in my experience. So how can it be that a full-colour vision of Ganesha appeared out of nowhere while I was minding my own business dancing round the fire? I'm a magician and weird things are my normal, but that was super-extra strange.

The day after the hot tub, Patrick and I were still in a state of post-festival bliss. When I looked into his eyes, I went all woozy and the same thing seemed to happen to him. He wanted to show me San Francisco, and after driving all over seeing the sights, we found a kooky vegan café by the Golden Gate Bridge and had a delicious supper of pan-fried veg with cashew-nut cheese. While stuck in a traffic jam on the way home, I outlined my options for staying in the country. I could hire a lawyer to acquire a visa, ask David Copperfield and a list of other notable magicians to vouch for me as an 'alien of extraordinary abilities,' or I could simply marry an American.

"I'll marry you," he said coolly.

The words, *Don't be ridiculous, you've only known me for two nights and most of that was spent chasing pigs,* were on my lips, when

I glanced up and saw an enormous brightly coloured mural on the wall of a building to our left.

"Stop!" I yelled. Patrick screeched to a halt.

"What?" He asked in surprise, looking around to see if he had hit anything.

"*Ganesha!*" I shouted, pointing to the huge blazing image of the Hindu God who removes all obstacles, the same guy with the elephant head of my vision at the fire.

"Huh?" Patrick didn't have a clue what I was talking about.

I shut my mouth, which, for a moment, had dropped open. When I told Patrick about my prayer and the vision of Ganesha at the fire, his jaw dropped open too.

We were to be married. Or so we told our friends. They didn't blink; nothing shocks a pagan. Patrick was going home that night to the eco-farm he lived on, and since I had two days left before I flew back to England, he invited me to join him. The night was pitch black. There was no light at all except for a few stars hidden by clouds.

"Take my hand," Patrick said, leading me through what felt like a field with a very scratchy crop. When we stopped, he flicked his lighter. In the light from the tiny flame, I could see that we were in the middle of a cornfield and a couple of paces away was a real, beautifully painted gypsy caravan.

"Is that yours?" I asked, astonished.

"Well, I live here for free while I'm working on the farm."

I was loving every unpredictable moment of this magical adventure. So many years of reading fantastic children's stories of gypsies and magicians and wish-granting genii, and now here I was in my very own fantastical tale. And if this sounds as if I'm making it all up, I swear I'm not. You can ask Patrick Pigeon Hawk himself; he's real, he's on Facebook.

Inside his caravan, Patrick lit candles in coloured glasses and made tea. As the kettle slowly boiled on his small wood-burning stove with the jewel-toned tinted candlelight reflecting off his silver samurai swords on the wall, he pulled down a book and read me his favourite Rumi poems. Then I recited my favourite poems to him. I'm wrinkling my nose now with the romantic soppiness of it all. My present-day husband, Johnny Walkabout, would rather have his leg cut off than listen to poetry. But Walkabout makes me magic props, mends my bike punctures and fixes the dishwasher. I've learnt that practical is better than poetic. But that night, in Patrick Pigeon Hawk's candlelit gypsy caravan, I was intoxicated by this handsome, idealistic eco-warrior. Even more so the next morning, when he led me to an algae-green freshwater pond in the next field to take a wake-up dip in our birthday suits. I was starting to get the hang of this Californian naked thing now. Plus, after two weeks of forest life, a whole week of sprinting round the fire through the night and enjoying myself enormously, those unwanted extra pounds had fallen off. I felt liberated and shiny. Eating was easy, even being naked with a lover was fine. The fire had worked its magic.

We lay on a sun-warmed wooden pier and soaked up the fresh bright morning sun, then threw on some clothes and walked through fields of wild flowers to the community kitchen. The colourful flowers were more than bright, as if I'd taken mescaline. Or maybe it was the effect of being so happy. In the wooden kitchen chalet, more wild flowers filled jam jars set on a long pine table. Steam rose from a large aluminium pan of porridge. A block of real honeycomb dripped a little pool of golden honey on a white plate, and next to the pan of porridge was a cobalt-blue earthenware bowl piled with purple grapes, green figs and blueberries. Other members of the eco-farm drifted in for breakfast, helped themselves and sat down around the table to eat.

"You're a magician, huh?" someone asked. I nodded, my mouth full of porridge. "Would you do us a little show later?"

Again, I nodded, happy to agree. I had enough props with me to pull something together.

"We've got a little open-air theatre down by the trees. We'll set some lights for you and invite a crowd."

As promised, when we walked down after breakfast, there was a woodland, half-circle mini amphitheatre with a little stage all set up in the forest with room for thirty people to sit on the wood-lined steps of dug-out earth. Tall fir trees formed a green backdrop. I spent the afternoon rehearsing while Patrick worked in the garden.

About seven o' clock, I heard a sound of jingling bells and voices. An odd assortment of folk were straggling down the winding path to the theatre: some wearing wizard's hats, some fairy wings, others long, brightly coloured cloaks. A few people carried lanterns with candles inside, which gleamed against the falling dusk of the summer night. Others held red Chinese parasols with golden symbols and swinging tassels. It was the most magical sight. They took their places in the tiny amphitheatre and waited expectantly.

These days I work on six-star luxury cruises in professional theatres with technicians and an audience of at least a couple of hundred well-heeled guests. It's very swish. But nothing, nothing can compare to the magic of that evening: the woodland setting, the golden glow of lanterns in the dusk and the scent of pine in the evening air. My act was the material I had worked on in Vegas and afterwards in my tiny room in Nicky's house. My performance was raw and unpolished, but it was everything I had. All my dreams.

When I finished and stood centre stage to take my applause, this kind audience rose to their feet cheering and applauding enthusiastically. My observing self, watching me, watching them, smiled and wondered about the odd, circuitous path I had taken to arrive here—how very odd it had been and how marvellous.

Heart full, I watched them feeling happy. This was what I'd always wanted. This.

My plan now was to marry Patrick Pigeon Hawk, get a green card and live in the States. The next day I flew home to England and planned to return to San Francisco in two months' time to get hitched. Back in Nicky's house, shutting the door of my cerise bedroom cell, I practiced magic all day, every day, chaste as a nun.

28

THAT'S LIFE

I was just about to book my flight to San Francisco, when Nicky, said, "Let's go to Provincetown for Women's Week first. We'll do street shows. I'll sing, you do magic. You can break your flight at Boston on the way to San Francisco. Provincetown is a ferry ride from there."

Wikipedia lists Provincetown, at the tip of Cape Cod, as a prime vacation destination for the LGBTQ[5] community. In summer, its population swells to sixty thousand. The high street is busy day and night, bars and shops crowded with tourists. During Women's Week, the town is full of female performers and female visitors—it's noisy and buzzing and fun. *Why not?* I thought, it sounded like an adventure. And you know how much I like an adventure.

When Nicky and I stepped off the ferry in Provincetown, we were met by a giant lobster. The lobster took our cases and carried them a little way down the jetty. He put them down and waited for a tip. We continued to bump into him through the next two weeks; the town is small, and a six foot four red lobster was hard to miss. He was a little odd, unless it's normal to be completely obsessed by all things crustacea.

---

[5]   Lesbian Gay Bisexual Transgender Queer

Extracting ourselves from Chris the lobster that first morning, we set off towards our rented apartment. Judging by the dense crowds of men strolling in pairs down the high street, all dressed or undressed in varying degrees of leather, this wasn't Women's Week at all but Leather Week. The street was jammed with moustachioed macho men in black biker jackets, peak leather caps, tattooed muscles and silver chains strung from leather belts to back pockets. Bare bums, hairy and smooth, peeked cheekily out from leather chaps. We had obviously got our dates wrong.

The High Street was crowded every day, and while Nicky played a mean slide guitar and sang the blues to the passing tourists, I performed classics of magic with cards and coins. One night we went to a karaoke bar, where a drag queen was holding court, singing most of the numbers herself. I can't hold a tune but Nicky can really sing.

"Go on. Sing Nicky, please," I urged.

"Nope, not a good idea, trust me."

"Go on. For me. Sing 'That's Life,' please. Please, for me." I wheedled. Finally, Nicky reluctantly got up and had a word with the drag queen.

"And now ladies and gentlemen, we have Nicky from England singing Frank Sinatra's 'That's Life.'"

Nicky was wearing scruffy jeans, a hoodie, and scuffed trainers. No one suspected a thing. People chatted and drank their beer. She started quietly, and the usual bar sounds hushed as people began to listen.

I said, that's life and as funny as it may seem
Some people get their kicks
Stompin' on a dream
But I don't let it, let it get me down
'Cause this fine old world it keeps spinnin' around

It's my favourite song and my favourite lyrics.

> *Each time I find myself flat on my face, I pick*
> *myself up and get back in the race.*

Before the end of the first verse, there was absolute silence. The crowd watched Nicky, transfixed. She can really sing. Everyone was now craned forward on the edges of their seats to hear better; they didn't know what to do with their hands; they wanted to clap, to wave them in the air, but it wasn't time yet. As she hit the final verse and soared into a crescendo, people leapt to their feet from their chairs. They jumped off their bar stools and whooped, throwing their hands into the air. I watched smugly. *See? That's my friend Nicky. That's talent, right there.* She hit the final triumphant note and the crowd erupted into loud cheers. She gave a modest smile, a shrug and handed the microphone back to the drag queen, who had a sour look on her face.

"When's the album out, honey?" the queen snapped.

For the remainder of our two weeks in Provincetown, we performed more street shows, swam in the warm sea and biked through the forest, getting a healthy salty tan, enjoying the last shout of summer. Finally, we returned our hired bikes to the bearded lady in the bike shop, and I said goodbye to Nicky. I boarded my plane to San Francisco and my future married life with Patrick Pigeon Hawk.

29

THIS IS HOW MAGIC WORKS

*T*his is how magic works. You set your intention. You let it go. Then the infinite wisdom of the universe, all the unknown wheels and machinations slowly grind into motion—precisely, accurately. Each cog slots perfectly into the space of the next. As momentum increases, the oil of one step after another lubricates the machinery, the sum of the parts spins faster and faster until there is a happy whirring and a humming of intention, pushing forward towards the end. Nothing will stop the machinery driving to the golden end point of desire. Unless you stick a bloody great foot in it and, to mix metaphors, upset the whole great apple-cart.

I asked, begged, implored the great Divine, God, Jehovah, Spirit, You Name It, year after year for my beautiful magic act. Left to my own devices, I traipsed like the tarot fool down one path after another. Finally, I found a clearing where a good fire was burning brightly and kindred spirits smiled a welcome. Sitting on a fallen tree trunk close to the fire, I stared into the flames, feeling myself drop away. I whispered to the flames, to the fierce heat and the sparks, *Let me serve. Let me be of use.* In a moment of thought-free inspiration, I threw my travelling bag containing my hopes and dreams, all my ambition and plans, all my doubts, bad habits and calcification of crap, slap bang into the middle of the fire. In a roar of supreme cosmic power, the flames flared brightly and burnt the whole kit and caboodle to ash. Nothing left. Or so it seemed.

But of course, as we know, everything is not as it appears.

In the magic of the fire, resistance, resignation and despair burnt to ash. Old corroded dreams and tired hopes stirred, reformed and lifted invisibly into golden notes. Somewhere in-between the nub of things, faint unheard music softly sang a new golden blueprint for the machinery. And from this base, no colour yet, not real in the sense of real but merely a thought, something new softly blossomed into being—a delicate waveform of new resolve, fresh courage, new shoes.

I had obeyed the command—or let's say, divine loving suggestion—to leave Martin. Cue beautiful Patrick Pigeon Hawk. More magical, mystical machinations involving visions of Hindu Gods, gypsy caravans and wild pigs. My compass pointed once more in the direction of Vegas. While I waited for Patrick to organise our marriage immigration paperwork, I spent two months in my cerise cell in Brighton hung with stars and ruby hearts, writing scripts and performing as many practice gigs as I could. The strange thing was that after all these months of excited transatlantic emails and phone calls between Patrick and myself, it was only in the last week, while I was in Provincetown with Nicky, that something had changed. The fairy dust had blown clean off the whole plan. When we met again, he was as handsome and lovely as ever, but the magic had simply got up and gone. There was no starlight, no cosmic visions, and definitely no wooze. I casually mentioned this, toe in water, just to see if he felt the same.

"Yup, last week," he agreed.

"So we won't get married, huh?"

"Guess not."

How strange. But there I was in San Francisco before going over to Vegas for a masterclass and another Firedance, with a show in my rucksack. Did I mention that? *A show in my rucksack!* The plan to keep me in my solitary cerise cell, practicing and rehearsing, safe from setting off on another fool's path and stepping off another cliff, had worked. Patrick called his friends, other friends called friends. Within an hour, I had a whole week of magic shows booked. In people's living rooms—nothing fancy, nothing paid even. But real shows. Shows!

After a week of doing my magic act in corners of people's living rooms in San Francisco, I left Patrick behind and flew to Vegas. We parted friends—we're still friends. Instead of getting married, I was off to do another magic masterclass with Jeff and Eugene Burger and yes, another Firedance, this time in the Vegas desert.

Magic has an odd but inevitable way of working out.

The trick I've learned is to let go and flow with it. Step, by step, by step.

30

INTRODUCING SEKHMET

$\mathcal{A}$ year after I had told Martin I was leaving, I was back in Vegas in late October, dancing round another fire with the Vegas Vortex pagans. The Vegas Vortex, as my friends from Firedance call themselves, hold their rituals at the temple of Sekhmet in the desert just outside town. This Goddess Sekhmet is a major player in my adventures. If you'd like to make yourself comfy with a nice cup of tea, I'll tell you a bit about her.

Sekhmet is a Goddess from the ancient Egyptian pantheon, the daughter of the sun God, Ra. She appears most often in a body of a woman with the head of a lioness. In ancient stories, she's both destructive and restorative—as the poet Rumi says, she is pain and what cures pain. Her mantra, *Sa Sekhem Sahu*, roughly translates as '*with each breath, divine strength enters my highest being.*' Her devotees believe that she weaves the magic of transformation, restores divine order and transmutes rage into strength. Very handy skills to have, if you ask me.

The Sekhmet temple in Nevada, built by Genevieve Vaughn in 1993, is about forty-five miles outside the outskirts of Vegas. It's built not only near the grounds of a nuclear test site, but also on land belonging to the Western Shoshone Native American Indian tribe that was taken by the government way back. In 1992, Genevieve purchased the land and returned it to the tribe.

Years ago, when struggling to have a child, Genevieve promised Sekhmet, who is also known as a goddess of fertility, that if she would help her have a child, she would build her a temple. Genevieve conceived a month later and commissioned the temple to be built. The tiny white building is made of stucco-covered straw bales with four large open arches on each side. It has a dome of seven interlacing copper pipes, making a canopy for a six-foot-high bronze statue of Sekhmet. Before meeting the Vegas Vortex, I'd never heard of Sekhmet. She didn't feature in my Catholic education.

As I stared into the fire, I wondered how I was legally going to stay in the States now that my potential husband had returned to his gypsy caravan without me. In the early hours of the morning, I noticed Earil, the high priestess with one leg, sitting near the fire, gazing intently into the flames, the purple streaks in her hair vivid in the firelight.

"Earil?"

"Uh huh?" She looked up.

"What do I have to do to stay in Vegas?"

Not missing a beat, she replied, "Fetch the water from the well in Glastonbury. Bring it to Sekhmet."

"Oh. Okay."

Warning: this is not an official US government-approved guideline.

Fetch the water from the well in Glastonbury and bring it to Sekhmet. I'd obviously been around pagans too much because this didn't sound odd at all.

A day after arriving back in England, I was astonished to open an email from a friend asking if anyone fancied going to a gathering in Glastonbury. Something about welcoming in the sixth constellation of a special planet or something. *That was quick*, I thought. Checking first on Google, I found that there was an actual well at Glastonbury, and indeed, it's one of the things the town is famous for. I took the address and drove down.

When I arrived, my friends were standing outside a large but normal looking-house looking a little embarrassed. It seems they'd misunderstood, this wasn't an official anything. The house belonged to a group of people who were gathered to celebrate this planetary constellation thing, but that was as official as it got and we were gate-crashing. When we knocked like the dwarves at Bilbo Baggins' hobbit hole, the owners of the house were puzzled, but after hearing our story, they welcomed us in and invited us to share a big pot of veggie stew before joining them in meditation.

We sat in a circle in their large living room on purple floor cushions around a large amethyst crystal and candles. Someone led a short guided mediation. That done, everyone trooped downstairs for more stew.

About ten o' clock, my friends made their excuses and disappeared back to London. But I still had to collect the water from the well. I asked if I could stay the night; I didn't mention my odd mission. They enthusiastically offered me a blanket and invited me to sleep on their living room floor. I fetched my toothbrush and found the bathroom. As I was brushing my teeth, something on a shelf caught my eye. A small bronze statue of Sekhmet! Sekhmet right there in a bathroom in a random house in Glastonbury! I was so surprised that I swallowed half a mouthful of foam and had to finish coughing before I could rush downstairs to the people in the kitchen.

"There's a statue of Sekhmet in your bathroom!" I shouted. They looked a little surprised.

"Yes, we're her devotees."

"But I'm here on a pilgrimage to collect water from the well in Glastonbury to bring it to Sekhmet's temple in Vegas! And you've got a Sekhmet statue in your bathroom!"

"Yup, that's weird," they agreed but they didn't seem overly surprised. I've said it before—but nothing shocks a pagan. I, however, was truly discombobulated. What were the chances? Among all the odd things that had happened, this was one of the strangest.

The next morning was my birthday. I thanked the people of the house for their hospitality and took myself off for breakfast. Glastonbury is full of charming little cafés. Choosing one, I ordered coffee and scrambled eggs and perched myself on a stool by the window. Buzzing on caffeine, enjoying the bright November sunshine and crisp air, I followed the signposts through town to the famous well.

In the gift shop on the way in, I noticed that there were small empty plastic bottles for sale so one could take some water from the well home. Who knew? Had Earil known? When I pulled out my little plastic bottle and crouched to gather the water, I looked closely at the tap. It was a tap in the form of a lion's head, water spouting from its mouth. Sekhmet is a lion goddess. Curious. I filled the bottle. Being a fan of Alice in Wonderland and open to change and magic, I drank it down then re-filled it and sat in the sunlight by the well. I pulled out a sheet of dark-blue paper and a pen with silver ink that I'd just bought myself as a birthday present from one of the little gift shops. Balancing it on my lap, I wrote down my hopes and wishes. I asked to make people happy with my show, and then to find a loving life partner and a happy home.

I'm sitting in that happy home today, more than ten years later. Wishes do come true. In the corner of my eye, I can see the cases of props that I haven't unpacked yet from yesterday's show. My husband Johnny Walkabout will be home soon for lunch, and Bongo the dog, snoring softly after his walk, is lying warm and relaxed on his back with his paws in the air. He must have been an extra special added bonus from the magic wishing fairies. Thank you!

Back in Glastonbury, I wrapped the blue paper around the bottle of magic water, secured it with a rubber band and took myself off for a birthday treat of coffee and chocolate cake in a café full of twinkling crystals.

31

WEIRD AND
WONDERFUL WAYS

*I*f you could have peeked through the window of my rented room in Brighton the two years following that trip to Glastonbury, you would have seen me sitting at a table with a sewing machine, surrounded by a pile of sequin fabric, magic books, tools of all descriptions and a constant, steaming mug of coffee. The little plastic bottle of water from the well sat wrapped in the same dark-blue paper on my altar on the window sill, slowly fading in the sunlight.

I'd moved to a room in a shared house in Brighton, where passengers on the top of the double-decker buses that passed my window could look right in and see me working if they'd only known. Sometimes, I was getting dressed as a bus went past and I gave them a full nude flash for free. They didn't see because their heads were deep in their phones, but it made me giggle. I propped a huge mirror against my headboard for magic practice and jacked up my bed on piles of books to squeeze boxes of props underneath. Feather headdresses and hanging costumes covered the walls, strings of fairy lights twinkled in the reflection of the mirror. I fixed a video camera above the doorway and had a tiny strip of practice room between my bed and the window. It wasn't ideal. To be honest, I didn't actually do any video practice because who likes seeing themselves on video? Me neither.

Peter, who owned the house, didn't allow me to bring glue or pins down to the shared living room, so I spent most of my time in my room, gluing and sticking and sewing, popping down to make coffee and have a quick chat with my housemates. Peter was a professional flamenco guitarist and had turned a large shop into a beautiful house with six bedrooms, polished wooden floors, a real fireplace and an ample kitchen with colourful Spanish tiles. He and a crowd of talented musicians hung out in the living room most evenings, drinking beer and smoking pot, jamming and drumming and chatting. I sat on the sofa, happily wrapped up in the music, admiring my talented friends and thinking how lucky I was to live there.

As for magic, I was trying to re-design the wheel. Stage magic has been predominantly invented and reinvented by men. In the old magic books, there are countless ways to make scarves vanish, send coins from one hand to the other or make rabbits appear, but nearly every technique is designed for male jackets, waistcoats, trousers and tailcoats. I could wear trousers and a jacket, but there's a good reason why women wear what they do. If I wear a loose-fitting jacket, I'll look bulky and shapeless; if I put anything in my pockets, I'll look even worse. Without any role models, I was inventing my own look—my own take on male magic.

At the end of that summer in 2003, I set off for another FISM, the world championships of magic, just to watch—I still didn't have an act good enough to compete. FISM is held every three years in a different country, and that year it was Holland. I couldn't afford a hotel, so I packed a tent, found a campsite and rented a bike. I chose a campsite that was a ninety-minute bike ride from the convention centre so I would be forced to cycle three hours a day. Three hours of daily exercise seemed to be what it took for me to stay in shape. Nothing much had improved eating disorder wise. I bumbled along, surviving. Only a handful of close friends with similar issues knew.

Each day, I swished along on trails through green leafy forests, then watched the stage magic competition in the huge convention theatre from morning until late afternoon before I cycled home through the dark. One morning, the skies opened and I arrived soaked through. I wrung out my knickers in the ladies' toilets and pondered the useless nature of card tricks. Not one of the thousand so-called magicians at the convention could magic me up a warm towel, a change of clothes or a dry pair of knickers. When I said as much to an interesting-looking man, dressed in black Japanese robes, his long black hair shaved into a widow's peak and plaited into a braid, he vanished, then appeared minutes later with a mug of hot coffee.

"But I can bring you this," he smiled.

This curious man was Max Maven, a huge star in the magic world. He is a man who knows everything—ask him a question, any question, he'll know the answer. Chatting with Max, finding him charming, and fearing that I wouldn't get another chance to talk to him, I said, "I would love to get your feedback on my act."

"Of course," he replied. "If ever I'm in England, I'll let you know and we'll arrange it." Max lives in Hollywood. He's in great demand as a performer, director and author. I had no real hope of ever hearing from him again.

Six months later, my phone rang. It was Max.

"Romany, I'm coming to London to meet up with some magic

friends. If you want to come by and do fifteen minutes, I'll give you some feedback." This was amazing. The people he was meeting were my friends too. Fantastic. We'd have a nice meal, I'd do my little act and get his notes. Great. Except that when I got to the address he'd given me, I found that it was a television studio. We weren't there for dinner; we were there for a magic convention for about a hundred magicians, and as I looked at the agenda, there was my name. *Cabaret with Romany—Diva of Magic.*

Oh, bloody hell.

Shaking with fright, I did my fifteen-minute act to the hundred magicians, and over dinner Max gave me notes. He flew back to Hollywood the next day.

The following week, my phone rang. It was Max again.

"Would you like to perform in the Hollywood Magic Castle for two weeks?" he asked. *Would I? Oh, yes.*

The Magic Castle is one of the most wonderful places to perform magic in the world, even if it's not a castle at all but a glorious Gothic mansion slap-bang in the middle of Hollywood. It's a private members' club, with a few Victorian-style theatres of different sizes, restaurant and bars. All sorts of celebrities pop by to watch the shows. I never dreamt that I would actually work there. But, thanks to getting drenched in a Dutch thunderstorm, thanks to the kindness of Max Maven, I was booked to do forty-four fifteen-minute shows in two weeks. Beside myself with anticipation and excitement, I rehearsed my act around the clock in the narrow strip of space between my bed and the window. Finally, feeling as ready as I would ever be, I flew off to Los Angeles, City of Angels.

Yes, I know you want to hear about Hollywood, I'll get to that. But first, I have this to say. It's important.

Magic works in weird and wonderful ways. There's no knowing how or why it works—it just does. The really important thing to know is that you have to be clear about what you want. For me, this was to have a great show that makes people happy. Then you have to start. Start anywhere, it doesn't matter. It doesn't matter because once you get started all manner of things will happen that will cause you to adjust your actions. You might get some help, you might encounter some obstacles, but you'll react to them as you go, and if you keep your destination in mind, then sooner or later you *will* get there. Think of the GPS system in your car. You put in your desired destination and it calculates the quickest and easiest route to get there. If you stop on the way for a coffee or a pee, it readjusts your arrival time and instructs you how to get back on the road. If you get lost, no problem, make a U-turn and you'll be back on course. However, if you don't switch the engine on and start to move, it can't tell you the next step of the journey. You have to have faith. You wouldn't drive for two hours following directions and then, five minutes before arriving, give up and say, "Oh, I'll just go back home—this is no good!" It's the same with magic. When you set your intention and start, all manner of weird and wonderful things will guide you to your destination, but *you have to keep moving.*

That being the case, I'll tell you a story.

In San Francisco, there is an artistic dinner theatre called Teatro ZinZanni, which plays nightly in a glorious spiegelzelt. The spiegelzelts, translated as 'mirror tents,' were built in Belgium in the 1930s as elaborate dance halls. Made of beautiful mahogany and filled with seats upholstered in crimson velvet, these moveable dance halls have multiple polished mirrors, colourful stained glass and sparkling crystal chandeliers. Each one is made up of six thousand separate pieces; only the Belgian families who have worked with them through the generations know how to put them together each time they're dismantled. There are only a handful of the original ones left, though some newer but less beautiful copies are about. The first time you enter a spiegelzelt and see its thick vermillion velvet draped from the top centre point of the roof to the stained-glass walls, tables covered in spotless white cloths set with shining silver cutlery, white candles flickering in candelabra, you too, I promise, will fall in love with them.

When such a spiegelzelt arrived in Brighton for the annual arts festival, I went *every* night for a month, danced until the early hours and even offered to entertain the queues for free. As far as the beautiful spiegelzelt was concerned, I would follow her wherever she would take me in a heartbeat. She didn't feel the same about me though, and neither did her owner. It wasn't personal—my act simply wasn't good enough for their show. But that didn't stop me looking about for other spiegelzelts that had dinner theatres, and I sent off enquiries to as many as I could find. They scattered unanswered like smoke in the wind.

While I was performing in Hollywood, a magician introduced me to a friend who'd come to see my show. He was a professional clown of Italian descent.

"I'm a member of the Guild of Italian-American actors," he told me in Italian. I knew my Italian degree would come in handy sooner or later. "We have Robert de Niro, Al Pacino and Danny DeVito among our members. We usually meet up for dinner on a Monday night." Star-struck as always, I was impressed. "I could pick you up this Monday and go for dinner," he offered.

It could have been my less than perfect Italian, or it could have been my staggering degree of naivety, but I truly understood that he was picking me up on Monday to have dinner with a gang of famous Italian-American actors. On Monday evening, as promised, he picked me up in his shiny black BMW from the Magic Castle car park. After a suitable time—I didn't want to appear too keen —I enquired casually,

"So who's going to be there tonight?" He looked puzzled.

"Just us. What do you mean?" *Damn.* Between my ridiculous imagination and my flawed Italian, I'd cooked up a whole restaurant full of movie stars. Now I was stuck for a whole evening with this guy whom I wouldn't have bothered meeting if I had thought Robert De Niro wasn't coming too. Yes, I'm an idiot. *Una idiota completa.*

Monday nights are quiet in most places, and Hollywood is no different. At the almost empty Italian restaurant, the owner welcomed my date like a long-lost brother and showed us upstairs to a private dining table. The clown did his best to entertain me with showbiz stories and jokes and was actually quite twinkly. Or maybe it was the wine. Even without Al Pacino popping in, I began to enjoy myself.

"Come to the circus tomorrow," he said, "bring your friends, stay for a drink after."

That week, I was sleeping on a friend's couch in Santa Monica. I'd hired a car so it was easy to drive to the outskirts of LA for the circus. Given the twinkle in his eye when he suggested I stay for a drink after, I told my friend I might not be home later. I was single, why not?

As I drove nearer the circus, each poster advertising the show featured my chap's face, huge and smiling in full clown make-up. He was obviously a big cheese. My friends and I had VIP seats, and I was in for a steamy night of Italian passion with the star. It was all very exciting.

At the end of the show, after signing autographs and meeting his fans, he came over to greet us. He chatted easily, then saying goodbye to my friends, said that he was off to have a quick shower and told me to wait for him in the car park. I waited. I re-applied my lipstick in the wing mirror of my car and brushed my hair. Thirty minutes later, I brushed it again. I waited until the huge parking lot was empty and the night sky was dark. I checked my watch.

Finally, after nearly an hour, there he was. He'd showered and changed, but he wasn't the same twinkly, attentive character he had been last night. He looked awkward and shifty and, without looking me in the eye, mumbled that he had an early morning start and needed to go back to his hotel. It wasn't an invitation. He turned and walked away. I was so surprised, I didn't say a word. I stood there dumbfounded, alone in the biggest, emptiest car park in the world, watching him retreat into the poster of his huge clown face, smiling in the gloom.

I'd been stood up by a bloody clown.

Well, at least I had wheels.

Slamming some music on loud, I revved furiously out of the car park towards Santa Monica. But the freeways out there are a tangle of confusion, and after three hours, I was still driving round in ever more frustrated circles, hungry and disappointed and lost on the stupid freeway. I finally drove to a quiet residential area and parked. Families were asleep in their houses with the curtains drawn; no one saw me when I peed behind a bush. As soon as morning broke, I headed back to Venice beach.

Venice beach felt like home. I went for a walk in the shallow waves, kicking through the warm water. After so little sleep I was tired, but more than that, I was angry. Not just angry, I was royally pissed off. What a complete idiot I was! What a complete twat to think that I was going to meet Robert De Niro! I walked along, kicking the water furiously. Well, not anymore! I was never going to be stood up by a stupid clown again! I was never going to be flattered by the stupid attention of someone famous! I was going to be the star! And while I'm about it, I thought, *I am going to get a gig in a spiegelzelt!*

I stomped along, half talking to myself, half talking to anyone who might be listening. It was still early. There wasn't a soul on the beach except for a few angels. Why wouldn't the director of a spiegelzelt hire me? Maybe my usual fee was too high. In that case, I told the angels, I'll do it for free. I went back to my towel on the beach and fished out my mobile phone. International calls charges were prohibitive then, but in that moment I was past caring. I was also phobic about using phones, thanks to British Telecom, but that morning? That morning, I was so annoyed and fired up that I didn't think twice. I phoned the director in Germany who I'd sent my showreel to a month ago. No one answered. I left a message.

"Hi, it's Romany, the magician from England. I sent you my showreel. I wanted to call and say that I think you should hire me." *Boom!*

Feeling much better, I stayed on the beach, looking out at the waves. Twenty minutes later my phone rang.

"Hello? Yes, we do want you to start in September. You'll be doing close-up magic in our dinner theatre in Hamburg five nights a week for six months. Call us when you get back and we'll give you the details."

What?! I sprang to my feet and jumped up and down. I stopped, breathing hard. Then I jumped up and down again. After that I sprinted up and down on the sand whooping *"YES!"* to the empty beach and the seagulls, *"YES!"* to the waves and the sunshine. What a difference a day makes. One moment I was sulking and sullen and full of resentment for that bloody clown, and the next—six months in a spiegelzelt! He was now my favourite clown in the whole world.

I got out my phone again. It was still early, but hey, he had said that he had an early start. He sounded sleepy and a little surprised to hear from me at seven in the morning.

"Guess what?" I almost shouted down the line. "I've just got a six-month contract in Germany and it's all thanks to you!"

You see? Magic works in weird and wonderful ways.

And if, like me, you're wondering why he suddenly changed his tune that night at the circus, let me tell you what he said when I asked him exactly that. I was so happy about the new booking that I didn't care that he had stood me up. But I was curious. I rang him later that day to find out.

"It's Romany."

"Uh huh?" He sounded wary.

"So the first night we went out, you were so charming."

"Uh huh?" Still wary.

"And then in the carpark at the circus, you said you had an early night and acted like a totally different person. Why?" He hesitated, pausing to pull an answer out of make-believe.

"When we met," he said, "there was such a strong attraction between us, it scared me. You must have felt it too. If I had followed it, I would have had to leave my life, my family, my work. The easiest thing was not to invite you to spend the night and not to see you again. Can you understand that?"

Yeah right. What I understood was that his wife or maybe his other mistress was waiting for him after his shower with his supper. Strong attraction, my arse.

But who cares? I'm going to Germany.

32

CAREFUL WHAT YOU
TELL THE ANGELS

*H*ere is a word of caution. You've heard the phrase, "Be careful what you wish for." Well, let me add, "Be especially careful what you tell the angels; they'll take you at your word."

Stomping along the beach in LA, I'd muttered angrily that I'd work in a spiegelzelt for free if that's what it took to get the gig. When I rang the office in Germany to ask how much my salary would be, I learnt that the angels had taken me at my word. The pay was a little more than nothing, but not much.

Back in the UK, I packed my car full. I could barely squeeze into the driver's seat. The gig came with accommodation in a hotel apartment, so at least I could save on rent. The theatre was in Hamburg, where I'd lived before with Martin, but he was now in America with his new girlfriend. Last time I was there,

I didn't have any friends or money or a job. This time, I was going to be part of a friendly gang of performers. I'd be busy performing magic, and even though my salary was peanuts, I'd have an apartment and meals provided at the theatre. It was all going to be great.

The first problem was that the billionaire owner of the spiegelzelt was a tight-fisted old bastard. He put the entire cast in a hotel on the opposite cheaper side of town from the theatre, a whole ninety minutes away by bike or bus. Because only a few people had cars, everyone rushed to get a lift as soon as the show was over. Every night, the people who failed to get a ride took the bus home after midnight, sulky and resentful.

Our dinner theatre was based on the model of *Teatro ZinZanni* in San Francisco, with a fine haute-cuisine seven-course meal and entertainment between courses. We had a high-quality team of artistes: two French-Canadian acrobats, a German juggler, an English visual comedienne, an American tap dancer, two East German clowns, a Polish tightrope walker, two Russian trapeze artists, a Russian hula hooper and an amazing Italian roller-skating trio to close the show. I was the bottom of the ladder, only there to do close-up magic around tables between courses. But at the first meeting to devise the show, the director said to me, "Hey, you can be mistress of ceremonies."

"Me?"

"Yup." Simple as that.

Simple, except that my audience was German. My German was passable after living in Germany for a year, three years ago, but 'passable' is not the same as being able to perform in it. There was just one week to write a script, translate and learn it. I'd been promoted from close-up magician to compere of the whole show, and since I was going to be on and off stage for four hours a night with three costumes changes, I asked the management if I could possibly, please, get a raise. Apparently not. I asked again, but the tight-fisted billionaire old bugger wouldn't budge.

"You've got a choice," Martin said when I asked for his advice on a transatlantic phone call. "Either work four hours a night, six nights a week getting great experience as mistress of ceremonies but earning peanuts, or leave. It's up to you."

I stayed. I wasn't confident about performing in my dodgy German on a central round stage, but the best thing about being paid peanuts is that if you disappoint, well, they should have paid more and hired someone better. What do they say? Pay peanuts, get monkeys? In this show, I was the monkey. I maxed out my credit card on three new gowns sparkling with crystal. If I was going to do this, I was doing it in style.

I had everything I'd wished for: a central role in a professional show in a beautiful spiegeltzelt, a paid-for apartment and an opportunity to gain experience as a compere. But everything, as I will continue to repeat, is never what it seems. As the weeks went by, the cracks in the dream began to show. Behind the sparkle and luxury of the spiegelzelt, the troupe was unhappy. The show could only be described as a right old cock-up. The artistes were some of the world's finest specialty acts, but the director hadn't given our show a structure. The opening number was all jumbled, and when the entire cast stood on stage at the end of the night to sing *When You Wish Upon a Star*, no one could actually sing and it wasn't clear who was more embarrassed, us or the audience.

It would be safe to say that I wasn't the most marvellous mistress of ceremonies. I'd never done it before, so it wasn't my fault. I tried my best, but I wasn't great. Backstage was a small, white prefab structure without enough space for the physical artistes to warm up. Our dressing rooms were stark and cold. I shared mine with two skinny French-Canadian acrobats who had one tiny sky-blue leotard each. I could feel their spiky resentment of my voluminous ball gowns, feathers and magic props, which spilled over the divide between our dressing tables. They chattered to each other in Quebequoise. I was convinced that they were bitching about me. They probably were. It was all a bit tense.

The food they gave us after the show was lukewarm, bland, and there wasn't enough to go round. For the first week, we grabbed leftovers from the audiences' dinners, but the menu was the same every night and there's a limit to how many times you can eat veal in cream sauce and pears in red wine.

The room where our food was served was stark white. The scant metal trays of anaemic pasta or basic pizza were stacked on an industrial metal shelf and there were fewer red plastic chairs than performers. People darted in, ate and vanished.

It would be fair to say that the troupe didn't bond. The Russian trapeze artistes whispered that the Russian hula-hoop girl was fat. She was. That was the point: she was a fat hula hooper. The East German clowns didn't like the West German juggler.

"He is *selbstgefällig*, how do you say? Ah, yes, smug."

Oliver, the West-German juggler, could throw a cigarette behind his back, catch it in his mouth, strike a match, throw that behind his back and light the cigarette. Why wouldn't he be smug? Monika, the strictly disciplined but rather homely Polish tightrope walker didn't like Candy, the beautiful American tap dancer. Monika said she was too full of herself. Candy from Michigan had flawless light brown skin and a Bond-girl figure, dreadlocked hair wrapped up in an ethnic wrap and a dazzling smile. She practiced her tap-dancing on a board for two hours each day: dripping with sweat, listening to her favourite music through ear-buds, lost in rhythm, looking like she'd stepped out of *Fame*. She sang like Billie Holliday. Yes, she was full of herself. If I were that beautiful and talented, I would be too. I remember her sitting on the step outside the theatre waiting for a lift home. The Polish cleaner, who worked all day every day for even less than my peanut pay, asked Candy if she would sing her a song. Candy's face lit up and, putting her arm around the Polish girl's shoulders, she crooned a jazz number into her ear. May everyone be so full of themselves.

We didn't see much of the Italian roller-skating trio. They had their own luxury trailer behind our dressing rooms and spent the evening of the show watching television and casually warming up. They only appeared at the end for twelve glorious minutes when Rudi, the handsome brother with impressive muscles and a heart-melting smile, stepped on stage on roller skates. It was hard to keep one's gaze from his tantalising Lycra-covered jock strap. When he spun tight circles faster and faster, his two sisters joined him— one blonde, one brunette—also dressed in white, their sparkling diamonds, beauty and professional smiles dazzling the audience. Rudi would fling one sister out in centrifugal force with her skates hooked around his neck so that she flew, her body parallel to the floor. As a finale, he held both sisters by one wrist each and did the same. The crowd went wild. By day, Rudi disappeared with his girlfriend, and both sisters stayed in their trailer watching daytime television. To me, once they switched off their electric smiles, they seemed lonely and sad.

The nicest person was the English comedienne whose act brought the house down every night. I watched her admiringly from the wings. That's what I wanted: a sure-fire act that worked every night. Krissie Illing had been honing the same six-minute act for the last twenty years. Hard work, focus and perseverance win every time. What do they say? Success is one percent talent and ninety-nine percent hard work. It's true. It really is.

It was a topsy-turvy schedule. After getting up at noon, there was just enough time to do some washing, buy some groceries or watch a bit of morning television to improve my German before heading off on my bike so that I could be at the theatre by six. I zoomed round the Alster Lake with the rest of the rush-hour bike traffic, then put on my false eyelashes, make-up and costume in the chilly pre-fab before checking my magic props.

I greeted the audience at 8 p.m. The show ran until 11.30 p.m., after which the guests stayed drinking and chatting in the bar until midnight when the theatre closed. After the show, I peeled off my lashes, hung up my gown and slid on my jeans for the ride home. Too wired after the show to sleep, I usually stopped on the way at a nightclub on the Reeperbahn. Slipping into the anonymous dark, I let the pumping music wash away the caustic backstage atmosphere.

After an hour, I'd cycle back, getting home about three. I wasn't having the best time, and bulimia was back in control. Like an unwanted vicious shadow, it followed me, unforgiving and tenacious. Sometimes if I was really having fun, like while I was working in LA or dancing with my friends in Vegas, it went to ground, but it always slithered back, toxic and destructive. In Hamburg, I didn't eat much all day; then I would buy sugary crap from a garage on the way home, stuff that down, throw up and finally sleep. It grew worse day by day. I couldn't find the way out. I tried everything—nothing worked.

If by chance you had looked out of your Hamburg window at two in the morning, you might have seen a young woman peddling furiously, head down, mouth open like one of those unhappy theatre masks, tears streaming down her face, flying through the deserted night. That was me. That winter I pedalled fast and wept for my mother, for losing Martin, for me, for everything that was broken.

We held that Hamburg show together for six months. In less than three hours after the last curtain call of the final show, everyone and everything vanished into thin air. We didn't have a party to celebrate—there wasn't anything to celebrate. I packed my costumes and props as the pre-fab dressing rooms were dismantled around me. By the time I'd finished, there wasn't a wall in sight. I went back to my hotel room to pack that up too.

Looking back at the path my life took then, in my thirties without children, a partner, a home or any debts, I was free-flowing: free to make my own decisions, where to go, what to do, how to live. What I wanted was that elusive sure-fire act. The idea of giving up didn't occur to me. I was committed, however long it took and whatever it cost.

But what was taking so long? I had little pieces of my act but nothing great, nothing bookable. In the spiegelzelt, there were nights when big act bookers came in from *Teatro ZinZanni*, *Cirque du Soleil*, or German variety theatres. In the bar after the show, they would approach the artistes to check their availability for future bookings. None of them were interested in me. I didn't expect them to be. I understood that I had nothing to offer. I saw how they talked to the best act first and then went down the pecking order of talent. A good act doesn't need to sell itself. We all want the best watch, the most beautiful clothes, the fastest car. We want the best we can afford, and if it's more than we can afford, we want it even more. If you're good, you'll be booked, it's as simple as that.

I watched and re-sculpted the shape of my ambition. Who would a booker want in his dream show? My ambition was to be on that list. It's a big ambition. But as Henry Moore said, "*The secret of life is to have a task, something you devote your entire life to, something you bring everything to, every minute of the day for the rest of your life.*"

Righty ho. We'd better keep going.

33

BERLIN

If you're game for another adventure, even if the last one sucked, if you believe that next time it will be better, more exciting, more successful—if you still desperately want to have a fantastic magic act, what do you do? You go to Berlin of course, capital city of cabaret. It seemed to be the logical next step. Maybe my act was waiting for me there, just around the corner.

Rooms were cheap in East Berlin. An airy room with a high ceiling, wooden floor and a balcony was half the price of the same in Brighton. I filled my little car with my belongings and drove east.

In Berlin in February, there was thick snow everywhere. I hadn't expected that. I hadn't expected the absolute cold. I had no income and no plan. What I did have was a large warm room in a flat shared with a friendly couple and their baby. I had my bike and a fitness centre at the top of the road. I was starting fresh, ready and enthusiastic to work on a new magic act.

The new act I'd thought up was going to be fantastic! This time, I'm a pert French housemaid, dressed in a figure-hugging black and white outfit, wide circle skirt with vertical alternating black and white panels, pulled in corseted black waist, a white cap-sleeved blouse and a little lace-trimmed maid's cap. As I tidy my mistress's bedroom, I'm surprised to find a hookah bubbling on the dressing room table, pink smoke curling upwards, reflected in the theatrical mirror with light bulbs set around the edge. Intrigued, I set my feather duster on the table and take a puff. I cough, pulling a wry face. The taste is sharp and sour. Curious. But I have chores to do so I ignore the hookah with the odd-smelling pink smoke and return to my work.

I stop dusting for a moment to yawn. A big yawn. I shut my mouth and then quickly open it in surprise. A pink ping pong ball pops out. Eyes wide with astonishment, I take it from my mouth, and—*pop!*—there's another! I remove that and—*pop!*—one more. Covering my mouth with my hand, I quickly look around the room to see if anyone is watching. I am alone. Slowly, carefully, I open my mouth again. Nothing. *Phew.* But then I feel something else coming up and I'm astonished to pull a long multi-coloured streamer from my mouth that goes on forever. I peer at the hookah pipe suspiciously and take another draw—it's really quite nice when you get used to it. I take yet another puff.

There's one light bulb missing from the set around the dressing-table mirror. My mistress keeps a small bottle of perfume just by the glass. Removing the stopper, I blow on the top of the bottle and make a bubble that floats up to eye-height in front of me. As I reach out to touch it, to my surprise, it changes into a lightbulb. I screw it into the empty socket and it glows brightly with the others. I pick up my mistress' antique silver hand mirror to give it a polish, and as I look in the mirror to check that my maid's cap is on straight, a vibrant pink rose blooms right out of the glass. I pin the rose on my cap, and when I blow on the mirror, the glass shatters into a thousand fragments, bursting high into the air, then fluttering down around me in a shower of silver.

One red shoe is lying in the middle of the room. The other is by the wardrobe. They glitter like Dorothy's from *The Wizard of Oz*. I shouldn't really, but I try them on for size. They fit. I turn my ankles this way and that, admiring the way they sparkle in the light. A slow gypsy violin starts to play. The red shoes, with my feet in them, begin to move in time with the music. This is unusual, but the third and fourth gulp of the intoxicating pink smoke has warped my sense of normal, and as the tempo increases, I allow my dancing feet to lead me around the room, the shoes keeping time with the rhythm of the violin. I dance, at first laughing and having a fine old time, but then as the music gets steadily faster, my dancing becomes manic, out of control, sending furniture and precious ornaments flying. Whirling faster, in a moment of magic, my black and white maid's uniform spins into a beautiful pink silk gown. I am more astonished than ever, but there's no stopping my dancing feet. I spin in a dervish swirl and, still spinning, rise towards the ceiling, lifted on the clouds of magical pink smoke now filling the stage. Just then, the sound of a car can be heard pulling up, footsteps crunch on the gravel outside, a key turns in the door. My mistress's voice sings out,

"I'm home!"

Abruptly, the music stops. I float down in silence, landing centre stage in a crumpled pile of pink silk. Snatching the red shoes from my feet, I hold them at arm's length, gazing at them with intoxicated incomprehension, preparing my most innocent expression to meet the anger of my mistress when she finds her room in chaos. Blackout.

Doesn't that sound fantastic? I thought it sounded fantastic.

Once the snow had melted, I cycled about Berlin searching the shops and flea markets for a pink hookah pipe. The perfect pink glass bong winked at me from a shop window selling guarana and other natural highs, and I triumphantly brought it home. I ordered ten pink ping-pong balls and multicoloured streamers from a magic shop. When I stuck the streamers in my cheeks, I looked like a French maid chipmunk. I practiced pulling them one after the other from my mouth, my room littered with soggy brightly coloured paper chains.

My housemates asked if I would I mind keeping an eye on their baby for one hour between the father going to work and the mother coming home from her night-shift. Just one hour? I had no experience with children—none—but surely I could manage one hour. How bad could it be? I agreed. I got in at six that morning after a salsa club, and while I was meant to be looking after the baby from seven until eight, I fell asleep again until woken by loud shrieks. Arriving home, my housemate had discovered her precious baby's face and cute little arms coloured bright yellow, blue and green, a couple of half-chewed multi-coloured streamers lying limp and wet on the floor beside her. The baby had crawled over to the pile of paper chains and had a little chew while I'd been snoozing. No one asked me to look after her again.

I worked on that act round the clock for four months. I had the black and white maid's costume made, covered a pair of shoes in red glitter and found a pink silk gown in a charity shop. I proudly worked out how to turn a bubble into a lightbulb. Pink balls popped from my mouth, no problem. I conjured a rose to blossom from a mirror and invented a way to get the glass to shatter in an explosion of silver shards. I hadn't managed to work out how to float to the ceiling on a cloud of pink smoke yet, but if generations of Peter Pans can fly, how hard could it be?

But before I got it finished, the absolute loneliness of living without friends or work in a foreign town defeated me. I hadn't made any friends apart from my housemates. I hadn't had a hug or a good giggle with anyone for months. Hamburg wasn't fun and Berlin was less. And yes, no matter how optimistic I tried to be, bulimia still had me on the ropes.

I gave up. Berlin might be the land of cabaret, but since I still didn't have a finished act, what did it matter? After a trip back to England where I spent time with my friends and laughed at nothing and everything, I decided it was time to call it quits and go home. I packed up my props and slipped quietly back to England, to my old room in Brighton, my beloved bright town, in the friendly house of musicians.

No one in Berlin even noticed I'd left.

34

IF AT FIRST YOU DON'T SUCCEED, FAILURE MIGHT BE YOUR STYLE

*C*hurchill said: *"Success consists of going from failure to failure without loss of enthusiasm."* By that definition, I've been super successful for decades.

I was soooo happy to be back in Brighton and England. Add another couple of 'o's and that's how happy I was. Back in my rented room in Peter's friendly house of musicians, I returned to work at double speed on my elusive stage act, half my double bed covered by piles of magic tricks in progress. I was literally sleeping with magic; there certainly wasn't any room for any other activity. Meanwhile, I was earning a living doing close-up tricks for corporate evenings, charity balls, and rich peoples' birthday parties.

I went to another masterclass with Jeff McBride. After watching my work for a while, Jeff seemed annoyed. Finally, he burst out, "You're cruising on your personality! You're not actually doing magic. What separates you from every actress out there? *Magic!* Everything we've worked on, where is it?"

I was shocked. I hadn't expected this criticism. As soon as I could escape the class, I sat on my hotel bed in tears of frustration.

Truth was, but how could he know that I *had* worked for months on his suggestions from our magic classes. I'd made the feather darts for a colourful opening, taping long bunches of bright ostrich feathers to real darts and throwing them about the room so they stuck upright in the floor. It was a great idea until you get to a theatre that has a concrete floor and the darts won't stick. I'd bought a magically appearing huge bunch of feather flowers for the finale of my act. I bought the best available, shipped over from America for hundreds of pounds. I commissioned a metal worker to fashion me a headpiece holder out of a Lavazza coffee tin so that I could put the flowers on my head like a giant flower hat. The result? Ridiculous, and not in a good way.

And what about that comedy magic act I had worked for months on with Sarah the director and then for more months in Vegas? I made the fatal mistake of performing it to seven hundred accountants in Alexander Palace for a corporate event and died so thoroughly and dramatically on my arse that the memory still makes my toes curl.

You want to hear about it? Ok, toes curled, here goes.

When a corporate contact asked if I could suggest a cabaret act for the entertainment at their annual ball, I said, "Yes. Me."

After dinner, seven hundred accountants sat back expectantly. Each year they enjoyed some slick, professional entertainment. This year they'd got me.

My act, if you remember, was the one where the Diva's props and costumes have been destroyed in a controlled explosion by over-zealous security guards at Heathrow Airport. On a huge stage at Alexandra Palace, I entered stage right in my newspaper outfit with matching hat. The accountants stared. This was unusual. I didn't have the polished look of their usual corporate entertainers. I explained that my luggage had been confiscated by Heathrow security guards and destroyed in a controlled explosion. The accountants continued to stare in blank incomprehension. Sadly,

I explained, my busty Brazilian dancers, including Leroy in his tight leather loincloth, had been stopped by immigration and were on their way back to Rio. More puzzled looks. As the act went on, the accountants looked embarrassed and started to talk among themselves. Horrendous. I got into a large fabric black bag and jumped about the stage shouting from inside that I was invisible. The hum of conversation quietened as the accountants stared at an obviously deranged woman jumping about the stage in a black sack. When I finally emerged in a red ball gown—*Ta-da!*—the silence was excruciating.

I ran off the stage, threw all my props into my case as quickly as I could, then walked through the guests to the exit. The accountants didn't see my hot, red face as I passed because they looked down at their feet or actually turned their backs. The backstage crew thought it was hilarious.

I never did that act again. Ever.

Then there was Glastonbury Festival. We might as well get all of my terrible cock-ups done with in one go.

I'd always wanted to sing. I can't hold a tune, but I decided to do a magic trick to music anyway. I hired a singing teacher, wrote new lyrics to Peggy Lee's song *Mañana* and commissioned a musician to make a backing track. The idea was to ask five people in the audience to pick a card, which I would discover and reveal while singing my song. What can I say?—This doesn't end well either.

I practiced. I applied to perform at Glastonbury in the cabaret tent. I assumed the cabaret tent would be a lovely little intimate theatre. It wasn't. It was a huge two thousand seater marquee packed with a stoned and/or drunk crowd of men. My new costume, inspired again by my beloved Carmen Miranda, was a cute peach number with frilled sleeves on a little top and a long skirt with more layers of white lace-edged frills. I looked like one of those old-fashioned toilet-roll holders my grandmother used to have.

On stage, I threw a pack of cards into the audience. I asked one person to pick a card and to throw the pack to the next person to do the same. This would have been achievable if the crowd hadn't been totally out of it. Getting the cards back was impossible. When the music started, I sang my song:

I go travelling through the world, on stages near and far.
I entertain the Queen herself, celebrities and stars,
You think I do not know your card, but that is not quite true,
Watch carefully my darling, I do this trick for you.
Oh magic! Oh magic! Oh magic is what I love to do!

As I sang, I danced about in my wellies —Glastonbury was wet that year—while two thousand men jeered and threw beer cans. If dying so completely at Alexandra Palace was bad, this was much, much worse.

I'd volunteered to do this act three times a day even though I only needed to do it once to get paid. Three times a day I died another excruciating theatrical death. The backstage crew was so embarrassed they couldn't look me in the eye. Years later I found the video tape of one of those shows. At the end of my act when I'd left the stage, the compere shouted to the jeering crowd, "Who the fuck booked her?" I never did that act again either. *That's* what took so long.

But never give up, that's my motto. You never know what might be round the corner.

35

IN THE STARS

A year after I returned from Berlin, I got a booking for the biggest gig of my career so far. I was hired to compere the cabaret tent at the Womad Festival in Reading. Despite my over-ambitious ideas for new theatrical stage acts dying as soon as they stuck their noses out of the creative womb, I did have a solid twenty minutes of tried and tested stage material that I'd played hundreds of times in my home theatre, at the Magic Castle and for corporate gigs. I was nervous but well-prepared and looking forward to it. On the drive there, my phone rang.

"It's Dad," my brother said, "he's had another heart attack."

That wasn't good. Dad had had two minor heart attacks in the last year. He'd had stents put in after the second one and had been doing moderately well.

"I'm on my way to a really big gig. Can't I come down after the weekend?"

"I wouldn't. This could be it."

Damn. I turned the car around and headed straight to the hospital. Dad was sleeping in a room by himself, a heart monitor attached to his chest, beeping quietly. I sat by his side. Looking round for his clothes, I noticed a large plastic bag in the corner.

"What's that?" I asked a nurse.

"His wetsuit."

I'd learnt not to be surprised by anything my father did. He was a charismatic, funny man. I like to think I take after him. I would be proud if anyone thought so. He once drove home with an ice-cream cornet stuck on his nose to see whether anyone would notice. Born in the East End of London, he left his family at the age of sixteen. By the time he was twenty-three, he'd bought three houses and created a bed and breakfast hostel for young men living on their own. He was an amateur ballroom dancer, windsurfer and could captain a yacht. He believed that he had special powers.

"I can move those clouds if I want," he would say, staring up at the sky, "but I won't unless I really have to."

He did have special powers. When Martin and I were in Hawaii on our world tour, we invited him to the Volcanic Circus juggling convention on the beach. He refused to learn how to juggle, but each time he went swimming, he was surrounded by pods of dolphins and the jugglers re-named him 'dolphin man.' That same time in Hawaii, he went on one of those tiny tourist trains and was the only westerner in a train full of Japanese. For some reason the train stopped in the middle of nowhere and didn't start again for ages. "Bullet train," my father said in perfect Japanese and the carriage rocked with laughter.

He'd put every effort into surviving my mother passing and had managed well for nine years, but his heart was literally broken and life wasn't getting any easier. When his heart began to cut out, forcing him to downscale from salsa to ballroom and give up windsurfing and skiing, he sat on the sofa watching TV, frustrated and bored.

"If I were to go now, I'd be ready," he'd told me a month before. With his damp wetsuit in the corner bringing the smell of the sea into the ward, it looked like he'd made the decision to take matters into his own hands. He'd gone to a salsa club and the next morning sailed out on his windsurf board and had a heart attack. Typical. But he wasn't done yet. Someone had rescued him, called an ambulance and now here he was. I spent the day with him while he slept—our last day.

"How long will it be?" I asked the nurse.

"I'm not sure. He has a strong life force."

The show must go on. Or so they say. I believed it then. I don't believe it now. Now I think that nothing, *nothing*, is more important than staying by your father's side while he is living his last few hours. If I could go back and change one single thing in my life, it would be that.

"I'm going off to do a show Dad," I whispered to him the next morning as he lay sleeping. "If you're still here tomorrow morning, I'll come back and see you." If you think that sounds astoundingly callous, believe me, that's nothing to what I think of myself. I can't bear to remember it even now. The cabaret would have carried without me. Or not. No one would have died.

Back at Womad, in the dressing room, I put on my stage make-up and costume and turned off my phone.

"This one's for you, Dad." I whispered.

It was a joyful show, full of fun and laughter. The audience was sweet and eager.

"We love you, Romany!" someone called out. In that moment, my heart ached to hear that more than anything. The moment the show was over, I went backstage and turned on my phone. There was a message from my brother who had arrived to stay with my dad, shortly after I had left the hospital.

"He's gone."

Time to break. Holding the dressing-room table, my knees buckled and my stage make-up dissolved in black runs down my face. My friend Anna came backstage to congratulate me on the show.

"Oh, my God! What's the matter?"

"My father just died." I whispered.

There was nothing to be done. I washed my face and joined Anna and my friends to walk through the late-night music crowd. I was glad I wasn't alone. My dad was there too. Each time I felt a slam of grief, I looked up into the night sky and saw him.

"You can be sad if you want," he cried, "but look—*Wheeee!*" In a night sky full of stars, my father dive-bombed, somersaulted and whizzed around the sky like a firework set free.

Stop all the clocks, cut off the telephone. Prevent the dog from barking with a juicy bone.

That's how it felt.

Because nothing now can ever come to any good.[6]

It was August and I'd been booked to perform in a variety show in the Edinburgh Festival. I cancelled. I sat on the warm stones on Brighton beach, doing precisely nothing, watching the waves sweep in and out, wondering why they still bothered. I wasn't in any mood to make anyone smile. This time, the show must *not* go on.

It didn't matter that my father told me he was ready to go, that I'd seen him joyfully zooming about the stars. He wasn't there any more to do silly dances in the kitchen, he wasn't there for me to tell him my odd adventures, or to get annoyed with when he talked over important plot points on the television. The man I admired and loved more than anyone, my dad who made me laugh, the

---

6   WH Auden Funeral Blues

only person in the world whom I resembled, was gone. I spent Christmas day alone that year, angrily doing my tax returns.

Bugger Christmas.

That was a bit bleak. Sorry. My father was a man who always made everyone smile. Don't worry, my story gets better from here. Honest.

36

BRING THE WATER!

"*Oh*, my God! Sekhmet!"

In one of those kooky New Age shops in Brighton, I was idly running my hand through a bowl of crystals, wondering whether I needed yet another to conjure more dancing beams of rainbow-refracted light around my studio. Relaxed, thinking of nothing in particular, I glanced up at the multi-coloured book spines on the shelf: manifestation, visualisation, chakras. One title jumped out: *Alchemical Healing* by Nicki Scully. I knew that name. I pulled the book free. Yes, I recognised her face from Firedance. I didn't need to read the book or even open it. It was a call, a shout from the desert. *Bring the water!*

I couldn't believe I'd forgotten about it for so long. Four years! The bottle with my wishes wrapped around it was still sat on the windowsill by my altar, faded from the sunlight and gathering dust. I had to take Sekhmet the water from Glastonbury immediately! I went straight home and booked a trip to Vegas. Or rather, I booked a flight to Los Angeles, because in the next phone call, I organised a week to perform at the Hollywood Magic Castle. I would drive to Vegas after that. I called my magic teacher, Jeff, to book a private coaching session and then I called my lovely friends Patti and Badger to ask if I could stay.

Suddenly, the wheel of momentum was in motion. I'd entered the stage competition of The Magic Circle that was to be held in October. The terrifying prospect of performing a fifteen-minute act on stage in front of my peers and a panel of professional judges was surely enough to force me to rehearse. I love most things about magic—writing scripts, inventing new techniques, sewing and sticking—but I really, *really*, don't like actual rehearsal. Why? Well, when you first try out your ideas, they don't work, they look ridiculous and it's very discouraging. Believing that the silk scarf you're fumbling to get out of your pocket will appear 'as if by magic' is a stretch. It takes a long time; it takes ME a long time to get it right. Stage magic only looks like magic when it's done flawlessly.

Back then, I only had my rented room in Brighton with the mirror against the headboard and the tiny space between the bed and the window to practice in, but it was enough. It had to be. It was time. It must have been time because someone lent me a freshly published book called *The Law of Attraction* by Abraham Hicks and my life changed. If you haven't read it or similar books like Napoleon Hill's *Think and Grow Rich* or anything by Dr. Wayne Dyer, you're seriously missing a trick. I'd definitely been missing a whole bunch of tricks for years.

The books say:

- *When you want to change your circumstances, you must first change your thinking.* – Rhonda Byrne

- *When you conceive something in your mind, know it is a fact, then there can be no question about its manifestation. In other words, that which we vividly imagine, ardently desire, enthusiastically act upon must inevitably come to pass.* – Elizabeth Gilbert

- *If one advances confidently in the direction of his dreams, and endeavours to live the life which he has imagined, he will meet with a success unexpected in common hours.* – Thoreau.

Basic magic. *Abracadabra,* meaning what I say becomes true. Surely, I should have known all this? I'm a magician, I should have. But I didn't. No wonder I'd been spinning my wheels, locked in a holding pattern, circling for years around my dreams. If we'd been chatting before reading these books, I would have told you that stage magic was difficult, that I didn't rehearse, that I wasn't ready. Suddenly, I saw the pattern and effect of my negative thinking.

I got to work. I changed my words to tell the new story as I wanted it to be. I changed my chronic statement from "my show isn't ready because I never rehearse" to "I love practicing and seeing my act get better." I changed my ten-year-old complaint that "magic is difficult to learn and a good act is hard to put together" to "I am joyful and excited about the marvellous shows I do." Each time I caught myself telling an old story, I stopped mid-sentence, shut my mouth, took a deep breath and started over with more positive words.

At first, it felt like lying to tell a different story from my current experience. I would say to my friends, "I'm loving rehearsal and my magic act is coming together nicely." They would look suitably impressed, although surprised. Then I'd whisper, "It's not really, I'm just saying that because I'm telling a different story." I continually had to bite my tongue when my old patterns of thought and speech came tripping out.

Reality, the now, feels so concrete. But 'reality' is merely a moment in time, and in the next moment everything can change. A belief is just a thought you keep thinking. We are the magicians of our own lives; we have the ability to change the old to something new and different. The first step is to change the words, then you can change the feeling, and the feeling is the *hocus pocus* that changes and influences what you actually experience. This is magic.

Little by little, my life really did begin to change. As my story became that I liked rehearsal, I began to rehearse. People don't believe me when I say I find rehearsal difficult. Shhh, don't tell that story. But it was true. I hadn't made much progress over the years because despite my great ideas, ambitious magical dreams and notebooks full of plans, I didn't take the next essential step of physical costumed rehearsal.

In the summer of 2006, with The Magic Circle stage competition approaching, armed with this new information, I finally knuckled down. Suddenly, but not suddenly at all, I was on my way to the Hollywood Magic Castle with the first version of the act that I perform today. Ten days after that, after a few days in Vegas to take the water to Sekhmet and take a private session with Jeff, I'd be performing it for The Magic Circle competition in London. Things were starting to move. *California here I come!*

37

TRUST A GODDESS
TO FIX THINGS

$\mathcal{C}$alifornia. That October, I stayed in Santa Monica and swam in the warm sea every morning. By lunchtime, I was in my dressing room in Hollywood, ready to rehearse my act through the afternoon before the evening shows began. The week was intense: three shows a night for seven nights. I was working hard on my competition routine, watching the video of it after every show and making changes. I loved setting out my props in the tiny dressing room by the side of the stage and hanging out with my magic colleagues after the shows.

In Hollywood, I was happy and healthy. I took refuge in the light of the warm Californian sun and the blaze of the bright spotlights on stage. My act was still new and raw, but I was working on it, in a real theatre, with my own dressing room with a star on the door with my name on it. Let me say that again: *A star on the door with my name on it!*

When the curtain came down on the final show, I had two

days left to take the water to Sekhmet in her temple outside Vegas and have a last-minute magic session with Jeff before returning to London for The Magic Circle stage competition. I drove my tiny rental car through the night on the busy I-15 freeway. Huge commercial trucks gleaming with silver radiator grills, pipes and bright multiple headlights drove close behind me, threatening to push my tiny car off the road. At five in the morning, I arrived at Patti and Badger's house. The water from the well at Glastonbury had travelled with me to Hamburg, then to Berlin, back to Brighton and now Vegas.

The wishes I had written in silver ink on the now ragged and faded blue paper were:

A beautiful magic act that makes people happy
To find my life partner
To have a happy home
Let me serve.

When I told my Vegas Vortex friends that I planed to ask Sekhmet to grant these wishes, they looked concerned.

"Be careful," one friend warned. "Sekhmet is a fierce and powerful goddess. If you offer her something, she'll take it. I offered her my voice once and the next day, I couldn't speak."

Hmmm.

As I drove out of town to the temple, I had plenty of time to reflect. The bottle of wishing water lay on the passenger seat beside me. I was nervous about visiting Sekhmet, but more worried about finding the temple at all. The freeway was busy and I was driving an American car on the wrong side of the road in a strange town without a GPS. My stress levels started to rise.

Since my fuel gauge was nearly at empty, I pulled in at a petrol station. In England, we fill up then pay—in America, you pay then fill. I mention this so that you don't think I'm a complete idiot when I paid for a full tank of petrol and drove off without getting any. A couple of miles down the freeway, I realised the fuel gauge was still on empty. My anxiety levels were now way past comfortable, and thoughts of giving up and turning back popped up each five minutes instead of every ten. It was only some stupid water after all.

Thirty minutes out of town, the Vegas desert stretched ahead, dull sand-brown empty land, dotted with clumps of blackbrush with tiny yellow flowers. The fuel needle dipped deeper into the red. There was nothing and no one about. My thoughts swung from panic that I would run out of fuel and be left stranded in the hot desert to worry about whether I should ask Sekhmet for my wishes—I didn't want to conjure up a whole new lot of trouble. The little bottle of wishing water was the only water I had with me. What if I had to drink it? That would be certain to attract some lion-flavoured celestial wrath.

By the time I saw the white dome of the temple, I'd decided that I was going to play it safe, deliver my gift from Glastonbury and not ask for anything at all.

I parked next to the small pre-fab hut belonging to the temple priestess. Her car was gone and no one was around. In the hot midday sun, I walked toward the temple carrying the water. The air was dry—I could feel the grit of the sandy ground crunch beneath my feet. I'd been anxious and unsure all the way here, worried about getting it wrong. But when I saw the large bronze statue of Sekhmet, I felt suddenly calm. Tears streamed from my eyes—I can't tell you why. I wasn't sad, I felt open, hopeful, safe. I knelt at the foot of her statue and waited.

"Pour the water over my head," Sekhmet said. Her voice was clear—as real as anything else. I'd already unwrapped my wishes from the bottle and folded them in my pocket. I unscrewed the lid and gently poured the water over Sekhmet's head. "These are my tears for the world," she said, her lion face marked with runs of water through the desert dust. I knelt again and put my forehead on the ground. Silence—not a sound, not a car, nothing moved.

After a while, the world turned again. I sat back on my heels and looked up at the statue. I wiped the dust and the water from the Sekhmet's face and shoulders with my scarf.

I wondered what to do next. My wishes wriggled in my pocket. I had expected a fierce, frightening goddess, but she had been calm, gentle and compassionate. My wishes were good wishes after all, I was simply asking to do a show to make people happy. Maybe it would be safe to wish for that. I unfolded the piece of paper from my pocket. Still kneeling, I lit the corner of it with a lighter. In the dry desert air, the paper caught easily. I dropped it into a mother of pearl shell on her altar and watched the words flame and shrivel to ash.

Something among the small pile of offerings at the base of her statue caught my eye. There was a white medallion, made of ivory, an inch across, with a symbol I didn't recognise on the front. On the back it said, 'To win a person's love.' In my imagination, Sekhmet offered it to me. I put it in my pocket and bowed my head in thanks. My heart felt curiously, freshly vulnerable.

I must have been kneeling there for an hour; when I got to my feet my legs were stiff. There was still nothing and no one about. I switched the car engine on, hoping the petrol would get me to the next petrol station. I turned on the radio and joyful Mexican music burst out. Feeling light and happy, I pressed my foot on the accelerator back to Vegas. Mission accomplished.

After filling up at the first garage I came to, I drove straight to Jeff's house for my private session. I showed him the footage from my shows at the Castle and he pointed out areas which I could improve. That done, I headed to Patti and Badger's and the next morning flew back to England.

The competition at The Magic Circle in London was in just two days' time.

The Magic Circle is a real society with real magicians who meet every Monday evening in a real building in a real street near Euston. Each week, the club room fills with magicians showing each other card tricks and talking earnestly about magic, followed by a lecture or a show in the theatre. The library is packed floor to ceiling with books full of methods to create mystery, and the museum is a treasure of props from the golden days of music halls when magicians were top of the bill. The exclusively male membership had a lovely time enjoying the peace and quiet of their clubroom right up to 1991 when they finally agreed to admit women as members too.

To enter the circle, you have to perform a selection of tricks in front of a panel of examiners. On the evening of my exam eleven years earlier, someone had announced to the clubroom that a young lady would be performing. Dust rose as a hundred magicians stampeded from the clubroom to the examination hall, jostling eagerly to catch sight of this new and very rare female member. I wore my salsa outfit with a high-cut sequinned leotard, fishnet tights and high heels. Tick, yes, she'll do. I performed my routine, it went wrong, the audience laughed and I became the newest and youngest female member of The Magic Circle.

And now, here I was, competing against my peers for the sought-after title of Stage Magician of the Year. Eight professional performers had been selected for the finals. We each had twelve minutes to impress the judges. I had no thought of winning—I'd only entered to force myself to rehearse.

Called back to the stage for the result, we waited nervously in a row.

"And the winner of The Magic Circle Stage Magician of the Year is—*Romany!*"

Still in shock, alone in the dressing room, I phoned Spinner, Jeff McBride's wife in Las Vegas. Spinner is a Sekhmet priestess. "Spinner?"

"Yeah?"

You know I took the water from Glastonbury to Sekhmet last week?" I said.

"Yup."

"You know I asked Sekhmet for success with my show?

"Yup."

"I've just won the Magic Circle competition!" I couldn't believe it.

"That's good. I'll tell Jeff."

"But do you reckon it was Sekhmet who fixed it?"

She laughed and hung up.

38

THAT MANIFESTATION
MALARKEY

*Gratitude and appreciation are the most efficient ways
to bring more of what you want into your life.
—Abraham-Hicks*

*M*y dream act, a happy home, and a loving partner. So far, wish one was in progress. Now that I had learnt the rules of manifestation, every morning I started the day with a practice of appreciation.

After making coffee, I lit a candle on my altar and wrote a list of the blessings in my life in my notebook: my colourful room full of costumes and fairy lights, my trusty little car, my talented musician friends, my strong healthy body, the fantastic freedom

I had to follow my dreams. Day after day, I filled that notebook with sketches and plans for the future. I wrote:

I am a successful performer,
I perform well-paid stage gigs around the world.
I work with a wonderful team of
loving and talented people.
I enjoy dancing, travelling and living by
the sea in my beautiful theatre house
where I create, love and am loved.
I am slim and fit, full of health and joy.
I bring laughter and encouragement to the world.
I enjoy a loving partnership with my beloved man.
ABRACADABRA.

Sitting in the early morning dark before sunrise, the room lit with a few chains of fairy-lights, I manufactured the happy feeling of all that being true.

A year after winning the Magic Circle competition, I bought my own dream house. I called it the "Sequin Palace of Dreams." Like the Magic Castle in Hollywood, which isn't a real castle, my house isn't really a palace. It's a four-bedroom house built in the 1930s, with roses in the garden. But what's in a name? Only what we understand it to be. I say that I am an itinerant spinner of dreams and magic. My name is Romany. I live in the Sequin Palace of Dreams. What I name and understand, so it is. *Abracadabra.*

Of course, explaining this to the gangly, pimple-faced young estate agent with black spiky hair who was showing me around several prospective houses was another matter.

"I was going to be a professional footballer," he confided wistfully. "But then I had trouble with my knees."

I nodded sympathetically and turned the conversation back to property.

"What I'm looking for is a house with a large living room that I can turn into a theatre," He stared at me blankly. Wearing jeans and no make-up, I looked very ordinary. If I had been dressed in purple flowing robes with a bejewelled golden turban, he might have understood quicker. But 'a large living room' is understandable in anyone's money and he dutifully showed me around a succession of houses with good-sized rooms.

As everyone says, you know it's the right house as soon as you step in the door. It's true and I did. My house-to-be had a large garage for props, a parking space for my future 'Divamobile' van and, yes, a huge L-shaped living room ready to transform into my very own tiny theatre.

That first summer, finally having my own home, finally being a bona-fide professional entertainer, I couldn't sleep. I was so excited, so grateful. I looked out the window at the quiet night in the early morning hours, watching a scrawny urban fox sniff hopefully at the bins, feeling heart-full thanks for my good fortune. My own house! I hired decorators to paint the walls a deep Moroccan cerise. I had a workshop with a mirrored practice wall built in the L-shaped part of the large living room, complete with a work-bench and shelves for my tools and props. In the rest of the room, I hung black velvet drapes to create the walls of the theatre. I gleefully collected heavy deep red vintage velvet curtains bought from eBay and sewed on rich gold braid and golden tassels by hand. My friends put up spotlights and helped me sand and varnish the floor to a beautiful polished wood sheen.

Fairy lights were coming into the shops early for Christmas. I hung as many of them as would fit every which way. I pressed a golden decal on the walls that stated, *Always believe that something WONDERFUL is about to happen.* I splurged on twenty-five chairs and fifty sequin cushions with golden elephants and monkeys on jewel-coloured silk backgrounds. I bought rich second-hand Turkish rugs and an antique Pianola that played old show tunes if you pedalled very hard. One day I pedalled a deafening *There's No Business Like Show Business* so energetically that I pulled my right hip flexor. I woke up in the night and couldn't turn over, because you need a working hip flexor to turn—who knew? I smiled in the dark; it had to be the most ridiculous sports injury ever. Finally, I commissioned a two-metre-wide hand-painted canvas backdrop that looked as though it came from an old-fashioned carnival tour that proclaimed, *Romany! —Magique Fantastique!* in gold letters on a pink and red background, bluebirds fluttering in the corners.

Eh voila! I now had my very own theatre. The little girl who dreamt of those gold-edged, crimson velvet curtains and her own star on the dressing room door was happy. My dream house was complete with everything I needed to work on magic. I had enough gigs to survive financially, good friends, a fun group of fellow fitness fanatics and the beautiful sea and hills of my adopted Brighton. Everything was finally coming together.

But something was missing. It had been six years since I'd left Martin to go to Vegas. Six years single.

It was time to manifest a man.

The Feng Shui book in the bookshop said: *Make physical space in your house to attract the love of your life.* I cleared out exactly half of the wardrobe in my bedroom. I slept only on 'my' side of the bed. The book continued: *Practice acting and feeling as if what you want already is.* I bought a large teddy bear and whispered in his furry ear, "I love you." I fell asleep each night cuddling him. I practiced the feeling of relief and happiness that I had finally found my love and gave Teddy an extra squeeze. You might laugh, but who is now held in the strong arms of a wonderful man every night? Me.

Finding him took a blooming long time. Magic doesn't happen instantaneously. There is a buffer of time, a cooling-off period between a wish being merely a thought and magic delivering it to your door. You can change your mind, retract or refine your order. It took a whole year of consistent practice before my husband, Johnny Walkabout, showed up. Teddy and I became very close. Dust gathered in the unused half of my wardrobe. I wrote daily in my notebook how happy I was to have found this man I intended to adore. *Adorare*—to venerate and hold as gold.

Where did I find him? He was dancing in a salsa club by the sea in Brighton, wearing a plain brown t-shirt, stonewashed jeans with ordinary short dark hair. He was definitely not a juggler. Thank God.

"Who's that?" I asked the girls.

"That's Buddhist John." *Interesting*, I thought. When the song ended, he walked off the dance floor through a door leading outside. Following him, I saw him sitting at a wooden picnic table chatting with another guy. I adjusted my cleavage into prime position, sauntered past, looking alluring, giving him the chance to look up, be immediately smitten and start our life together. He didn't. Nada, not a glance.

Six whole months later, I was back at the same club. There he was again. I wasn't going to miss my second chance, so I marched right up to him and asked for a dance. We danced. Or rather I moved straight in for a full-on cuddle. He felt gorgeous, six foot two, nice muscles, exactly what I had ordered.

"Would you like to meet for a coffee?" he asked.

"Yes," I said firmly.

"What's your number?"

"Google me."

"What?"

"Put 'Romany' into Google and you'll find my number." It's a lot easier then searching for a pen and paper in a busy nightclub, plus he'd get a chance to see what I did for a living and could exit pronto if a stage magician in feathers wasn't his idea of a perfect mate.

My website hadn't seemed to put him off because he rang the next morning and arranged to meet by the sea that same afternoon. When I arrived on my bike, he said, "Let's walk." Walk? You don't burn calories by walking; I wanted to ride and said so.

"Lock up your bike, we're walking." he said firmly. It's not that I'm *very* bossy, but I am, perhaps, a little bossy. When a man comes along who has no problem saying what he wants, that works for me. After thirty minutes strolling along the prom, I threw my arms around him in a great big full-frontal bear hug.

"What's that for?" he asked, confused. I was not confused. I knew that I had found him. I just knew.

He, however, didn't know anything of the kind. He had no idea that he had been manifested. He was also extremely slow to realise it in the weeks and months that followed. He liked me well enough, but he had no idea that he was in it for the long haul. I gave him time. I rode my bike and whispered to the faithful, listening wind, "He loves me," manufacturing the feeling that he did. *Poco a poco*, slowly, slowly. After a lovely year of fun and bike rides and dancing, I asked him to move in. He was rather surprised to find so much room in my wardrobe for his clothes.

But life, even with magic, doesn't give you exactly what you ask for, and usually not in the time frame you demand. John is three years younger than me, and for seven years he had been a Buddhist monk. A real ordained English monk living in Southampton. I say this because people usually imagine a Tibetan monk fresh out of a cave. Then he gave up being a monk. If you ask him why, he'll tell you—that's his story. I met him two years after he'd disrobed. He'd lost his direction and didn't know what to do with himself. Excellent, I had just the job for him. He could be my roadie, my stooge, my stage technician. I would stick swords in him and make him vanish. Perfect. I didn't tell him that, of course. Instead

I invited him along to my gigs, which he found boring beyond belief. Show business is a lot of hanging about. You have to arrive at the venue early to avoid any traffic, then you wait around until it's time to set up, then you do a tech run and wait again for perhaps four or five hours until it's time for the show. I'm excited and nervous, it's not dull for me. I need a good couple of hours in the dressing room to practice and concentrate—time leaving John bored with nothing to do.

"It's like going with your mum to work," he stated flatly and refused to come with me again.

I was really disappointed. I used to love working and touring with Martin. Plus, I had a three-month booking of ninety shows coming up in Dubai and I had hoped that John would come with me. It wasn't looking likely. Not looking likely at all.

39

YOU CAN HAVE ANYTHING YOU WANT BUT NOT EVERYTHING

*T*he heat in Dubai is unbearable in August. The temperature swells to above forty degrees Celsius or a hundred Fahrenheit, with extreme humidity. Because anyone in their right mind would escape to cooler climes, the government spends a sizeable amount on entertainment to keep locals amused in their huge air-conditioned shopping centres. This year they shipped an original spiegelzelt from Belgium so that they could put on a dinner theatre for the summer months. The English manager of one of the huge shopping centres was a former agent that I'd worked with years before. He had followed my career and offered me the job of mistress of ceremonies for ninety shows over three months. Here we go, take two. But this time, I was to speak English and get paid real money.

Back in the cool green of England before I left, I was excited. I was going to earn a good stack of money while having the perfect opportunity to polish my magic. Emails flew back and forth with plans for the show. Buddhist John booked flights to visit me halfway through the run for ten days. The other artistes were Andrew Van Buren and his wife Allyson, a well-known illusion act. We'd been promised an orchestra to play our music live. My act was packed. I was ready.

When we arrived, the Belgians were still putting the spiegelzelt together. We were due to open the show in a week and time was tight. The theatre was outside the shopping centre, which meant that extra air-conditioning was essential but since, it's a vintage wooden building made up of three thousand separate parts, it's impossible to seal, and making the air-con work properly was super tricky. No one seemed to have thought of this.

It had all sounded so glamorous, but our apartments were basic. No internet, no gym and no swimming pool. A gym or pool is standard for most apartments since the heat and humidity is so extreme that even a walk outside is uncomfortable for much of the year. We were not alone in our apartment. One night we were awakened by a shriek when Andrew's wife Allyson woke up to find a two-inch-long cockroach crawling over her face.

Finally, four days before the opening night, the theatre was ready, except the air-conditioning that was still causing problems. Andrew and I were worried about the music. We hadn't met the orchestra yet. Obviously, we needed to rehearse. Two days before we opened, the 'orchestra' arrived. Great. Except that they were a five-piece Arabic band. I mean, an authentic Arabic group of musicians that played Arabic music. Not cabaret, not jazz standards, not anything other than Arabic classics.

But we had bigger problems. Without consulting the artists, the management had had the stage built in the shape of a penis. They'd commissioned the builders to put together a chip board stage with a wide top for the orchestra, a narrow walkway for the acts and a round bulb on the end for my announcements. It was too narrow for my birdcage act or for Andrew's plate spinning routine. We were watching a train crash in slow motion, powerless to do anything about it.

Opening night. My routine went well despite having to perform it on the narrow stage. I invited two men up to the stage to help with my escape act. The crowd, made up of local Emirati people, gasped and applauded. Andrew finished with a squashed version of his big plate spinning finale, thirty plates precariously spinning on wooden sticks. For our first night, it hadn't been too bad.

After the show, I was summoned to the back of the now-empty theatre. A good-looking Emirati guy wearing a traditional white dish dash robe stood talking to our director. Judging by the deferential style our director had adopted he must have been important. He was. Apparently, he was funding our show. It was also his job to see that we didn't offend any Emirati laws or customs.

"You can't do that act," he said to me abruptly. "You must not talk to the men, you must not look at the men. You must never invite them onto the stage."

I was lost for words. *Had anyone actually seen my act before they booked me?* I thought.

"And you must not do the trick with the bottle."

Part of my act is to produce a bottle of champagne from a popped balloon. Alcohol wasn't allowed in the theatre but I'd been clever and found a bottle of grape juice that looked like champagne. But no, the veto stood. All that remained of my repertoire was my appearing birdcages and linking silver rings routine. Eight minutes. No comedy, no audience participation.

We rumbled on for the next three months. Ninety shows, two shows a day and one day off a week. Thank God we enjoyed each other's company. I set up a video camera, filmed each performance and watched it back twice daily, making tiny improvements each time.

As I stood backstage in feathers listening to the last bars of Arabic music before I went on, I asked Joe the stage manager the same question. "How many shows left now?"

"Forty-three."

"Oh God."

Soon, halfway through the run, John was coming to visit. I couldn't wait. In my head, he would love my little showbiz world so much that he would eagerly volunteer to travel with me. Andrew and Allyson travelled everywhere together and had a fantastic life, why not us?

It was wonderful to see him again. We did all the tourist things: a visit to the Zouk, a splash in the Wild Wadi waterpark and meals out in delicious restaurants, but even so, it was tedious for him to wait for me from mid-afternoon to midnight while I worked. After a week, it was very clear that he was bored. Andrew, Allyson and I could talk showbiz stories 24/7, but John wasn't interested. I could see that he wasn't going to be happy following me around the world. All my plans, my excitement that I'd finally found the man of my dreams, was on the line. I sat in a café pretending to read but really thinking hard. The best work in showbiz is on cruise ships or abroad for months at a time. I wanted an act *and* I wanted a life partner. I was used to going wherever a booking would take me, but maybe that was what I had to surrender. I knew what it was like to be lonely in luxurious hotel rooms. I didn't want that. Good men are hard to find—I was determined I wasn't going to lose this one. I made my decision. I decided to commit to our relationship and refuse any booking that would take me away from home for more than two weeks at a time.

When I told John about my dilemma and decision, my future

husband, being the most laid-back, undramatic, un-showbiz man ever, just nodded. "Okay."

Which leads me to this. People often ask me why there are so few female magicians. This is my opinion. A female magician needs to have the *chutzpah*, guts and tenacity to create an original act and then walk into a new environment over and over to face a fresh audience each time. She has to be physically strong to carry her props and organised enough to arrive at the right place at the right time with everything prepared and working, ready to fix things herself if they aren't. She will have to drive long distances through the early hours after gigs, usually alone, or if travelling internationally, arrive at far-flung destinations ready to schlep herself and her props to unknown venues and audiences.

If you're a strong enough character to be a successful professional female magician, you're going to want a man who is equally strong by your side. Not some sap who is happy to follow you about, twiddling his thumbs while you're working. Many male magicians have found themselves wonderful women who take care of more than half of the business. Andrew has Allyson, who not only makes their costumes, packs the props before and after the show, creates the choreography and is the glamour of the act, but also does all the catering and housework *and* takes care of their daughter. I wouldn't mind having a wife like Allyson.

It just doesn't work the other way round. There are only a tiny number of professional female magicians in the whole world performing *and* travelling with a husband. And what about children? I was putting all my creativity and energy into creating my act when I was thirty. As street performers, Martin and I could barely pay our rent; we didn't have any extra money to bring up kids. *You can have anything you want but you can't have everything.*

After ninety shows in three months, watching the video of my act back twice each night, talking magic and show business all day, every day, I arrived back in Brighton with a satisfying amount of cash in my pocket and no desire to do magic ever again.

It's true: I'd put every ounce of effort into each performance in Dubai and I was done. Instead, released from the arid city landscape of Dubai, I spent a fortune on flowers for my garden. John and I bought mountain bikes and zoomed about on the green local hills.

One week after getting home, John asked, out of the blue,

"Shall we get a dog?" *A dog! A DOG!* I love dogs but never thought I would ever be able to have one. Now that I'd made the commitment to stay home, it was totally possible. I wanted a black curly dog—only a black curly dog would do, don't ask me why. When we visited a breeder, a tiny black curly miniature labradoodle jumped onto my lap. I was suddenly, deeply, irreversibly in love with every bit of him.

"What are we going to call him?" I asked. "Pom-pom? Twinkle? Treacle Bottom?"

"What was the name of your magic friend who just died?" John asked.

"Ali Bongo?" My wonderful, eccentric magic friend who everyone loved? Perfect. That's it. Bongo.

For the next two months, I planted more flowers in my garden, played with our tiny black curly puppy on the beach and waited for my love of magic to return.

40

WHERE NOTHING IS IMPOSSIBLE, NOTHING IS WONDERFUL

*F*rom six-years-old, running along the garden path, whispering, *I want to be a fairy, I want to be a fairy*, to this moment, right here, right now, I've believed—*I believe*—in magic.

If I hadn't become a real fairy **or a** ballerina, or if Hamburg, Berlin and Dubai weren't the cabaret wonderlands I'd hoped they would be, that didn't mean that something wonderful wasn't or isn't about to happen. It's about having faith that the pieces will fall into their perfect **place.** *You cannot get it wrong and you cannot get it done.*[7] Magic has its own timing, its own quirky way of things working out in perfect time and space.

If you're becoming impatient, wondering if I'm ever going to get to Broadway, either metaphorically or literally, hold your

---

[7]   Abraham-Hicks' *Law of Attraction*

horses, keep the faith. The stage is all set to erupt in a sparkling display of jubilant fireworks. Any minute now. Make yourself a cup of tea. Put the kettle on. Have a biscuit. Have two. These things take time.

While I played with Bongo on the beach, while I went swing dancing with John, while I concentrated on having fun just like all the personal development books advised, a potent cloud of shimmering magic dust was gathering above my Sequin Palace of Dreams. All those spells I'd cast, all those fire-fuelled prayers I'd whispered, all my fervent hopes and wishes made over decades, gathered and hung, waiting. Week followed week, my props still packed in my cases from Dubai. After precisely eight weeks, a speck of magic dust tickled my nose, I sneezed and—*hey presto!*—I was back in love with magic. Just like that.

Which was handy because before I left for Dubai I had entered the International Brotherhood of Magicians stage competition and the finals were in exactly four weeks' time. The competition was eight minutes of pure stage magic. No talking, no flouncing about with feathers, no getting by with comedy, just pure, proper, technical magic, requiring real, technical rehearsal.

In my little Sequin Theatre, I had everything I needed: a video camera, a wall of mirrors plus four weeks of free time and magic friends to help and advise. Not an obstacle in sight. Except me.

"I suppose you could actually rehearse." John suggested one day. I looked at him sharply to see exactly how sarcastic he was being. He knew me well enough to know that I would do *anything* to avoid rehearsal. Stay inside on a brand-new morning? Not me! He looked serious. "If you don't rehearse, it won't happen. You need to put your costume on in the morning and perform the act three times to the camera and then watch it back. You can go out on your bike after." I glared at him like a stroppy five-year-old. I didn't want to put on my uncomfortable costume, tight corset and feathers first thing in the morning. I didn't *ever* want to put it on. I definitely didn't want to watch myself back on video.

But he was right. He usually is. I pinned a card on the studio wall with a quote from one of my magic heroes, Doug Henning:

> *The hard must become habit.*
> *The habit must become easy.*
> *The easy must become beautiful.*

I began. Before I did anything else in the morning, I did my act once, twice, three times to camera. Even though the act I was rehearsing was only eight minutes long, the process of loading the props, performing it, watching it back, making notes on what was wrong, re-loading the props and doing it all over again took three hours. Taking off the corset at the end was a glorious moment. The feeling of satisfaction after rehearsal rather than my usual daily guilt was a wonderful feeling too. After a week, things started to improve. After two weeks, my technical skills increased, after three weeks, everything was so much easier. Funny that—who knew?

Four weeks of daily practice later, I won the IBM stage competition, a huge trophy and another thousand pounds.

Now what? I'd won two major magic competitions and I had gigs coming in, but I still didn't have a world-class act that international variety show producers were banging on my door to book. How would I find the key? I had a little think. And when I'd had a little think, I remembered Siegfried and Roy. Siegfried and Roy had been heroes of mine since I saw the movie of their transformation from two young German boys in post-war Germany to mega stars of Vegas with their own spectacular show featuring lions, elephants and amazing theatrical illusions. In the last show that they would ever do, Roy's tiger dragged him off-stage by the neck, severing an artery, causing Roy to have a massive stroke. Their show was cancelled that night and never re-opened.

I'd always had the feeling that if I could only meet them, some of their magic would rub off on me. But how?

Every year in Vegas, Siegfried and Roy held a competition called the World Magic Seminar. Each year, one magician won the highly respected Golden Lion Award and a cheque for five thousand dollars. If I entered the competition, I would be sure to meet them backstage. I wrote to the organiser asking whether there was still time to enter.

"You can have the last of seven places and we'll give you $500 travel expenses," the organiser replied. What? Seven places? Travel expenses? I'd assumed that there would be at least thirty entrants. I Googled the list of competitors. Each one was a hotshot magic technician and top award winner of his country. Technically, I was a British award winner too, but I felt I'd won my titles with comedy, not magic.

What I needed was *real* magic. What did all the past winners have in common? More Googling. Photos of the winners smiled at me holding a giant cheque sandwiched between Siegfried and Roy. I photoshopped my face over the previous winners and pinned the images around my studio. Each afternoon while I walked Bongo in the forest, I whipped up the exultant feeling that I'd actually won. *Winner of the Las Vegas World Magic Seminar! Me!* I walked along pretending to hold the oversized cheque in my hands, Siegfried and Roy on each side, posing for the cameras.

"I know! I can't believe it! I won!" I told the trees. Bongo turned to look at me with surprise. With my flight to Vegas paid for, my hotel room booked and my competition place confirmed, I put my head down and rehearsed.

The competition was in February. By January, the act wasn't

looking too bad. But two weeks before the competition, I got an email from the organiser.

"Due to changes concerning the use of pyrotechnics, no fire of any sort is permitted," it declared. *What?* I was doing an eight-minute act and three of those minutes used fire. I wrote back desperately, pleading my case.

"We understand if you want to pull out," the organiser replied. Pull out? I've bought my flight, I've booked my hotel. I *have* to meet Siegfried and Roy.

"What am I going to do?" I asked my magician friends in a panic.

"Do your comedy coin routine. We like that." This coin routine was the first trick I ever learnt and not something to impress one thousand magicians in a prestigious Vegas magic competition.

"I can't do that!" I wailed.

"What else are you going to do?" they pointed out. Fair point.

Backstage in the theatre, the competitors nervously put on make-up, checked props, checked again and re-checked. One thousand magicians waited eagerly in the auditorium of the Las Vegas showroom, each clutching their voting paper. The atmosphere was intense.

It was time.

I was first on after the interval. I walked out onto the huge stage into the spotlights. I performed my opening routine: silk scarves fluttering to reveal a suddenly appearing birdcage, plumes of cerise feathers materialising from nothing, a large diamond necklace held in my hand which I had shown empty seconds before. So far, so good. Now for my coin routine. I chose two men from the audience. Both men jumped up as instructed and followed me to the front of the auditorium and up four steps to the stage. One chap bounded up the stairs energetically. But when the other reached the stage, he collapsed on all fours, breathing heavily. Over the music I could hear him wheezing, gasping for breath. Something was wrong. The sound technician cut the track and now the rasp of his laboured breathing filled the auditorium. It was a big stage, and before I could get to him, six men from the audience jumped from their seats and crouched around him, looking worried. He continued to gasp, still on all fours, his back humped. A thousand pairs of eyes were fixed on him—a thousand and one including mine. There was nothing I could do. I stood there thinking, *Oh God, I've killed him.*

Finally, his breathing quietened and, taking the arms of the men around him, he slowly struggled to his feet. The six men stayed, watching him warily, ready to catch him if he fell again. I approached and, in character, said sternly, "Young man—" He wasn't young. "This show isn't all about you, you know." My stage character has a certain way of thinking and speaking. In her world, if someone *is* going to have a heart attack on stage, they should do it quickly and quietly so she can get on with her act. "The choice is yours. Are you going to stay or are you going to go?"

A long pause. He took a deep breath and wheezed, "I'll stay." A great cheer went up. Everything from that point on was comedy gold. You couldn't have written it better: the tension, the relief, the characters. My act was *much* funnier than it had *ever* been before. As I walked off stage I knew I'd won, I just knew.

To say I was relieved would be an understatement. I was pleased that the technical magic in my act went as planned, but I was really amazed with the success of the comedy adventure in the middle. I walked back down the long hotel corridor to my room, fell on my bed and gazed at the ceiling. It was all so very strange. There seemed to be too many coincidences happening. Was Sekhmet still spinning her magic and answering my wishes?

While I was lying on my Las Vegas hotel bed lost in my

thoughts, the magicians back in the theatre were voting for the act they liked best. One magician, one vote. One thousand votes. The results would be announced tomorrow afternoon.

The next day, I put on my hot-pink, full-length satin gown and diamond necklace for the awards ceremony and walked past the flashing slot machines in the lobby of the hotel to the showroom theatre. It was still afternoon, everyone else was wearing jeans, but I had a funny feeling that I might have won. And if I was going to get that photograph with Siegfried and Roy, I was damn well going to be dressed for it. No one seemed to notice I was overdressed. It's Vegas—no one is ever surprised at anything.

I took a seat at the back.

"And the winner is—"

Drumroll.

That pause. Anything could happen.

"*Romany—Diva of Magic!*" Wow. Hard to get out of my seat. Hard to take it in. I didn't move. I couldn't move. The auditorium was full of applause. I forced myself to get up and floated on cheers and applause to the stage and up the steps. At the top, I pretended to trip and collapse on all fours as my volunteer had done, my bum facing the audience, and a great laugh went up. On stage I stood between Siegfried and Roy holding the cheque, just like in the forest with Bongo. Except this time, it was real.

Magic is strange. It swirls, lifts and blows on currents of thought and feeling. You can hold it in your hands and mould it this way or that. You can say, "I will this to be so," or in magical language, "*Abracadabra*"; then you have to inhabit the *will*, as if it is, as if it is *already*. When you really, *truly* feel as if it is, then it IS. When you decide and commit, believe and act as it if is *already*, all sorts of things you couldn't have dreamed possible come into play.

Goethe had it right. He said:

"Until one is committed, there is hesitancy, the chance to draw back, always ineffectiveness. Concerning all acts of initiative and

creation, there is one elementary truth the ignorance of which kills countless ideas and splendid plans: that the moment one definitely commits oneself, then providence moves too. All sorts of things occur to help one that would never otherwise have occurred. A whole stream of events issues from the decision, raising in one's favour all manner of unforeseen incidents, meetings and material assistance which no man could have dreamed would have come his way. Whatever you can do or dream you can, begin it.

Boldness has genius, power and magic in it. Begin it now."

I now had five thousand sparkling new dollars in my bank account, thank you, and a big trophy with a Golden Lion Head on my wall. That made a hat-trick of three major magic competitions, and finally my stage magic was beginning to shape up. But hang on. *Lion head?* Sekhmet is a lion-headed goddess. The bronze taps on the well in Glastonbury were lion heads too. Was this all Sekhmet's secret lion-themed joke?

I had a few more days to spend in Vegas before my flight home. Back at Patti and Badger's house, I opened an email. Would I like to join David Copperfield for a private tour of his magic museum meeting at midnight in a secret designation in Vegas? *Are you kidding?* Could this trip get any more exciting? Oh, wait, it could. When a large black limousine picked me up at my hotel, I saw it contained four other magicians: Sylvan, legendary TV star magician of Italy, Juan Tamariz, mega-star of Spain, Jonathan Pendragon, American superstar illusionist and performer of countless presidential performances and Paul Stone, big-time show producer. And me, not mega anything at all. But they had all watched my performance yesterday and were very complimentary.

The car stopped in the middle of a dark car park. When I got out, all I could see was a large industrial unit with a normal-looking shopfront. There were a couple of male mannequins dressed in sharp suits in the window. Strange. I turned back to see what the others were doing and there, *right there* in front of me was David Copperfield. Not a waxwork, not a poster, the *real* David Copperfield. He held out his hand to shake mine. I was so shocked that I said, "You look young."

Smooth as silk, he replied, "Good. It must be working." He turned to greet his other guests while I gave myself a slap. *You look young? Idiot.* We followed him across the car park into the little shop.

"My parents," he began, when our little group were gathered in what seemed to be a little tailor's shop, complete with shelves of dark cloth, "owned a little haberdashery shop in New Jersey just like this one. I started performing magic when I was ten." He handed us each a white business card. It said, Davino—Boy Magician. "At twelve, I was a shy kid. Magic was my way to fit in." David led us through the back door of the haberdashery shop and into another room, filled floor to ceiling with glass cases packed full of ventriloquist dolls. Stubbornly open eyes stared at us from behind the glass. Onwards to a large dark room full of huge black drawers. Every show he's ever done has been filmed and catalogued, every reference to him in every article and book recorded. Eleven Guinness world records, twenty-one Emmy awards, thirty-three million tickets sold, a knighthood from the French government, a star on the Hollywood walk of fame, listed by Forbes in the list of twenty highest earning celebrities in the world. He's even got his own flipping Caribbean island. Extraordinary.

Onward. On through a huge industrial warehouse housing his famous illusions. He shows us the water tank of his escape from death illusion. Once while rehearsing, shackled and handcuffed, he'd gotten tangled in the chains and started breathing in water. After banging on the sides of the tank, he was pulled out hyperventilating and taken to hospital with pulled tendons in his arms and legs. He was in a wheelchair for a week.

I suddenly understood. This was a show, a carefully scripted one-man show not on stage, but in his very own magic museum. David was taking us on a tour of his life, his passion for magic and his mega success. The tour had begun at midnight and it was now 3 a.m. I was getting hungry. At 4 a.m., while the other four world-famous magicians were having conniptions over an extremely rare antique magic mechanical clock, all I was thinking about was how I could really murder a large portion of hot salty McDonald's fries.

Finally, the tour complete, we were escorted through another mysterious door and suddenly we were back in the car park where our limo was waiting. I looked back at the haberdashery shop. I blinked; the shopfront was different. I shook my head and stared hard again but it had definitely changed. In the place of the two mannequins dressed in pinstriped suits, there was a beautiful showgirl standing on a low podium. Not a mannequin but a real live moving showgirl. Wearing a sparkling diamanté bikini and a diamond-studded feather crown, with high heels and long, long legs, she slowly fanned two huge turquoise feather fans. My mega-star magic colleagues were chatting to each other and hadn't noticed a thing. As I stared in wonder, she caught my gaze, gave me an especially dazzling smile and winked.

Costume design and illustration by Kevin Freeman

41

OPEN SESAME

*E*ighteen years on from my first magic class at the City Lit in Covent Garden, two summers after winning the Golden Lion Award in Vegas, and one after my stint in Dubai, I watched in amazement as five hundred people rose to their feet, clapping and cheering.

I was performing a solo forty-five-minute show in a professional theatre on a six-star cruise ship for the very first time. After the show, I went to the bar to meet the cruise director.

"That was the most original, freshest show I've seen on a ship in years," he said, beaming, "and I've written to the entertainment booker of the whole cruise line to tell her so." Blimey. High praise. To say I was relieved was an understatement.

Just after the Vegas competition, I'd got a call from the production company putting together ITV's *Penn & Teller: Fool Us*. Penn and Teller are big magic stars with their own long-running Vegas show. In it, they challenge professional magicians to come up with something that will surprise them. The point is not actually to fool Penn & Teller, but to create some great magic for television. The day filming in the TV studio was light and straightforward. Jonathan Ross, the presenter, was friendly and helpful. I did my thing in front of an enthusiastic TV audience, and it was all great fun. When your stars align, everything is easy. The show went out on ITV in May to four million viewers. The next week I got a call.

"I'm Gary Parkes; I put acts on cruise ships. I think yours would work very well." Gary is one of the biggest agents for international cruise ship entertainment and I was flattered. But after eighteen years, I still only had thirty minutes of solid stage material. The ships need two forty-five minute complete shows that you can perform to hundreds of people in a professional theatre. When I explained this over the phone, Gary said, "Come in and we'll talk it over."

In his office, I liked Gary immediately. He might be one of the most important agents around, but he was warm and down to earth. But however enthusiastic he was, I didn't see how I could accept his offer to put me on the ships since coming up with another hour of material seemed impossible.

"I don't think you understand," Gary said. "Push open that door." He pointed to a large cupboard next to my chair. It was rammed full of DVD's and brochures. "Ten entertainers ask to be on my books every week; you don't seem like you want the work."

What could I say? Over the next year, he rang every couple of months and asked, "Have you got that new material yet?" Finally, a whole year later, he called to say that the six-star luxury cruise ship was willing to give me a trial with just one forty-five-minute show. I nervously agreed.

A driver was waiting at Santorini airport to drive me to the dock. Two crew members put my luggage in a tender boat and we zoomed off over the cobalt blue waves towards a beautiful white ship, its tinted windows glinting golden in the sun. I was impressed. On board I was shown to a spacious airy cabin with a large window, a double bed and luxurious bathroom, a fridge stocked with champagne and flowers on the table. The letter on the bed said that my show would be the next day.

Wandering around the ship, everyone was extremely well dressed: the women glamorous, manicured and coiffured. Apparently, each female guest was a top beauty consultant with Mary Kay, an American network marketing company selling beauty products.

"Are you the new entertainer?" a petite redhead asked me at lunch. She would have raised an eyebrow if she could. "We didn't like the entertainer last night. We didn't find him at all funny."

She wasn't kidding. Not only had the crowd not found him funny, but they had decided his jokes were in bad taste and walked out of the showroom en-masse in the middle of his show. Ouch. But she was warm and friendly to me, and the next morning I got a phone call.

"Romany, I would like to invite you to my suite for a beauty consultation." In her suite, she stared at my skin intently. "Tell me, what is your usual beauty routine?"

"I brush my teeth and splash cold water on my face."

"And then?" she asked.

"That's it."

Horrified, she set to work. Her dressing table was covered with creams and cosmetics. In minutes, I was plastered in goo. She held up a mirror. I was beige all over. I thanked her and returned to my suite to prepare for my show.

Gary had called several times. Head office in Seattle had heard from the furious Mary Kay boss about the off-colour jokes from last night's comic and was now understandably worried about my act. The comic wasn't from Gary's agency, but the situation was still tense.

"Remember Romany," Gary said, "no swearing." I reminded myself not to say 'bugger' more than once.

But no one needed to have worried, the crowd of exquisitely dressed ladies and their obedient husbands were a dream audience, and here they were at the end of the show, on their feet, cheering and yelling for more. With all this magic swirling about, the Mary Kay crowd told the booker that they loved my show and the cruise director did the same. The next thing I knew, I was booked for as many weeks as I requested on luxury cruise ships with passenger status, which means the finest food, a luxury suite and full passenger privileges. All I had to do was one forty-five-minute show once a week and host a table in the restaurant a couple of times per cruise. And yes, they flew me everywhere and paid generously too—it was astonishing.

But where was Johnny Walkabout? I'd promised him I wouldn't travel for more than two weeks at a time. As a guest entertainer on cruises, one contract is typically only one week, and you let the company know when you are available. This meant I could sail for one or two weeks and then go home before I missed Bongo too much. Or Walkabout.

For the next couple of years, I rode camels in Petra, donkeys in Greece and wandered around exotic spice bazaars in Istanbul. I marvelled at markets selling fat olives and goat cheese in France, climbed mountains in Norway and snorkelled in turquoise waters full of brightly coloured fish in Antigua. I had three massages in one day in Thailand because, at seven quid a massage, it seemed rude not to. I narrowly escaped being dive bombed by angry arctic terns in Svalbard above the Arctic Circle and got lost for a couple of panicked hours in a labyrinthine olive grove in Greece. My shows went well, passengers were charming, cruise directors friendly, and both the bookers and my agent were happy.

But what have I repeatedly said? Nothing is what it appears. Nothing. Ask any cruise entertainer and they will tell you that not everything is as perfect as it seems. The first time my ship hit stormy waters, I discovered that I suffer from seasickness. All I could do was take refuge in my bed and hope the winds would be calm again by the night of my show. Even if the seas are rough and you're as sick as a dog, entertainers are still expected to perform. Five minutes before my performance, dressed in full feathers, I was on my knees retching into a bucket.

"I can do it. I can." I promised the cruise director who was watching me doubtfully. With three minutes to go, the cruise director made a snap decision.

"Bring on the Sinatra!" he yelled. A young guy in a smart suit and gelled black sticky-up hair ran in to take my place.

There's another glitch. It's not rocket science to imagine that a cruise is not the best place to be if you have an eating disorder. I'd had three whole years after meeting John of being so happy that the bulimia seemed to have vanished. But on the ships, I put on ten pounds and couldn't get into my costume. I took six weeks off and hired a nutritionist and personal trainer.

I counted steps, measured portions and never ate a carb unless I'd earned it. I got down to my 'perfect' weight. Good. However, my perfect weight is not where my body likes to stay. The stricter the rules of what I can and can't eat, the louder my brain shrieks at me to sabotage my hard work. Just when I managed to get my costume to fit again, bulimia came crashing back through the door and stayed.

Then there's the travel. For a guest entertainer who flies to the ship wherever it is, performs for two nights in one week and then flies off again, travel is a whole other adventure. You'd think it would be simple. If you only flew once or twice a year, it might be. But multiply your flights by fifty, add in two maximum-weight cases containing priceless props and costumes and the necessity that both you and your luggage have to arrive together at the ship before it sails, the chances of something going pear-shaped increase dramatically.

On each trip, when the plane lands, the first question is whether the luggage has arrived too. Two cases? Success. Next challenge is to get through customs without being asked to unpack my whole caboodle of birdcages, silk scarves and rubber eggs. I've learnt to keep a couple of tricks on the top of my suitcase, as one suddenly appearing birdcage is usually enough to encourage the customs officers to wave me through. The cruise company organise a driver to meet me at the airport. Or rather, they *book* a driver to meet me at the airport. Whether he shows up or not is another matter. Once, after the longest flight in the world, I landed in Peru at two in the morning. At the exit, nada, no one, not a soul. There wasn't even anyone to ask where the ship might be. All I could do was to take a taxi and hope that the driver might know. After driving through one of the most dangerous areas in Peru, we arrived at a random port that just happened to be mine. I boarded the ship in the dead of night, and by the time I woke up, we were on our way to Tahiti with a stop for a quick extremely expensive cup of coffee on Easter Island. It's all a bit hit and miss.

One morning, arriving in Cairo, just a few months before the June 2013 uprising, it was a miss. No driver. Not panicking just yet, I found the information desk.

"Excuse me, could you tell me how to get to the port?" The girl on the desk spoke perfect English but she seemed to have a little trouble with the last word.

"Port?" she repeated.

"Yes, port. Where the cruise ship docks. Do you know how to get there?" She didn't. She didn't because there wasn't one. There wasn't one because Cairo is about one hundred miles from the coast. No, I hadn't looked at a map before leaving home. Where was my ship? Not in Cairo, that was for sure.

Next stop for the confused cruise entertainer is the emergency hotline to the twenty-four-hour Seattle help desk. My phone helpfully told me that I had exceeded my credit limit and would be without service until I topped it up, which I couldn't do offline. Great. I found a kiosk offering business services and put in a call to

Seattle. A helpful lady answered with the important information that the ship was leaving from Alexandria, a five-hour car journey from Cairo.

"Wait there, I'll find you another driver," she said. I found a café and sat down with a book. It was now 2 p.m., and the ship was leaving at 10 p.m. I still had plenty of time. But three hours later, there was still no sign of my driver. Finally, I spotted a guy hurrying towards me, waving a piece of paper with my name on it. He was about sixty, with deep brown skin, baked-in wrinkles and wiry grey hair, his clothes were crumpled and his toes in his open-toe sandals were dirty.

"Come, come," he cried, seizing my cases. In the car park, he threw them into his scruffy mud-green car, which was as crumpled as his clothes. He could have been anyone, taking me anywhere; without my phone I had no way of calling for help if needed. But he seemed friendly enough, and soon we were on the motorway, my feet fighting for space with a pile of empty crisp packets. I soon understood why it was going to take five hours to reach Alexandria. The roads were chaotically full, busy with cars driven by drivers crossing lanes with determined creativity, beeping their horns with great passion. I'd never seen anything like it. The road trailed off to each side into dust and litter, peppered along the way with tiny corrugated iron-roofed shacks selling watermelons and snacks.

My driver leapt into the fray with kamikaze vigour. As our speed and the number of times we narrowly missed other cars increased, I realised how long it had been since I had properly prayed. Getting irreversibly squished in an Egyptian road crash looked more and more likely, so I abandoned my misgivings about the Catholic Church.

"Dear Father, it is a very long time since I last confessed. I haven't got time to remember all the sins I've committed, but could we cut to the chase and get my gold VIP Catholic get-into-heaven-first card sorted please?"

Miraculously, we arrived in Alexandria in one piece. The ship was scheduled to leave at 10 p.m.

My driver was now on a mission. It was 9.15; if he didn't get me to the ship before it sailed, he was going to be in trouble. But he didn't know his way around Alexandria, nor where the ship might be. His old car didn't have a GPS, and he didn't have a map. Plus, Friday night in Alexandria was obviously a party night. We were stuck in gridlocked traffic. Every restaurant was full of people enjoying a night out. In the dark, beautiful Moroccan lanterns in every colour hung from shop entrances, swinging in the light breeze. Locals puffed on glittering shisha pipes in pavement cafés, and the hot air was fragrant with sweet scented smoke.

At 9.30 p.m., with grim James Bond determination, my driver asked, window to window, for directions. Finally, with five minutes to spare, we saw the white glimmer of the ship. Screeching to a halt just below the gangway, we jumped out. I noticed that about ten officers in white uniforms were standing by the gangway looking anxious. The chief purser ran to shake my hand.

"We didn't know where you were," he said. "We tried calling; your phone is off. You've been missing for six hours." I hadn't thought that they might have been worried. I suppose a woman on her own in Egypt not answering her phone and nowhere to be found might well cause Seattle head office some worry. The captain gave the order to draw up the gangway, and off we sailed. I had a mental picture of my brown-wrinkled determined driver, watching the ship depart, punching the steering wheel in triumph before starting back on his long journey back to Cairo.

If you ask any cruise entertainer, he or she will have a suitcase full of similar hair-raising stories: arrested in Brazil, lost luggage in Antarctica, ship already left port in Australia. Amongst ourselves, entertainers say that we get paid to travel, our show we'll do for free. What keeps us packing and unpacking, lugging our heavy cases through airports and spending solitary weeks in far-flung corners of the world far from home is the opportunity to do a proper show in a real theatre to a real audience that is rare to find anywhere else. And if the waves are quiet, your time on the ship visiting fascinating ports, year-round sunshine and interesting fellow guests is as luxurious as one would expect.

42

A DIVA MEETS A PRINCE

*I*n kooky vegetarian, liberal Brighton, in my forties, I was enjoying the life I had spun so often in my manifestation notebook—I mean in the exact detail that I had written it. I had my little family made up of Walkabout and Bongo and good friends, the house of my dreams and even the VW camper van that I had sketched over and over in so many notebooks. I was performing well-paid cabaret magic up and down the country as well as working in beautiful theatres on cruise ships. As long as I took good care of my nutrition and mental health, I was relatively free from anxiety. No, I hadn't kicked that pesky eating disorder, but you can't have everything.

My gigs became more golden. I was invited to perform on a ginormous stage at a ball in Dubai for a thousand of the wealthiest people in town and flown over for one night to perform for a Saudi princess in Abu Dhabi. I was hired as mistress of ceremonies for a huge ball for two thousand people in the beautiful Blackpool Tower ballroom, complete with my own troupe of feathered show dancers.[8] A super-talented costume designer called Kevin Freeman created extraordinarily beautiful costumes for me that satisfied even my inexhaustible demand for sparkle and sequins.

I returned to Vegas and booked the amazing Joanie Spina, lead dancer and choreographer for David Copperfield's show, to give me director's notes. She was beautiful in every way, as a dancer, a person and as a magician. She died recently. Look up her on YouTube to watch the way magic *should* be performed. I'm so glad I had the chance to meet and work with her.

She sat in the bathroom of my hotel room watching me do my act between the beds.

"You look as if you're in another world. You need to be present with the audience. Why are you standing in fifth position with your legs crossed most of the time?" She asked.

"If I put one leg in front of the other, it makes my thighs look thinner." I replied.

"Well, don't. You look like you need to pee."

I had written "I hire Bob Fitch to help me improve my show" in my manifestation notebook for at least ten years. Bob spent forty years dancing and acting on Broadway, was Liza Minelli's chief dancer and has been a legendary magic adviser for many great magicians. He's 82. I figured it was time. Some dreams you just have to make happen yourself.

I booked a private four-day session with Bob in his beautiful studio in Canada. Outside, the snow was two feet deep. Inside, warmed by the huge wood burner, we went through every line and every movement of my show, looking for ways to make it better, to make me a better performer. He asked me what I wanted to do

---

[8] Thanks to the apparently barmy but actually 'undercover genius' Professor Vanessa Toulmin.

with my magic— as always, to make people smile, to soothe tired hearts. He really listened—and really helped. Those four days weren't cheap; but for me, *nothing* could be more valuable.

Each night, too excited to sleep, I sat in the window seat, looking out at the snow still falling in the dark, marvelling that my long-held dream was in motion.

It was all coming together, the wheel of momentum turning faster.

One ordinary Tuesday, the phone rang.

"Could you come and entertain at the palace?" a well-spoken voice enquired.[9]

"Err, yes. Who for?"

"His Royal Highness Prince Charles, the Duchess of Cornwall and their friends. Could you do ten minutes?"

"Could I do fifteen?"

And that is how I found myself in a huge elegant room, papered with dark red flock wallpaper and hung with oil paintings in golden frames. There was a stage built just for me at one end of the room with a dusky pink velvet backdrop lit with magenta spotlights. Abundant bunches of silver helium balloons floated on each side.

I stood on stage looking out at the elegant crowd. This was my moment. Fifteen minutes? *Bugger that*, I thought, *I'm doing thirty.*

I wasn't nervous. I knew they would be an appreciative crowd. The organiser insisted that I use Prince Charles' personal policeman and head of security to tie me up for my signature escape trick. *Really?* But it all went well and Prince Charles and his friends clapped and laughed.

Afterwards, I stood in the next room catching my breath.

"Quick! Quick! They're waiting for you!" someone shouted.

I sprinted down the length of the hallway, past portraits of

---

[9] Actually the heavy French accent of Etienne Pradier, who kindly put me forward. Merci Etienne!

forgotten kings and queens, to take my place in the presentation line. When Prince Charles reached me, he smiled broadly.

"That was absolute genius!" he chuckled. "But I was rather worried you might pick me."

"I wanted to, they wouldn't let me."

"I liked it when you did this—" He put both arms straight up above his head in a perfect impersonation of my act.

"I'll do it just for you." I did. We laughed. The Prince and me. Just us. Everything was twinkly. Top bloke our Prince.

And then he was on to the next person, making them feel golden too.

If I can be invited to perform for royalty, then anything is possible.

43

SPUN INTO GOLD

*I*t's time to go. It's time to let you get on with your dreams while I carry on with mine. I've told you all I know; it's your turn now.

One last thing. When I was watching a Dr. Strange movie recently, some words jumped out at me as true:

We never lose our demons, we only learn to live above them.

I think that's important to know—that even if we never defeat our demons, there is no shame in living above them. No one said life would be easy. Or perfect.

Leonard Cohen sang,

There is a crack in everything, that's how the light gets in.

I still grapple with bulimia and its controlling self-critical thought patterns every day. I'm still ashamed to admit it; I wish it weren't true. I am hardwired by my childhood, the media and my industry to always desire to lose those extra ten pounds that stand between me and feeling slim. My mind fights constantly to make me believe that being slim is more important than anything else. But I know that that struggle belongs to my ego and my mind and not to my soul. My soul knows better. My soul knows it's just the old resistance training: weights in the gym, sprints uphill. These days, most days, I'm winning.

A few years ago, when I was having a really bad time, I asked myself, "What if I never shake this iron hook that keeps me wriggling?"

"Keep walking," my angel whispered. "Keep walking because who knows what new and wonderful places you will see. Each time you get up and put one foot in front of the other, I promise you will find your joy along the way."

There is a great TED talk on YouTube by Amy Purdy. Amy recently won a double gold for snowboarding in the Paralympics Games and competed on *Dancing with the Stars* despite having had both legs amputated below the knee. One moment she was a healthy nineteen-year-old woman, the next she was in a near fatal coma with meningitis. When she came out of hospital, she stayed in bed for months with her head under the covers, her clumsy prosthetic legs resting against her bedside table. Her angel must have whispered to her too because now she not only keeps walking but she dances, she snowboards, she flies Olympic-fast through powdered snow, inspiring the whole world.

In her talk, Amy Purdy asks, "If your life was a book and you were the author, how would you want your story to go?"

It's a good question. I decided that if my life were a book, I would tell the world my truth. I would tell it to put one defiant middle finger up to this millstone around my neck that has had a damn good crack at keeping me small and slow. I would tell my beautiful sisters and the fewer brothers trapped in the ravaging cycle of an eating disorder: *You have to find the way to your joy.* And if you're way out of control and your life seems really crap—if you're lost in deep shame and despair—I'm truly sorry. The only way out that I know is this: if you can remember the little things to be grateful for; that you can blink, that the sun is shining or the rain is falling and the wind is blowing, it will make you feel a little better. Just this. Try to practice gratitude as often as you can and find what makes you happy. Then do it. Do more of it. Life will get better. Trust me.

And another thing. This battle wasn't started by you. This food/body-image crap isn't your fault. You just happened to be born at a time when the pressure to be slim and look young is increasing exponentially. It's become normal for women everywhere to have regular toxic injections to prevent wrinkles, get breast implants or have their lips swollen by expensive fillers. Young girls are bombarded by insidious photoshopped images of perfect women they can never be, not because they are lazy or greedy but because *those women don't exist.* Our ordinary human bodies can't compete with those air-brushed images we see on the media that are lengthened and sculpted by computers. Add into the mix the highly processed addictive foods pushed at us daily by giant food corporations, it's no wonder that obesity is on the rise and with it the number of women caught up in the poisonous swirl of body–mind crap. Can you imagine the freeing up of brain power and energy and simple happiness if women weren't obsessed with counting calories and steps and feeling bad about their bodies?

In my childhood, there was a cartoon superhero called He-Man. He stood with his feet wide apart brandishing his longsword above his head.

"By the power of Greyskull!" he shouts to the universe. *"I have the power!"*

In a shower of joyful golden sparks, I seize my staff of bright pure gold, the one spun by magic from that grey, boring millstone of shame that I have carried for so long. Raising it high into the air with both hands, I shout:

By the power of joy and magic!

By the power of imagination and faith and stubborn tenacious persistence!

I have the power!

Step by joyful, golden, determined step, I move towards the Light.

Costume design and illustration by Kevin Freeman

44

BROADWAY
~ Some Day Soon ~

*F*inally.

Beneath the window of my dressing room, far below on street level, figures bustle in a snow globe, swaddled against the cold in thick coats, hats and gloves. Above, on the wall of the theatre, a rectangle of single bulbs shine in sequence around a name. Over the years, the names burn bright then change on a breath to new ones: 'Minelli,' 'Fosse,' 'Garland'—all the greats. Tonight, the bulbs blaze white around 'Romany!' How is that possible? I am a nobody, a seller of telephones, a dreamer. And yet, there it is— electric real in a world of magic.

I have saved you until last, New York. I have saved you for the last, tastiest bite. I have chosen your stage for my tremulous, victorious shaking out of wings.

I never thought this Broadway dressing room would be so cramped, the windows small and dingy with cracked panes and peeling paint. The mirror is cracked, the floor has bare boards, the hooks on the door have lost one screw apiece; they hang upside down forlorn.

My show starts in fifteen minutes. I need to focus, breathe. I stare at my reflection in the mirror. The Diva of Magic stares back. Her costume is black and cerise, straight out of Victorian vaudeville: waist drawn in by the steel-boned corset, bosom pushed up, diamonds around her throat, her crown a quivering plume of dark pink feathers. Imperious. She sparkles and glitters as she turns to check that everything is in place. Her face is theatrical, arched eyebrows, thick eyelashes, rouged cheeks and red lips. She smiles at me, coquettishly, admiring herself in the glass. I have hand-sewn diamonds and jewels and sequins onto every spare inch of fabric.

"More," she demanded, "more!"

The magic props are arranged in order, reflected in the mirror. Bunches of cerise ostrich feathers, piles of silk scarves, raspberry-pink balloons, candlestick and candle, pointed balloon popper with ruby handle, a birdcage. Inside the cage, a silver sequin bird with scarlet tail-feathers sits quietly. It's the bird's first time in New York too. To be honest, he never thought he'd get here either, it's taken so long. A couple of repair jobs with hot glue, some fresh Swarovski's and he's looking chirpy. It might be nice to take a flutter about Central Park, see the sights, but firmly glued to his perch, it's not looking hopeful. But you never know. He'd heard there was magic here on Broadway, golden magic in the very air of the theatre that could give him real wings, could set him free.

My heart is beating fast, I feel light-headed. I haven't eaten for hours. Props loaded, costume checked, microphone wire tucked in, I step carefully downstairs. I can hear the orchestra tuning up. I watch the stage manager talk in her headset to the technicians. Suddenly I am six years old, feet dangling in my plush velvet theatre seat, hearing those jumbled sounds for the first time in the Royal Opera House—eyes wide, surrounded by gold and amazed by the huge red velvet stage curtains. The curtains here are as rich and ruby red as in my memory, but from where I stand I can only see their old worn lining, brown with the stamp of the fabric manufacturer repeated across its width. I know both sides now.

This is it. I am about to step off this ledge and hope that all the angels are there ready to catch me. I hope they laugh—the audience I mean. I hope the magic works. With my finger, I draw two interlocking electric blue triangles, making a six-pointed star and imagine myself inside, protected in blue light. My own magic.

I close my eyes and say my usual prayer: *Let Love flow through.* I imagine rays of cerise light entering the crown of my head and radiating out from my heart in a joyful arc right to the very back row, right up to furthest corner of the balcony.

Ready?

It's time.

Let's go.

45

GOLDEN

ABRACADABRA
ABRACADABR
ABRACADAB
ABRACADA
ABRACAD
ABRACA
ABRAC
ABRA
ABR
AB
A

*I*f I gave you a cedar wood box, inlaid with carved curves of bright gold, lined with ruby velvet and said, "This is the box of your greatest treasure, the box of your heart," what would you put inside? Think for a moment.

I put inside, first, always, Bongo. My black, curly-haired, soft brown eyes always by my side, always eager for a snack, ready to chase a ball, to sniff about the woods—loved more than anything Bongo. Then Johnny Walkabout, who holds me in his strong arms as I've always dreamed of being held. Who calls me "little pickle head," and shows me his love in daily small acts of kindness. I put inside my friends who know me in and out and love me regardless.

I put inside the box my tiny homemade Sequin Theatre, its worn red-velvet curtains trimmed with thick gold braid, my little workshop with its muddle of tools, glue and paint and the sewing machine my mother bought me brand new only weeks before she died, after years of struggling with a second-hand one that always broke the night before a costume had to be ready.

I put in the box an endless supply of good coffee and my favourite mug—the big pale turquoise one with the scratched gold leaf handle. I put inside England's cool, damp then sunny weather that everyone complains about but which I wouldn't change for anything. That curious feeling when you look out in the morning: what will it be today? Dry, crunching toffee brown leaves as autumn turns, winter rain against the window as you snuggle into a rug. The exhilaration and surprise of a really hot day when the sea is actually warm, or at least not freezing, and after a swim you can plonk down on the beach's sun-warmed stones: first front, then find another dry patch for your back.

I put in the box the dusty smell of a theatre, the quiet, excited and nervous preparation backstage. I put in that feeling when your act has gone well and you huddle with the other performers at the side of the stage, peering through the curtain to watch your friend triumph and the audience cheer: that feeling when you stand in the finale line-up and watch the audience all smiles, clapping until their hands ache.

I put in the box a morning, tiptoeing down through the dark house before sunrise to switch on a string of circus-coloured bulbs, set some incense smoking, a little perfume to greet the Gods. I sit in my mother's favourite Queen Anne antique chair with a mug of fresh coffee warming my hands, Bongo snoring softly at my feet. I look out at the garden, watching the sun warm colour back to the flowers.

Through the window, a bronze Buddha sits serene in a clump of pink-purple fuchsias. A polished rose quartz rock with the word *Spirit* painted by Julie Woods in gold leaf lies on his open upturned palms. Julie Woods who, without a stitch on and supremely happy in her skin, played her guitar and sung us to sleep after the hot tub in Berkeley. I see the golden threads spun from the people I love most, web woven strong around my heart.

Or rather my good mind feels—knows—I am held, just like I felt this morning in Walkabout's arms. The misery of the Half Lady is only a memory now. And if the scared, fragile part of my mind sees the fall below, the cry and the darkness, then here in this morning, here now, my heart is light and joyful.

More coffee? Always more coffee.

I am safe. Safe within the Divine. Golden.

I shut the lid of my box and hold it tight.

So may it be. And so it is.

Epilogue

BIG MAGIC

"It's not fair, everyone else is out at the beach enjoying the summer but I have to stay in and practice," I whined. "It's so stupid, I make things appear then vanish then appear again. It's so boring." I was in the middle of a session with Matthew, my life-coach.

Probably fed up with me moaning, Matthew asked innocently, "Romany, if you weren't practicing magic, what would you rather be doing?"

And this is what I said: "I'd rather be writing. I'd like to get up in the morning and write. I'd like to write all day."

This was odd because I'd never thought of that before.

"So what's stopping you?" he asked.

"No one wants to read my writing. No one's going to pay me for writing."

"How do you know?"

I've said it before: careful what you wish for; the angels are always listening.

As the words left my lips, magic swirled into action, forming a perfect golden spiral. Those golden cogs of momentum began to grind and whir, just like they always do.

After our session, I biked to the market for some veg. Cycling past a book shop, I saw a brightly coloured book with the words *BIG MAGIC*[10] – 'Creative Living Beyond Fear' on the front. I screeched to a stop. It called to me as if it had a Buy Me label on it. I didn't even bother flicking through. I paid for it, dropped it in my panniers, bought some fruit and went home. I made coffee, opened the book and didn't stop reading until I had gulped down the last page at a silly hour in the morning. *BIG MAGIC* is a urgent call to arms to create. Write your book, dance your dance, let paint spatter. Ignore the mean inner voice that whispers, it's too late, you're too old, not talented or skilful, not worthy.

After a good chunk of sleep, I got up, made some coffee, got comfortable in my mother's favourite antique Queen Anne chair, and started writing.

And now here we are, you and me.

To the detriment of my magic practice and the firmness of my perky posterior, I wrote all summer. I got up at 5 a.m. and wrote until late. I sat in the corner of the garden under the shade of the ivy and wrote, and then when the summer cooled, I went inside and carried on, looking out at the garden as the roses faded and dropped. Apart from my ever more numbing bum, I was happy. I wasn't bothered about getting shows in the diary; I wanted to write more than anything else. So I did.

I started in August. By November, I'd written eighty-two thousand words. Only a first draft, but still.

Then, because it was Christmas, which is a busy time for magicians, I laid the book gently down and returned to my day job of making birdcages appear and silk scarves vanish. And that was the end of that.

Almost.

My book sat patiently untouched and unloved for the next six months while I went back on the ships. In June, my friend Pemma left me a WhatsApp.

---

[10] Written by Elizabeth Gilbert, author of *Eat Pray Love*.

"Do you want to come to a workshop with me?" she asked. Pemma is my friend with whizzy corkscrew shoulder-length blonde curls. I have serious hair envy—everyone does. "It's with Elizabeth Gilbert and I know how you love her."

Elizabeth Gilbert is the author of *Big Magic,* that book that gave me the courage to start writing. It's true that I admire her; I'd been listening to her TED talks and watching her on Oprah and been encouraged by her podcast called, ironically, Magic Lessons. When the nasty stick-thin perfectionist in my head whispered, *You're wasting your time, no one wants to read your story, what makes you think you're any good at writing?* I took refuge in Liz's encouragement and got back on.

I clicked on the link to the workshop that Pemma had given me. It was in London, in September, three months away. A little voice whispered, *Go!* Then the same little voice said, *Since you're going, you could give her your book.*

Oh.

And then my imagination jumped up and imagined giving Liz Gilbert a thick stack of paper wrapped up in beautiful swirls of gold organza and curling ribbons.

Oh, and gold helium balloons! Squeaked my five-year-old inner child. *I bet she'd love balloons! Please, please, balloons! Balloons!*

How am I going to get on the tube with a huge bunch of balloons? asked my older practical self. But getting excited about making a beautiful gift to Liz that her book and podcasts had inspired was enough to silence my inner critic. It wasn't about me anymore; it was about honouring Liz's inspiring work and spirit with a book in return.

Suddenly I was writing again. I felt an extreme cosmic sense of urgency to get it finished.

And while I was putting in every hour to get it ready, not for me but for Liz, I listened to Oprah's Super Soul Sessions on YouTube. Her speakers are amazing: Marianne Williamson, Glennon Doyle Melton, Brené Brown, Pastor John Gray. Powerful warriors of truth and light. I'd like to be like them. But I haven't got anything to say. But what if my show could speak? What if the story of my life might help? Someone, anyone?

I remembered my childhood hymn:

All that I am, all that I do, all that I ever have, I offer to you.

In the garden, sitting with my laptop, I put my head down and prayed. *Take my hands, take my feet, take my wishing and my ego. Take my shame and my failing. Take my incompetence and my small victories. Take my crap and my glory. I surrender.*

And in the way that magic happens—I swear to you this is true—literally *five seconds* after I typed the final re-write of the final chapter and sat back in my chair to breathe a sigh of relief, my email pinged.

"We are sorry to inform you that due to a family illness, the workshop with Elizabeth Gilbert is postponed until May."

A wave of disappointment swept over me. But then I thought the timing was actually perfect. Now I had seven months to re-write, make a cover, do all the many practical things to make this book real.

And then, as if my compassionate, powerful angel was leading me on, saying, *Come, come, this way, this way to your happiness,* circumstance after circumstance unravelled.

Working in my studio, I had YouTube on auto-play. My attention was caught by a video of Louise L. Hay's work with young men who had HIV in the 80s. Louise Hay is the author of *You Can Heal Your Life*, and the founder of Hay House, which is now a huge international publishing house. She recently passed away aged ninety-two, after a lifetime of inspirational teaching. I couldn't help but watch the documentary to the end. So many beautiful young men diagnosed with HIV were told by doctors that there was no hope for them. Louise was one of the first and few people to offer them a positive alternative solution. As I watched the documentary, I was so moved by her love and compassion that, in tears, I went out into the garden. Shutting my eyes, I asked Louise for help with my book, with this book in your hands. And then I got back on with some magic practice.

Two days later—*two!*—I got an email from my singer-songwriter friend Nicky, with a link to Hay House's online writing course. By now, I've learnt not to ignore flashing neon signs from the angels. I bought the course immediately and—*bam!*—suddenly hours and hours of on-point information about publishing and marketing a book came streaming through the internet into my magic studio. *Astonishing.* There is always another step and there is always help. As the golden decal on my studio wall says, "Always believe that something WONDERFUL is just about to happen."

And here we are. Marvellous adventures are yet to unfold. Step by step.

If you've got this book in your hands, then magic is real and you should go out right now and do some yourself.

Because nothing serious is happening here.

And the 'there' you dream of will always become 'here,' and another 'there' will pop up and all exist in the same moment anyway.

Find your joy, pay close attention to the cosmic signs and remember, be careful what you tell the angels, because I swear they're always listening.

Happiness is a journey not a destination.

Romany
The Adventure Continues!

Did I ever give this book to my hero Liz Gilbert? Did my gorgeous Prince Charles call back for a repeat performance? Did I really make it to the bright lights of Broadway?

To find out and join me on more sequinned adventures, ridiculous exploits and crazy cosmic co-incidences, please go to:

www.romanyromany.com

Or follow me on any or all of the following:

Author site	www.romanyromany.com
Magic site	www.romanymagic.com
Facebook	Romany
Twitter	@romanysequin
Instagram	@magicromany

I'd really love to have your company!

More detailed information and resources about any of the topics in my book can be found on www.romanyromany.com

More information and background to the transformational fire work in this book can be found on www.vegasvortex.com

Thank You

My Marvellous Believers, Editors & Patrons!

Of course, firstly Walkabout. He is VERY patient.

My first believers for their loving support and encouragement; Betty Greene, Carole Unter, Marty Hill, Ian Rowland, Liz Shorrocks, Patricia Rawden, Joanne Frazer, Robb Schinnour, Hal Meyers, Paul Romhany, Nicky Mitchell, Julie Woods, Abigail & Jeff McBride, David Reed-Brown & Rev David Trefault.

My clever editors, Parthenia Hicks of kn literary arts, Patricia Rawden, Jeff Gardiner, Susannah Walters, Nick May & Georgina Melaris.

Kevin Freeman for illustrations and gorgeous costumes.
Neil 'Nez' Kendall for the back photo, and Glo Mason of InaGlo Photography for extra sparkle!

My patrons who donated towards the publication process. Thank you for believing in me! Thank you so much for being in my life!

Patricia Rawden, Owen & Jasmine Jefferson, Dolly Rocket, Gina Jourard, George Scott, Dave Andrews, John Lenahan, Maike Ahlers, Kay Trayford, Caroline Fry, Caroline Porter, Sandy & Ingrid Waterfield, Chris Ayers, Jez Rose, Robin Sol Lieberman, Sandie Williams, Nikki Hooper, Gordon Astley, Bob & Sue Hamilton, Wendy McRae-Smith, Aidan Heritage, Elsa Sandmark, Matthew Painton, Alan Twomey, Jane Oz, Rob Norman, Pete

Lloyd, Sally Carter Tobasso, Sophie Leach, Linda Puttock, Eva Garay, Helen Diedrich, Matthew Van Zee, Mandy Davis, David & Tracy Whittle, Kim Willis, Samina Pitrello, David Oakley, Barry Cooper, Craig Davidson, Marc Thompson, Tracey Rowland, Robb Schinnour, Zoe Lewis, Andrew Van Buren & Allyson, Klive Humberstone, Cara Hamilton, Christopher Howell, Belinda Sinclair, Charlotte Braithwaite, Michael Parks, Colin Richardson, Neal & Sian Udeen, Lewis Orchard, Mandy Fletcher, Stacy Smith, Tobias Oliver, Paul Goodbody, Roy Marsh, Dave Cumins, Gay Ljungberg, Tom Stone, Matthew Field, Brian Watson, Ren Thackham, Patti & Badger Decker, Graham Lee, Lola Chica, Stephen Scott, Loredana Cerrato, Alexander Crawford, Matt Hobson, Kim and Nichola Robinson, Ian & Carol Dronsfield, Karolina Bartnik, Austin Gannon, Mark Watson, Philip Haynes, Kelly Gregory, Marty & Sandy Hill, Nicky McAllister, Richard Parsons, Nick Ralls, Brian Sibley & David Weeks, Charlie Burgess, Marcel Leipoldt, David Reed-Brown, Tim Converse, Colin Dymond, Ally Riley, Careena Fenton, Andrew Johnson, Susie Latta, Mike McErlain, The Widow Stanton: Liz and Adrian, Corinne Ott, Ian Fraser, Veronique Faber, Jeff & Abigail McBride, Sue Oakley, Luise Frazer, Laura White, Richard Pinner, Sarah Lowe, Julie Woods, Sylvia Brailier, Ronald Elliott, Chris Pobjoy, Francesca Sansalone & Movin'Melvin Brown, Matt Wainwright, Jana Bundy, Sarah & Rex Boyd, Christina Nyman, Sheba & Simon Cassini, Paul Craven, Jon Orrell, Paul Coopes, Jannek Saebo, Hayley Stones, Caroline Blencowe, Fiona Condie, Antonia Frances, Susan J West, Jenny Hearn, Gaia Germani, Raven Marquez, Steven Bargatze, Johnny Slap, Michael McCabe, Todd Carr, Paul Regan, Kitty Olson, Matthrew Dowden, Amanda Collier, John Gordon, Sue Popper, Clare Turner & all my friends who gave anonymously.

Nam-myoho-renge-kyo
May All Beings Know Peace